Developing Information Systems Accurately

Bert de Brock

Developing Information Systems Accurately

A Wholistic Approach

Bert de Brock
Faculty of Economics and Business
University of Groningen
Groningen, The Netherlands

ISBN 978-3-031-16861-1 ISBN 978-3-031-16862-8 (eBook)
https://doi.org/10.1007/978-3-031-16862-8

This Springer imprint is published by the registered company Springer Nature Switzerland AG
The registered company address is: Gewerbestrasse 11, 6330 Cham, Switzerland

This book is dedicated to my late wife Audrey
and our children
Cherelien, Daniëlle, Nelson, and Kimberley

Foreword

I have met Bert de Brock, the author of this book, several times at REFSQ (Requirements Engineering: Foundation for Software Quality) conferences, both in person and online. I found that he and I attended the same sessions, which tended to focus on practical applications of RE and its methods. His questions of the speakers always addressed this practical applicability. His questions showed that he has had lots of in-the-trenches experience developing large-scale industrial and commercial information systems (ISs) on which people's lives, safety, and well-being depend. This impression was confirmed when I read in this book about his 40 years of experience. Bert brings this experience to bear in this book.

The book describes a stepwise and iterative method for developing ISs. A method must be both process- and data-oriented and at the same time, because an IS has both processes and data, and they must be properly related to each other in order for the IS to work as required.

The method is described in Part I as a step-by-step process for producing functional requirements for an IS, starting with user wishes, converting them to user stories (USs), use cases, and then system sequence descriptions (SSDs). To promote the methodological accuracy called for by the book's title, all the key artefacts, including SSDS, are in highly structured natural language. Generated natural language and graphical SSDs are used in validation discussions with the IS's stakeholders. The structure comes from keyworded templates with free-form natural language text in between the keywords. The book shows also how to implement the specifications in the SQL database language.

In the method, as new artefacts are derived from existing artefacts, the free-form text from the existing artefacts is carefully duplicated into the new artefacts to maintain traceability between related artefacts. That is, the natural language is manipulated accurately!

For each step, the book shows how to use textual artefacts to accurately model the requirements for an IS. The book shows a number of analyses that can be conducted on the artefacts to help understand what the models say, to discover exceptions and new requirements, and to help validate the correctness of the artefacts with respect to stakeholders' requirements.

An overarching theme of the book is using accurate manipulation of highly structured natural language artefacts to overcome the difficulties of communication that exist when converting up to thousands of imprecise and vague natural language requirements for an IS into precise models and specifications that will allow an orderly implementation of the IS, in the face of continual changes in requirements, the organization, and personnel, with the added pressure of reducing time to market.

Part II guides the reader through three case studies of applying the method to three substantial examples. Each case study focuses on a different development problem. The first shows the stepwise development of a complete conceptual model from a simple domain model. The complete conceptual model is subsequently developed into a design for an SQL implementation.

The second case study shows the conversion of a natural-language use-case and user-story model to a textual system sequence description (SSD) and then from the textual SSD back to natural language, and finally to a graphical SSD. The third case study shows the development of a control system in a context in which the control system's requirements are continually changing, partially due to deployment of earlier versions of the control system.

In conclusion, I think that this book is a must-read for any practitioner who, having been burnt in the trenches once too often, feels that 'there's gotta be a better way'.

Daniel M. Berry

Professor of Software Engineering,
Cheriton School of Computer Science,
University of Waterloo,
Waterloo, ON, Canada

Preface

Even after decades of numerous bad experiences, many software development projects are still failing on at least one or even all three basic requirements for a project:

- Too little: The project delivers inadequate functionality
- Too late: The project is not within time
- Too costly: The project is not within budget

Or, even worse, the project has been ended prematurely, usually after a lot of time and money have been spent, and without delivering any working functionality…

The reasons for those failures usually lie at the very beginning: There is no clarity in what the customer really wants and needs, leading to incomplete and even wrong specifications, and subsequently programmers who fill in the functional gaps to the best of their own understanding. So, it is very important to get really clear what the customer wants and exactly needs and to make unambiguous, correct, and complete functional specifications. As a consequence, the programmers do not have to fill in functional gaps themselves anymore, thus avoiding many of the misunderstandings.

As the title and subtitle of the textbook already indicate, this textbook is about developing information systems in an accurate way, taking a wholistic approach. The approach is also very pragmatically oriented. The emphasis of the book is on the *functional* requirements.

Why I Wrote This Book

Thanks to my mathematical logical background and after writing my PhD thesis on database models and retrieval languages, I was very well able to model and develop databases in a professional way, also for complex practical situations. I developed a direct way from a conceptual model to a working system.

However, finding out what the customer really wanted and needed was very difficult, each time again. And although I was said to be good at it—at what I now know is called *requirements engineering*—it was more art than science, as opposed to the modelling. An unsatisfactory situation. The problem was to get grip on that very early development stage in a professional way.

Starting in the early 1980s, we already carried out site visits, had continuous (close) interaction with the client, made specs of what has to be built—in particular the conceptual data model—, worked with on-site developers, used prototyping, and applied modular development. We never applied waterfall methods. But still it stayed very elusive to get a clear view on the problem space and on the (origin of) user wishes and to come to a conceptual model.

All this schematically summarized in a picture:

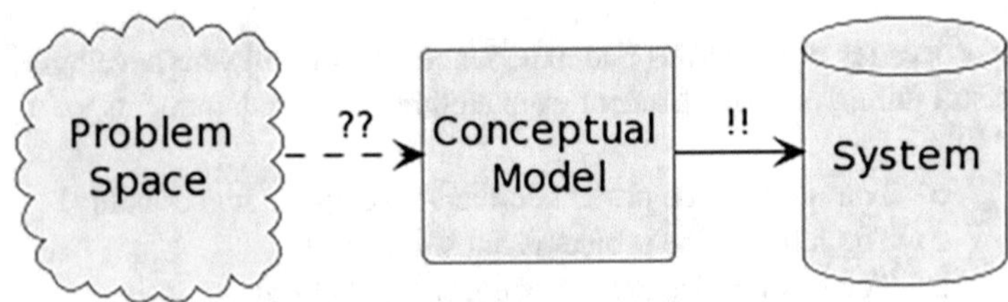

Over the years, I have experienced, seen, and read about many problems in developing information systems and read many solutions for each isolated problem. However, usually the solutions to the isolated problems along the complete development path were not aligned to each other.

Based on more than 40 years of intensive experience in various roles in developing information systems—within theory as well as within practice—I was able to arrange a straightforward development path for functional requirements, starting from elementary user wishes all the way to working systems. It was pivotal to align and improve the complete development *path*: not only the individual development *steps* but also their proper combination and alignment.

Therefore, I decided to write a book on how to develop information systems accurately and in a straightforward way, following a *wholistic* approach. The used theory aligns with and supports practice. I hope that this book will help develop and deliver properly designed, adequately working, and highly manageable information systems.

Leek, The Netherlands
July 2022

Bert de Brock

Organization of the Book

The book consists of two parts: Part I presents the underlying theory while Part II contains various illustrative case studies.

Part I starts with an introduction to the topic (Chap. 1). Then it explains how to develop functional requirements that represent the conceptual *dynamics* of an information system (Chaps. 2 and 3). Chapters 4 and 5 explain how to model the conceptual *statics* of an information system. Chapter 6 gives some directions for implementation. Finally, Chap. 7 explains how a 'technical manager' can organize and manage the development process.

As an illustration of the theory, Part II contains three substantial (use) case studies. The first one (Chap. 8) presents a stepwise development starting from an informal situation sketch via a simple domain model towards a precisely specified, full-fledged conceptual data model, which finally is translated to an SQL database. In the second case study (Chap. 9), we convert the well-known nontrivial use case *Process Sale* from Larman into a textual System Sequence Description (SSD). For validation purposes, we subsequently translate that textual SSD (back) into natural language and into a graphical SSD. The third case study (Chap. 10) shows the applicability of our approach to a *control system* and also illustrates the typical situation that the requirements are constantly changing during development.

Each chapter starts with an overview and ends with a summary. Although we often introduce a new topic by using a concrete example and illustrate our approach with various practical examples, we also express it in general terms, say in terms of 'x' and 'y' and 'A' and 'B'. Hence, no 'Theory-by-Example'.

Our objective is to treat only what we need for our approach (*Ockham's razor*) and not to mention each and every alternative theory in the field. Therefore, we will not treat and hardly mention the visual modelling language UML and treat only very few—but relevant—normal forms for databases, to mention just a few examples.

Additional course material—such as slides, additional exercises, solutions to exercises, and the code for the figures used in the book—can be found on the companion website of the book: Accurate-IS-development.com. For questions, suggestions, and other matters, the author can be reached by e-mail via e.o.de.brock@rug.nl.

Acknowledgments

I want to thank several people. First of all, I want to thank Frans Remmen, who introduced me to the area of databases and also taught me a lot about its practical applications. I also want to thank my 'sparring partners' Herman Balsters, Rein Smedinga, Wilco Wijbrandi, and Coen Suurmond for the many discussions we had. I want to thank Rein Smedinga, Ghica van Emde Boas–Lubsen, and especially Coen Suurmond for their careful proofreading of the book and Toon Koppelaars for his careful proofreading of the SQL parts. Furthermore, I want to thank all my students over the years, who made my unclarities clear. Last but not least, I want to thank my wife, Audrey, and our children, Cherelien, Daniëlle, Nelson, and Kimberley, who allowed me to be a workaholic.

Global Contents

Contents

About the Author

Bert de Brock is Professor Emeritus of Business Information Modelling at the Faculty of Economics and Business of the University of Groningen, The Netherlands, a position he held for 15 years. Prior to that, he was Associate Professor of Information Technology, in particular Software Engineering, for more than 10 years.

Before moving into academia, Bert had worked as a senior researcher at Philips Research, developing generators for generic workflow software for instance, and he was founder, owner, and director of Remmen & De Brock, a software and consultancy firm specialized in requirements engineering and designing and building dedicated information systems for various customers.

Bert has taught Information Systems Development, Databases, Business Intelligence, E-venturing, and Programming for several decades, both to students and to practitioners.

He holds an MSc in Mathematics (Specialization: Logic and Foundations of Mathematics) from the University of Groningen and a PhD in Computing Science from the Eindhoven University of Technology. His PhD thesis was on database models and retrieval languages.

Abbreviations

Here we recall the abbreviations used in this book.

1NF	First normal form
2NF	Second normal form
3NF	Third normal form
AS	Alternative Scenario
a.k.a.	Also known as
BCNF	Boyce-Codd normal form
BOM	Bill Of Material
BPM	Business Process Modelling
CASE	Computer-Aided Software Engineering
CDM	Conceptual Data Model
CRUD	Create, Read, Update, Delete
CRUDA	Create, Read, Update, Delete, Archive
CSA	Central Student Administration
DBMS	Database Management System
EMA	*European Medicines Agency*
eUW	Elementary User Wish
FDA	Food and Drug Administration (USA)
FR	Functional Requirement
FURPS	Functionality, Usability, Reliability, Performance, Supportability
gSSD	Graphical SSD
IOU	'*I owe you*', an official acknowledgement of a debt
IS	Information system
MSS	Main Success Scenario
MVC	Model-View-Controller
NIST	National Institute of Standards and Technology
NL	Natural language
PC	Postal code

POS	Point of sale
pUW	Parameterized User Wish
SQL	Structured Query Language
SSD	System Sequence Description
SSL	Structured Scroll Language
SSN	Social Security Number
SW	Software
tSSD	Textual SSD
UC	Use Case
UI	User Interface
u.i.	Uniquely identifying
UML	Unified Modeling Language
US	User Story
UW	User Wish
XP	eXtreme Programming

Symbols

A1 ➡ A2: X	Actor A1 sends X to actor A2 (if A1 ≠ A2)
A1 ➡ A1: X	Actor A1 does X
▼	in a form: indication of a list to choose a value from
📅	in a form: indication of a calendar to choose a value from
⏱	in a form: indication of a list of times to choose a value from
▶, ◀, ▲, ▼	in a domain model: reading direction of an association
R^{-1}	the *inverse* of a relation R, i.e., { (b;a) | (a;b) ∈ R }
⊖	non-commutativity of a diagram
A ⟶ B in C	property set B is *functionally dependent* on property set A within concept C

Chapter 1
Introduction

Abstract This initial chapter presents quite diverse topics. It introduces the subject of the textbook (Sect. 1.1), its scope (Sect. 1.2), globally its contents (Sect. 1.3), its position in terms of computing curricula (Sect. 1.4), its intended audience (Sect. 1.5), and its learning outcomes (Sect. 1.6).

This chapter subsequently sketches the problem area (Sect. 1.7) and our approach to it (Sect. 1.8) while it distinguishes goals on different levels (Sect. 1.9). Moreover, we distinguish between functional requirements and quality requirements for a system (Sect. 1.10). The emphasis of the book will be on functional requirements.

1.1 Subject of the Book

The main subject of this textbook is how to develop the *functional requirements* of (information) systems. The book emphasizes that it is important to consider the *complete development path* of a functional requirement. Our main message is to consider the whole development path, not only the individual development steps but also their proper combination and their alignment.

To elucidate the main message: Usually, the theoretical (and practical) proposals for solving the individual problems along the development path are not mutually aligned. For instance, certain development steps tend to have *textual* contents (e.g., use cases from users/customers), while other intermediate steps have *graphical* contents (e.g., UML-diagrams), and the final steps have *textual* contents again (e.g., software programs). In the 'symbolic' Fig. 1.1, each arrow represents a development step. The figure expresses that the different development steps are based on different paradigms and that the development path switches between textual contents and graphical contents.

There is also the (old) basic question whether you should be 'process-oriented' or 'data-oriented'; see, for instance, the blog https://analyticsdemystified.com/analysis/are-you-data-oriented-or-process-oriented. Well, our message is that you should be both: You should approach the development of an information system from both perspectives, *and* in combination! The reason is that an information system must support processes, a.k.a. its *dynamics*, and it must also contain data—its

B. de Brock, *Developing Information Systems Accurately*,
https://doi.org/10.1007/978-3-031-16862-8_1

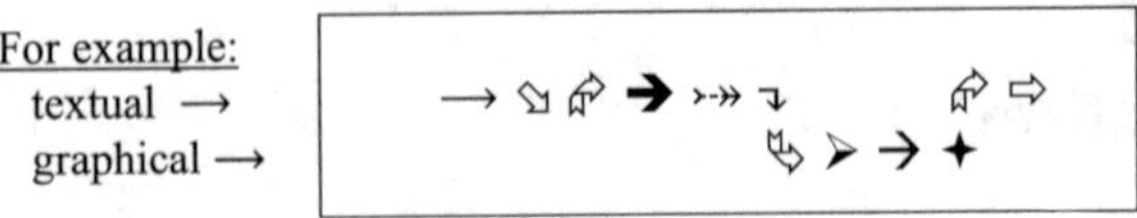

Fig. 1.1 No proper combination and no alignment of the development steps

statics—in order to work properly, *and* they must be tuned to each other. They are the two sides of the same coin, so to speak.

Therefore, the book shows how to develop *data structures* (the statics) as well as *processes* (the dynamics) and how to *integrate* them concurrently and in a consistent way. In the meantime, we also pay attention to development *patterns*.

The book specifically discusses the question how to uncover (initial) user wishes and come up with a conceptual design, in such a way that the development has certain 'desirable' properties. The most important property is that the conceptual design is *accurate*, i.e., that it exactly covers the customer needs. Other desirable properties are, among others, that the development is straightforward, traceable, modular, flexible, declarative, transparent, incremental/agile, practically applicable, and implementation-independent. We will return to these properties later on.

Since user wishes usually start vague, incomplete, or even inconsistent, you cannot start with clearly formulated problems. Moreover, initial user wishes might change over time, for instance, due to new insights or external or internal changes. Nevertheless, the resulting conceptual design must be clear, consistent, and precise. Given the vagueness and uncertainties in the beginning versus the required preciseness in the later stages, you must apply a *wholistic* approach that considers the complete development path.

This book does not treat real implementations in depth, but Chap. 6 contains *directions* for implementation, e.g., directions for a realization using SQL, a standard language for databases.

Although we claim the applicability of this approach to the development of the functional requirements for an *information* system (IS), we think that our approach is applicable to the development of the functional requirements for various other systems as well, for instance, applicable to *control* systems; see Chap. 10.

1.2 Scope of the Book

What will be treated in the book and what not? The textbook covers the development of functional requirements, both the *dynamics* (Chaps. 2 and 3) and the *statics* (Chaps. 4 and 5). The book starts from elementary user wishes all the way to directions for implementation (Chap. 6). Moreover, Chap. 7 explains how a 'technical manager' can organize and manage such a development process.

The book does not study business processes. For a good book on business processes, we refer to Fundamentals of Business Process Management of Dumas et al. [Dum]. Also, the book does not treat *quality* requirements, a.k.a. 'non-functional'

Table 1.1 Scope of the book

	Business processes	**Elementary User Wishes**	**...**	**Directions for Implementation**	**Implementation ... deployment**
Functional Requirements (both statics and dynamics)		+	+	+	
Quality Requirements					

requirements. Table 1.1 gives an overview of the scope of the book. The book is about the colored part of Table 1.1, which is explained globally in the next section.

1.3 Global Contents of the Book

Essentially, the results of an analysis phase for a system to be developed consist of a description of the dynamics, describing the relevant *processes*, and a description of the statics, describing the relevant *data structures*. Chapter 2 presents the dynamics in the form of *textual System Sequence Descriptions* (textual SSDs), and Chap. 5 presents the statics in the form of a *Conceptual Data Model*.

When it comes to implementation design (Chap. 6), the conceptual data model is mapped to a data model according to the envisaged platform, while each interaction with the system expressed in a textual SSD might be implemented using a *procedure* or *method* according to the envisaged platform.

Together, the statics and the dynamics constitute a complete conceptual 'blueprint' of the system to be developed, as summarized in Table 1.2.

Chapters 2 and 3 explain how to model the *dynamics*. Chapter 2 works out a development path starting from an *elementary user wish* up to a *textual system sequence description*, while Chap. 3 sketches some *development patterns*.

Chapters 4 and 5 explain how to model the *statics*. Chapter 4 discusses *Domain Models*, which might be useful in an early stage of development, while Chap. 5 treats *Conceptual Data Models*.

Chapter 6 gives some *directions for implementation*, for the statics (via data models) as well as for the dynamics (via procedures).

Chapter 7 is of an organizational nature discussing how to organize and manage all this, from the point of view of a *technical manager*, not that of a general manager.

Part II of the book contains three illustrative case studies. In the first case study, the emphasis is on the *statics*, and in the second one, the emphasis is on the *dynamics*. The third case study illustrates the *interplay* between the dynamics and the statics.

Table 1.2 Overview of analysis and design results per aspect

	Aspect	Analysis results	Design results
Functional Requirements	Dynamics / Processes	Textual SSDs	Procedures or Methods
	Statics / Data structure	Conceptual Data Model	Data Model for implementation

1.4 Contents in Terms of Computing Disciplines and ACM Curricula

We can position the textbook in terms of computing curricula as well, say as mentioned by the Association for Computing Machinery on [ACM1]. Their Overview Report *Computing Curricula 2020* [CC20] distinguishes seven computing disciplines, of which three are relevant for us:

(a) Software engineering
(b) Computer science
(c) Information systems

In particular:

(a1) For *undergraduate* programs in *software engineering*, the textbook covers the knowledge area *Requirements Analysis and Specification* ([SE14], p.28 and p.31/32).
(a2) For *graduate* programs in *software engineering*, the textbook covers much of the knowledge area *Requirements Engineering* ([GSE09], p.37/38).
(b) For *undergraduate* programs in *computer science*, the textbook covers part of the knowledge area *Software Engineering*, in particular the knowledge unit *Requirements Engineering* ([CS13], p.178/179).
(c) For *undergraduate* programs in *information systems*, the textbook deepens some parts of the course *IS Project Management* ([IS10], p.48–50), e.g., regarding agile projects, not so much for the general (software) manager but more for the (technical) manager of a development project.

1.5 Intended Audience

The textbook is meant for:

- (Under)graduate students who want to learn how to carry out adequate problem analysis, to make good system specifications, and/or to understand how to organize and manage an IS development process
- Practitioners who want to improve their problem analysis abilities and/or their ability to make good system specifications.

1.6 Intended Learning Outcomes

After reading this textbook, the reader will be able to:

- Clarify, structure, and redefine inadequate—and changing—problem statements
- Ask adequate questions to the problem owner
- Make a precise, consistent, and complete system specification that can serve as a starting point for an implementation
- Make a design for an implementation using SQL
- Know how to organize and manage an IS development process, from the point of view of a technical manager

The first two learning outcomes relate to *problem analysis*, the third one to *specification*, the fourth one to *implementation*, and the last one to the *organization and management* of the development process.

All in all, the book helps the reader develop information systems accurately.

1.7 Sketch of the Problem Area

Developing an information system (IS) is a difficult and often elusive process, for several reasons. For instance:

(A) The language and way of thinking of the users is usually quite different from the language and way of thinking of developers:

- Users normally use imprecise unbounded natural language, with a lot of domain specific terms, and users often think in terms of only (business) processes, neglecting the underlying data structures.
- Developers, on the other hand, usually think in terms of abstract schema's, models, data, input/output, parameters, procedures/methods, etc.

(B) The set of user wishes is unclear, at least in the beginning (even though the requester might think it is clear): The set of user wishes is most likely incomplete and also growing over time, and the individual user wishes within the set might be unclear/vague and prone to changes as well. Reasons might be:

- Undefined or moving scope of the system: What are the boundaries of the system? Which (functional) part of the organization should be covered? In other words, what should be in the system, and what should be left out?
- Unclear functionality: What exactly should the system do, e.g., only registration, or also planning, or even automatic ordering of extra supplies?
- Which actors—people (user groups), sensors, and/or (software) systems—should interact with the system?
- Vague/undefined notions, especially the central ones in an organization. Typical examples are 'flight' in an airline company, 'study' and 'exam' in

a university, and 'bed' in a hospital. They are often *homonyms* as well, i.e., having several different meanings, though often closely related meanings.
- Confusion between closely related notions which, as a consequence, are not consistently used, at least initially (e.g., *base lot* versus *base stock*).

(C) Moreover, there might be dozens, hundreds, or even thousands of requirements. One of the largest numbers of requirements we heard about was more than 50,000 (in the automotive branch).

(D) Usually, a new system has to interact with other systems, existing or also under development. However, existing systems often have no, or poor, or only outdated documentation.

(E) On top of this, the development/introduction of the system might change the organization itself: People wake up, and the requirements analysis and/or (pilot) system might trigger new possibilities and new requirements.

As mentioned under (B), user wishes might initially be unclear, for instance, containing vague, subjective terms like 'suitable', 'useful', 'good', 'adequate', 'reasonable', etc. It is then up to the requirements analyst to ask the customer what they mean by those terms and, together with the customer, come to concretely checkable criteria that can be determined by the system or by the user or by the system and user in collaboration. For instance, the requirements analyst can ask the customer '*When do you consider it suitable?*' and try to come to checkable criteria.

On the other hand, concrete criteria might turn out to be used a bit 'fuzzy' after all, as illustrated in Example 1.1, taken from practice.

Example 1.1: Seemingly Concrete Criterion That Is Used 'Flexible'
In a production environment, say in the food industry, each produced item might get a *production date*. Well, the system can of course determine the date very easily. But those items might be produced in batches. If the production of a batch ends some minutes after midnight, then—for practical reasons—the few items produced after midnight might be given the date before midnight, just as the other items in the same batch ... 'But how long after midnight can this go on?' the requirements analyst might ask. 'Well, not too long', the customer might answer. Then the imprecise term 'not too long' must be made more concrete. The answer might be 'At most 25 minutes' or something like 'At most 25 minutes but for roast beef at most 10 minutes'. The customer might also add that the operator on duty must be able to decide whether or not to use this extension option and, if so, at which moment within the allowed time interval.

All in all, it seems that the system should, by default, use the 'current date' as the production date, but that the operator on duty must be able to instruct the system whether or not (and when) to use the extension option, while the system must guard the length: 'At most 25 minutes but for roast beef at most 10 minutes'.

What Example 1.1 also illustrates is that a decision might be entirely up to the user or entirely up to the system or a mixture in between. For example, maybe the system must check some boundaries, which might result in a refusal plus an error message, a warning ('*Then you will lose all your . . . !*'), or a consideration call ('*Are you sure?*') issued by the system. In the case of refusal, nothing will happen, but in the other two cases, the user might still let it happen. The choice for a solution type is primarily an organizational choice.

Problems (A)–(E) are relatively 'old' problems, which are already encountered for many decades. In the beginning of computerization, say roughly after World War II, well-established, stable, and well-understood *manual* processes were automated. However, later on, *new* processes in existing organizations had to be automated as well. But such new processes were often not yet well established and not yet so well understood. And nowadays, you often have to develop information systems for businesses that still have to be developed themselves. So, you then have *concurrent development* of a business (model) and its enabling information systems. Or, to rephrase this point shortly:

(F) Developing information systems went from automating well-known processes—say, which used to be paper-based before—to enabling entirely new business models, often even yet to start.

Therefore, the theme of Chaps. 2–5 of the book is:

How to overcome such 'communication' problems?

The following problems, (G) and (H), are newer problems too. They are managerial problems that are becoming stronger and stronger:

(G) The 'times to market' should become shorter and shorter, putting pressure on the development:

- Product variation and personalization is rapidly increasing nowadays.
- The speed with which new product versions appear increases constantly (mobile phones, etc.).

(H) Circumstances within the organization and in its professional or social environment might change during development and consequently also the set of requests, the individual requests themselves, and/or the conceptual data model. Example 4.5 is a nice illustration of a social change leading to a change in the conceptual data model.

So there are many uncertainties and unclarities. When developing an information system for an organization, you really have to understand that (changing) organization! When it is unclear what the customer really wants and needs, this might cause problems at the programmers' side as well. For example, programmers might fill in the functional gaps to the best of their own limited understanding/guessing.

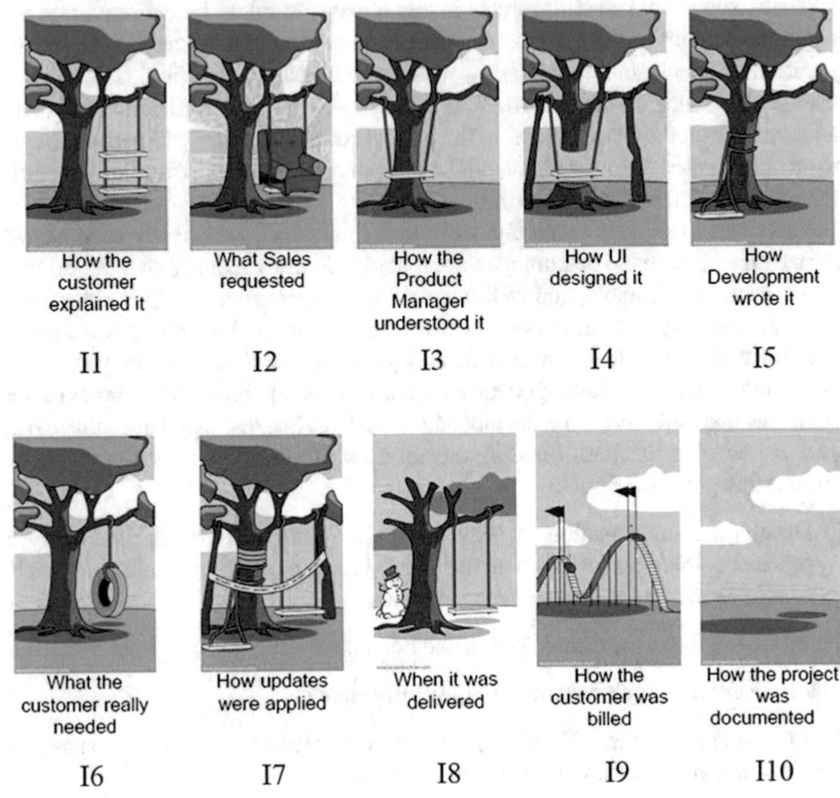

Fig. 1.2 The problem area

All these problems can have severe consequences for an IS development project, which might therefore be failing on all three *basic requirements* for a project:

(1)	The project delivers inadequate functionality	(too little)
(2)	The project is not within time	(too late)
(3)	The project is not within budget	(too costly)

Or even worse: The project has to be ended prematurely, usually after a lot of time and money has been spent, and without delivering any working functionality. Even after decades of experience, this still happens very frequently.

All in all, the problems ask *for high flexibility in development,* and the requirements are actually clear only *by the end* of the project.

Therefore, the theme of Chap. 7, the last chapter of Part I of the book, is:

How to organize and manage an IS development process?

Figure 1.2 illustrates some of the problems very nicely. For instance:

The five pictures I1–I5 illustrate problem (A): The users' language and way of thinking is often quite different from the language and way of thinking in the development organization. The pictures also illustrate another problem, namely, that the original customer info passes several 'noisy' intermediate stations before it reaches the actual designers and developers, who don't seem to have direct contacts with the customer. (You may know the game of *Hear-Say*, where a player whispers a sentence in the ear of the next player, who then whispers that sentence in the ear of the next player, etc. After a few steps, it becomes something completely different.)

Pictures I1 and I6 (*How the customer explained it* and *What the customer really needed*) illustrate problem (B): The real user wishes might be explained wrongly.

Pictures I5 and I7 (*How Development wrote it* and *How updates were applied*) illustrate Project Problem (1): The project delivered inadequate functionality.

Picture I8 (*When it was delivered*) illustrates Project Problem (2): The project is not within time.

Picture I9 (*How the customer was billed*) illustrates Project Problem (3): The project is not within budget.

Picture I10 (*How the project was documented*) illustrates how problem (D) can live on: There is no—or poor—documentation of the new system.

1.8 Our Approach

We emphasize *stepwise clarification*, *stepwise refinement*, *stepwise specification*, and (very) *iterative and incremental development* when developing an information system. Some of the reasons are that the user wishes might still be unclear and maybe prone to change as well and that the set of user wishes is most likely incomplete, at least initially, and growing over time; see Sect. 1.7. Another important reason is that the circumstances within the user organization and in its environment might change quickly and consequently also the set of user wishes itself. Therefore, developing an information system can better be done incrementally and (very) iteratively. We will illustrate our approach with various practical examples.

1.9 Goals on Different Levels

We can distinguish goals on different levels. We respectively explicate the goals:

1. of an *information system*
2. of *system development*
3. of *problem analysis*

1. Usually, the consecutive goals of an information system (IS) are:

   (a) Registration of (many) elementary transactions (*operational* level)
   (b) Support tactical tasks (*middle management* level)
   (c) Support strategic decision-making/decision-makers (*top management* level)

Explanation per goal of an information system:

(a) Usually, the first goal of an IS is the registration of elementary transactions, e.g., the student enrolments, the course enrolments, the exam results, etc.
(b) Then middle management (e.g., course coordinators and program directors) can use that elementary data for their purposes, e.g., retrieve the number of enrolments for a course, or the average grade per course in a program.
(c) Also top management (e.g., faculty board and university board) can use that data for their purposes, e.g., retrieve the number of students (or courses) per program, the number of students (or courses) per faculty, or the 'success rate' per program or faculty.

In general, the goal is to increase the efficiency, effectivity, and possibilities of the organization.

2. The primary goal and primary condition of system development are:

   (a) The primary goal: create value for the organization and deliver value quickly.
   (b) The primary condition: the system must be *useful for*, *useable by*, and also *used by* the user.

3. The goals of problem analysis are:

   (a) Find out what the users want and need: the *requirements*
   (b) Create a model as a basis for the design of the system
   (c) Produce (intermediate) products that contain everything needed for the designer

1.10 Functional and Quality Requirements

We can distinguish many types of requirements for an information system. A well-known acronym in this context is **FURPS**, which stands for:

- Functionality
- Usability
- Reliability
- Performance
- Supportability

Then there is the notion of **FURPS+** as well, i.e., FURPS plus some other requirements, such as:

- Design requirements
- Interface requirements
- Implementation requirements
- Physical requirements

- Legal requirements
- Ethical requirements

There exist other requirements classifications as well.

A main distinction is often made between the *functional requirements* for a system and the other requirements. Those other requirements are called *quality requirements* or *non-functional requirements* (a strange name, frankly speaking).

Although we sometimes touch upon some quality requirements, we do not really treat them. The focus of this book is on **functional requirements**, i.e., the functionality the system should provide. In other words: What the system must be able to do. Or, more concretely, its input/output behavior: Which inputs should the system accept and what should the corresponding outputs and state changes be?

1.11 Summary

The subject of the book is how to develop the functional requirements of an (information) system or, in other words, how to uncover (initial) user wishes and come to a conceptual design. Since user wishes usually start vague, incomplete, and sometimes even inconsistent, you will not start with clearly formulated problems. Moreover, initial user wishes might change during the development project, e.g., due to new insights or due to external or internal changes.

We distinguish between functional requirements and quality requirements for a system. The focus of the book is on **functional requirements**, i.e., which functionality the system should provide (what the system must be able to do) or, more concretely, its input/output behavior (which inputs should the system accept and what should the corresponding outputs and state changes be?).

The main intended audience for the book consists of

- (Under)graduate students who want to learn to carry out adequate problem analyses, to make good system specifications, and/or to understand how to organize and manage IS development processes
- Practitioners who want to improve and streamline their problem analysis and/or specifications skills

The intended learning outcomes of the textbook are that the reader will be able to:

- Clarify, structure, and redefine inadequate—and changing—problem statements
- Ask adequate questions to the problem owner
- Make a good system design that can serve as a starting point for implementation
- Make a design for an implementation using SQL
- Know how to organize and manage an IS development process, from the point of view of a technical manager

Some of the problems of developing an information system are the following:

(A) The language and way of thinking of users and of developers are (very) different.
(B) The set of user wishes is initially unclear, most likely incomplete, and growing and changing over time and might be(come) inconsistent.
(C) There might be very many requirements.
(D) Often there is no, or poor, or only outdated documentation of other systems with which the new system has to interact.
(E) The requirements analysis and/or (pilot) system might trigger new opportunities, new wishes, new requirements, and changes in the organization itself.
(F) Developing information systems went from supporting well-understood processes to enabling entirely new business models, often even yet to start.
(G) The times to market should become shorter and shorter.
(H) Meanwhile, circumstances in the organization and environment might change.

All in all, the requirements might be clear only *by the end of the project...*

We will approach these problems by stepwise clarification, stepwise refinement, stepwise specification, and (very) iterative and incremental development when developing an information system.

The contents of Part I of the book summarized in a nutshell: Chaps. 2–5 of the book treat how to overcome the communication problems, Chap. 6 sketches some directions for implementation, and Chap. 7 sketches how to organize and manage all this.

Part I
Theory

Part I is organized as follows:

- Chapters 2 and 3 explain how to develop the functional requirements that represent the conceptual *dynamics* of an information system.
- Chapters 4 and 5 explain how to model the conceptual *statics* of an information system.
- Chapter 6 gives some directions for implementation.
- Chapter 7 explains how a 'technical manager' can organize and manage the development process.

The chapters of Part I in an overview:

Analysis and Specification	*Directions for Implementation*
Ch. 2 & 3: Dynamics Ch. 4 & 5: Statics	Ch. 6
Ch. 7: Organization and management	

Chapter 2
Developing a Functional Requirement

Abstract This chapter treats the development path of an individual *functional requirement* (FR). Chapter 7 discusses how to manage a (large) set of functional requirements, a set which will (initially) not be delimited clearly and is also constantly changing.

This chapter starts with an *overview* of the development path of an FR (Sect. 2.1). Then it delves deeper into the notions concerned: *user wishes* (Sect. 2.2), *user stories* (Sect. 2.3), *use cases* (Sect. 2.4), (textual) *system sequence descriptions* (SSDs, Sect. 2.5), *forms* (Sect. 2.6), and *scenario integration* (Sect. 2.7). Section 2.8 works out how to map *textual* SSDs to natural language and to *graphical* SSDs in a systematic way. This is useful for validation, for explanation, and also for customer-friendly documentation.

Finally, Sect. 2.9 summarizes our approach to develop a functional requirement and writes it out as an *IS development* business process.

2.1 Development Path for an Individual FR: An Overview

Section 2.1 sketches, in a nutshell, the beginning of a development path for an individual functional requirement (FR), summarized in Table 2.1 and Fig. 2.1.

The basic ideas behind the development path for a functional requirement are *stepwise clarification*, *stepwise refinement*, and *stepwise specification*. Moreover, we gradually go from users' language and way of thinking to developers' language and way of thinking.

As the starting point for developing an FR, we came up with the notion of an **elementary user wish** (eUW), a 'half-liner' in natural language expressing an FR. For example, in case of an administration system for a university, user wishes might be *Register a Student*, *Handle an Enrolment*, or *Update the info about a Course*. It should be relatively easy for users to come up with such elementary user wishes.

Another clarification question is: *Who*—or *which systems*—will need this FR [and *why*]? The answer should not be on the level of individual persons, for example, 'John Smith and Mary Jones', but on the level of roles, say a 'Student administrator'.

B. de Brock, *Developing Information Systems Accurately*,
https://doi.org/10.1007/978-3-031-16862-8_2

Table 2.1 Introduced notions, their abbreviations, and some comparisons

FR	Functional Requirement	
UW	User wish, either an eUW or a pUW	
eUW	Elementary user wish (without parameters)	
pUW	Parameterized user wish	pUW ≡ eUW + input parameters
US	User Story	US ≡ UW + actor [+ benefit(s)]
UC	Use Case	UC ≡ MSS + AS*
MSS	Main Success Scenario	
AS	Alternative Scenario	
SSD	System Sequence Description	
tSSD	textual SSD	
gSSD	graphical SSD	

eUW => US => UC = MSS + AS* => tSSD => software procedures

⇙ ⇘

For validation: NL-text gSSD

Fig. 2.1 The development path of a functional requirement

As indicated by the square brackets, the why-part might be left out. The combination of a user wish, a role, and an optional benefit part constitutes what is known as a **user story** (US). The most popular template for a user story is:

As a <role>**, I want to** <user wish> [**so that** <benefit>]

As Cohn says in his blog Why the Three-Part User Story Template Works So Well [Cohn3], it indicates the *who* (<role>), *what* (<user wish>), and *why* (<benefit>).

The template originated with Rachel Davies while working at the company Connextra. This template is now known under the name *Connextra template* [Cohn]. For our example, this template would lead to:

> ***As a*** *Student administrator,* ***I want to*** *Register a Student*
> ***so that*** *(s)he can follow a study*

Although the benefit part is optional, it helps to distinguish the important from the frivolous user stories, as Cohn puts it in User Stories Applied: For Agile Software Development [Cohn].

The next clarification question could be: Which *input parameters* are needed? In the example, it could be *name*, *address*, *birth date*, *phone number*, *gender* (?), and *social security number*. The *student number* and *university e-mail address* of the student might not be *input* parameters but values to be generated by the system upon registration. It is up to the user organization to say what they want. We call an elementary user wish plus input parameters a **parameterized user wish** (pUW). In our example, the parameterized user wish would be:

Register a Student with a given name, address, birth date, phone number, gender, and social security number where the original *elementary* user wish is underlined.

The next step is that the customer writes a *use case* for the FR. A **use case** (UC) is a text in natural language that describes the sequence of steps in a typical usage of the system. A use case corresponds roughly to an *elementary business process* in business process modelling. In our example, the use case could run as follows:

1. The *Student administrator* asks the system to *Register a Student* with a given name, address, birth date, phone number, gender, and social security number.
2. The system generates a new *student number* and *university e-mail address* based on the name of the student.
3. The system registers the student with the name, address, birth date, phone number, gender, and social security number, together with the generated student number and university e-mail address.
4. The system informs the student administrator about the generated student number and university e-mail address.

Actually, this is only what is usually called its **Main Success Scenario** (MSS) or sometimes its *happy path scenario* or its *sunny-day scenario*. More neutral names are *Main Scenario*, *Basic Scenario*, and *Basic Flow*. Anyway, it is a typical or 'standard' flow in which everything goes 'well', without any complications.

Which complications could occur in our student registration example? Well, the phone number might be unknown or absent, the mentioned phone number and/or social security number might have a wrong format, or the registration is simply too late, or too early, to name just a few possibilities.

In general, a use case can have various so-called *alternative scenarios* as well. An **alternative scenario** (AS) describes the alternative sequence of steps for such a case. So, a use case consists of an MSS plus several alternative scenarios. Or, in a 'formula', where '*' indicates zero or more:

$$\boxed{\text{UC} = \text{MSS} + \text{AS}^*}$$

Since alternative scenarios describe the *correct* completion of alternative situations, you might call them *successful* as well, e.g., the correct refusal of a late registration. Therefore, we would prefer a more neutral name for *Main Success Scenario*, such as *Main Scenario*, *Basic Scenario*, or *Basic Flow*, but *Main Success Scenario* (MSS) is the established name.

It is important to note that until now everything was expressed in natural language: user wishes, user stories, and use cases. That means that they can be written by, discussed with, and checked by the people in the user organization.

Our next step is to *integrate* the MSS and the ASs of a use case. Moreover, we want to represent the use case in a schematic way. Therefore, we introduce *system sequence descriptions*. A **system sequence description** (SSD) of a use case schematically depicts the interactions between the primary actor (user), the system (as a black box), and other actors (if any), including the messages between them. The *primary actor* of a use case is the one (i.e., the role) that starts the use case. We will introduce the notion of a ***textual* SSD** (tSSD) for these schematic descriptions.

A basic step in a textual SSD has the form:

$$X \rightarrow Y: M$$

which has to be read as '*Actor X sends M to actor Y*' when Y≠X and as '*Actor X does/executes M*' when Y=X.

As an illustration of our textual SSDs, we work out the textual SSD for our student registration example, integrating the MSS plus one AS, namely, the AS where the registration period might be over. In that scenario, the original steps 2–4 will not be executed, and the user will be informed accordingly. The textual SSD might be as follows, where U stands for User and S for System:

U ➡ S: Register a Student with the given parameter values [(1)];
S ➡ S: Check whether the registration period is over ;
if the registration period is over
  then S ➡ U: 'Sorry, but the registration period is over'
  else S ➡ S: Generate a new *student number* and *university e-mail address* ;
    S ➡ S: Register the student with the given [(1)] and generated [(2)] values ;
    S ➡ U: The generated student number and university e-mail address
end

[(1)] name, address, birth date, phone number, gender, and social security number
[(2)] student number and university e-mail address

For our convenience, we enumerated the parameters in isolated footnotes because those lists of parameters may 'grow' during the development of the system.

The basic step of the form 'U ➡ S: ...' expresses what the user sends to the system, the two basic steps of the form 'S ➡ U: ...' express what the system sends to the user, and the three basic steps of the form 'S ➡ S: ...' express what the system must do internally.

So, from the elementary user wish *Register a Student*, we arrived at a textual SSD that spells out and structures the sequence of steps to be taken by the user and by the system, with the MSS and the alternative scenario integrated.

Sometimes the same use case might turn out to be relevant for several other roles as well. In case of our—fictitious—university, for instance, it might turn out that also a secretary can register a student, not only the student administrator. Therefore, we prefer to use the word 'User' instead of mentioning specific roles in an SSD. The applicable roles can be denoted separately elsewhere.

The development path for an FR so far can now be summarized as follows:

$$\boxed{\text{eUW} \Rightarrow \text{US} \Rightarrow \text{UC} = \text{MSS} + \text{AS}^* \Rightarrow \text{tSSD}}$$

For validation purposes, it would be useful to validate the resulting textual SSD with the user organization. For that purpose, Sect. 2.8.1 contains *generation* rules to translate the textual SSDs step by step to *natural language* (NL), in this case to English.

Some people are used to—and comfortable with—*graphical* SSDs, also known as (*system*) *sequence diagrams*, for instance, in UML (see https://www.uml.org). A graphical SSD (gSSD) can give a quick overview, e.g., of the actors involved. Graphical SSDs might support validation too. Therefore, Sect. 2.8.2 contains rules to systematically *generate* graphical SSDs from our textual SSDs.

Chapter 6 explains that a textual SSD can be implemented by one or more software procedures.

Table 2.1 and Fig. 2.1 summarize this overview: Table 2.1 recalls the introduced notions with their abbreviations as well as some comparisons between them, while Fig. 2.1 recalls the complete development path of a functional requirement.

Sections 2.2–2.8 work out these individual notions and the steps of the development path in more detail.

2.2 User Wishes

This section zooms in on user wishes. We distinguish between *elementary* user wishes and *parameterized* user wishes.

2.2.1 Elementary User Wishes

An **elementary user wish** (eUW) is a 'wish' of a (future) user which the system should be able to fulfil. An elementary user wish is typically a 'half-liner' expressed in natural language (so, even shorter than a one-liner), for example, *Register a Student* or *Process a Sale*. An elementary user wish can be the starting point of the development of a functional requirement (FR). An elementary user wish might end up as an option in a menu structure; see Sect. 2.3. An elementary user wish can originate from the prospective user, his/her boss, a domain expert, (important) customers, 'the public', or other (internal or external) stakeholders.

A user wish often has the form:

<(action) verb> **a** <noun (phrase)>

such as the two examples given in the previous paragraph. Examples in a registration system for a university could be any combination of:

Register / Retrieve / Update / Remove **a**
Student / Lecturer / Course / Course Enrolment / Exam Enrolment / Exam / Grading

As you can see from the previous examples, the *noun phrases* heavily depend on the application area: They are *application specific*. They usually hint at the relevant *concepts* and *properties* in the application under consideration. Therefore, the noun phrases typically are related to the *statics*.

Table 2.2 Some alternatively used CRUD verbs

CRUD	Some alternatively used action verbs
Create	Register, Add, Enter, Insert, Store
Read	Retrieve, View, See, Search, Select, Get
Update	Refresh, Change, Modify, Edit, Alter, Adapt, Replace, Rename
Delete	Remove, Erase, Destroy

The *action verbs*, on the other hand, are often more generally applicable and usually are related to the *dynamics*.

The literature recognizes four general basic functions applicable to *data* in a system:

- add data to the system (Create)
- only look at data in the system (Read)
- change data in the system (Update)
- remove data from the system (Delete)

In the literature, the acronym **CRUD** (Create, Read, Update, and Delete) refers to these four general basic functions. Although this acronym might be associated with databases and computer programming, it already makes sense on conceptual level.

Preferably, the action verb in the elementary user wish should already indicate what should be done with the data (CRUD). The action verb should indicate *what* should be done with the data (i.e., the intent), not *how* it should be done. So, *Enter* is better than *Scan* or *Type in* (or *Speak in*). The way the data is entered might change over time, but the intent stays the same. Table 2.2 contains some alternative action verbs you might encounter.

When a course will no longer be given, or a student leaves the university, the corresponding data can be deleted, it seems. However, that data might be needed later, say for monthly or yearly reporting. Archiving might then be needed, and even obligatory, due to legal retention periods, e.g., in governmental situations. Therefore, instead of *deleting* certain data, it might be needed to *archive* that data. Therefore, we add a fifth basic function to CRUD:

- archive data in the system (Archive)

replacing CRUD by **CRUDA**.

In a sense, the CRUDA-functions are a kind of basic functions. However, a user wish might be more complicated, consisting of a combination of basic functions. In that case, verbs like *Handle* (a Measurement, an Order, etc.) or *Process* (a Sale, a Request, etc.) might be used.

2.2.2 Parameterized User Wishes

We call a 'half-liner' as described in Sect. 2.2.1 an ***elementary* user wish** (eUW). What is still missing are the necessary *input parameters*. Together with the user organization, you have to find out what the relevant input parameters for a user wish are. We will call an elementary user wish plus input parameters a ***parameterized* user wish** (pUW). In a simple 'formula':

pUW = eUW + input parameters

For instance, what are the relevant input parameters for the elementary user wish *Update a Student address*? The *new address*, of course. The *student number*, or the *social security number* (to identify the student)? It might turn out that not all (foreign) students have a social security number but that all students do have a student number. The *current address*? No, not necessarily. Moreover, once the student is identified, you can probably find the student info and check his/her current address, if you want. So, all in all, the parameterized user wish could be:

Update the address of a Student with a given student number and a given new address

You have to distinguish whether a value for a parameter is *required* (i.e., never absent) or *optional* (i.e., might be absent). For instance, the user wish *Register a Student* in Sect. 2.1 had the input parameters *name*, *address*, *birth date*, *phone number*, *gender*, and *social security number*. However, since not all (international) students have a social security number (SSN), the SSN might be optional. And maybe students are not obliged to mention their gender. And also the phone number might be optional. So, all in all, for the elementary user wish *Register a Student*, the parameterized user wish could become:

Register a Student *with a given name, address, birth date, maybe phone number, maybe gender, and maybe social security number*

As pointed out for the elementary user wish *Register a Student* in Sect. 2.1, the *student number* and *university e-mail address* might be generated by the system upon registration and, hence, are not *input* parameters in that case.

Retrieval means requesting the system for information without changing the state. With retrieval, there can be *optional* parameters too, as the next example illustrates:

Retrieve total sales amount [over a given period] [per department] [per product]

where the parts between brackets are optional. Here, *period* could even be split into *since b* and *until e*, each of them being optional as well. That would lead to:

Retrieve total sales amount [since <begin date>] [until <end date>] [per department] [per product]

Actually, the options account for several retrievals, 2 * 2 * 2 * 2 in this case (when neglecting the parameters *begin date* and *end date*).

2.3 User Stories

A clarification question about a user wish might be: *Who*—or *which systems*—are the ones that need this user wish [and why]? As indicated, the why-part might be left out. The combination of an elementary user wish, a role, and an optional benefit part constitutes what is known as a **user story** (US). User stories originate from Kent Beck, back in 1997, and are popular as a method for representing requirements, especially in agile development environments. According to Lucassen in Understanding User Stories [Luc], the most popular template for a user story is:

As a <role>**, I want to** <user wish> [**so that** <benefit>]

As mentioned in Sect. 2.1, this template is commonly known under the name *Connextra template* [Cohn]. The role might also be something like 'Guest'. Some examples of user stories, sometimes without a benefit part:

- **As a** *Student administrator*, **I want to** *Register a Student*
- **As a** *Course coordinator*, **I want to** *Retrieve the number of enrolments for a course* **so that** *I can plan a room*
- **As a** *Planner*, **I want to** *Update the availability of a room* **so that** *we don't get double bookings*
- **As a** *Planner*, **I want to** *Delete a room reservation* **so that** *the room is available for bookings again*

From a set of user wishes and the corresponding roles, you can simply derive a 'user wish menu' for each role. Suppose you have the user wishes and corresponding roles as indicated in Table 2.3, where *CSA* stands for *Central Student Administration* and where UW8 has associated two roles.

On the main menu level hereafter, we neglect the options such as in UW6 and UW7. They could appear on submenu level. Table 2.4 indicates the user wishes per role.

Some people like to depict this information in a so-called **use case diagram**, a graphical representation of the possible interactions of users with the system. In its simplest form, part of the use case diagram for this example would be as shown in Fig. 2.2. For more drawing options, see https://Plantuml.com/use-case-diagram.

2.4 Use Cases

A **use case** (UC) is a text in natural language that describes a sequence of actions in a typical usage of the system. A use case should describe one session with the system. A use case should be written by the user. A use case can be considered as a further elaboration of a *user wish*, with much more detail. Use cases originate from Ivar Jacobson, back in 1987. Section 2.1 already contains a small example.

Table 2.3 Some sample roles and user wishes

	Role(s)	Elementary user wish
UW1	Sysadmin	Initialize the state
UW2	CSA-employee	Create a Student
UW3	Program director	Create a Course
UW4	Program secretary	Create a Course Registration
UW5	Student	Create a Course Registration for me
UW6	CSA-employee	Retrieve the number of students [per gender] [registered since date d]
UW7	Program director	Retrieve the set of my Courses [each with the number of Course Registrations]
UW8	Program director, Program secretary	Retrieve the Registrations for a Course
UW9	Student	Retrieve all my Course Registrations
UW10	CSA-employee	Update a Student address
UW11	Student	Update my address
UW12	Program director	Update a Course name
UW13	CSA-employee	Delete a Student (plus his/her registrations)
UW14	Program director	Delete a Course
UW15	Program secretary	Delete a Course Registration
UW16	Student	Delete my Registration for a Course
UW17	Guest	Show all Courses

Table 2.4 The 'user wish menu' per role

Sysadmin	**Guest**
• Initialize the state	• Show all Courses
CSA-employee • Create a Student • Retrieve the number of students • Update a Student address • Delete a Student (plus his/her registrations)	**Program director** • Create a Course • Retrieve the set of my Courses • Update a Course name • Delete a Course • Retrieve the Registrations for a Course
Program secretary • Create a Course Registration • Retrieve the Registrations for a Course • Delete a Course Registration	**Student** • Create a Course Registration for me • Retrieve all my Course Registrations • Update my address • Delete my Registration for a Course

A use case roughly corresponds to an *elementary business process* in business process modelling (BPM). What we call a use case is sometimes known as a *system use case*, as opposed to a so-called *business use case*, which in general has a broader scope and describes a business process even if the process does not have any interaction with a (software) system.

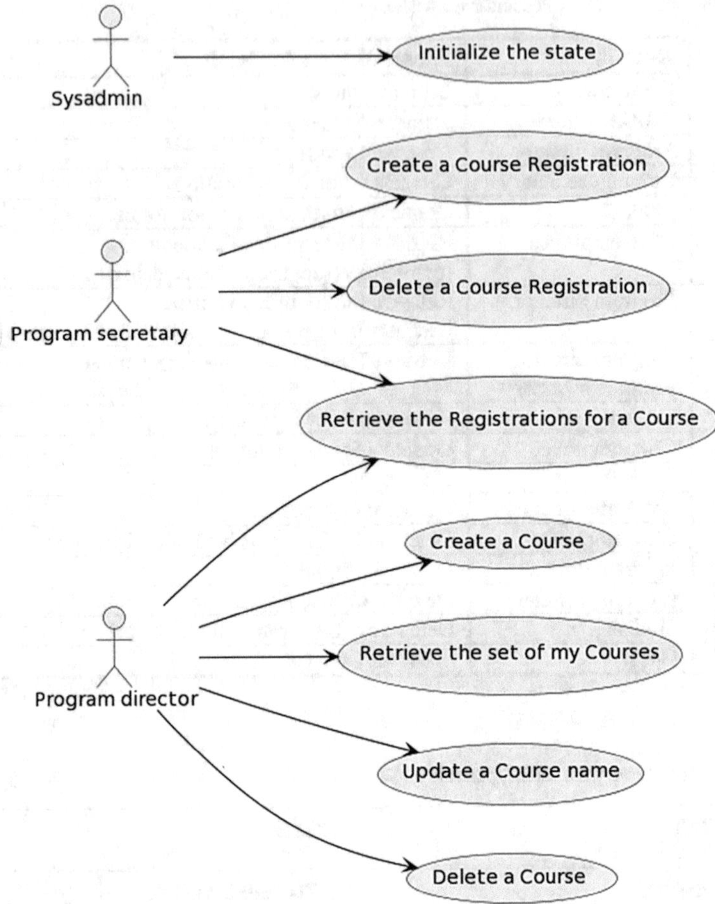

Fig. 2.2 Part of a simple use case diagram

2.4.1 *Main Success Scenario and Alternative Scenarios*

A use case usually consists of a *main success scenario* (MSS) and zero or more *alternative scenarios*. Or, in a simple 'formula', where AS stands for alternative scenario and '*' for zero or more:

$$\boxed{UC = MSS + AS^*}$$

The **main success scenario** (MSS) of a use case describes its normal 'success' path, i.e., when all conditions are satisfied, all (silent) presuppositions are true, no errors occur, and no exceptional situations show up, in other words, the scenario in which everything goes 'well'.

As explained in Sect. 2.1, we would prefer a more neutral name, such as *main scenario* or *basic scenario*, but *main success scenario* is the established name, and we will use the abbreviation MSS for it.

A pattern for a (very) simple MSS could be:

1. **The User asks the System to** <parameterized User Wish>**.**
2. **The System tries to do** <parameterized User Wish>**.**
3. **The System sends** <Result> **to the User.**

where the User has the role as was mentioned in the user story. Upon successful execution, <Result> might be:

- In case of a *mutation* (Create, Update, Delete, Archive):
  'Done' and maybe some more information, e.g., any system-generated values
- In case of a retrieval (Read): the information asked for

If the execution is not successful, <Result> might contain the reason(s) why the user wish could not be executed.

An **Alternative Scenario** (AS)—a.k.a. an **Extension**—of a use case describes another potential *execution path* of the use case, besides its MSS. In practice, various alternative scenarios for a use case will turn up, e.g., because some input parameter values might refer to a non-existing entity ('*Unknown student number*') or might have a wrong format, or because there might be special cases (exceptions) which have to be treated differently, e.g., foreign students or students from a different faculty. Or in our sample user wish *Register a Student*, it could be that the registration attempt happens outside the registration period and so might be too late, or too early. What to do then? Here, we might need two alternative scenarios describing an alternative path: one for 'too late' and one for 'too early'. As noted in Sect. 2.1, since alternative scenarios describe the *correct* completion of alternative situations, you might call them *successful* too.

A straightforward scenario—say, without branching—could consist of a sequence of sentences of one of the following forms, among other possibilities:

S1. The User asks the System to <parameterized User Wish>.
S2. The System checks <condition(s)>.
S3. The System asks the User for <extra info>.
S4. The User does <own action>.
S5. The User sends back <requested info>.
S6. The System does <subsequent action(s)>.
S7. The System sends <result/request> to <secondary actor>.
S8. The System sends <result> to the User.

Some clarification:

S1: The user—i.e., the primary actor—'triggers' the use case.
This step is a typical candidate for the first step in an MSS.
S2: The system might need to check all kinds of conditions;
this might lead to the need for alternative scenarios.

S3: The system might need some extra information, e.g., based on the checks.
S4: Sometimes the user must do something without using the system.
S5: The user sends back the requested information.
S6: Might be CRUDA-action(s).
S7: <secondary actor> could be another person or another system.
S8: A typical candidate for the last step in an MSS.

In summary: A use case is a text in natural language (written by the user organization), describes functionalities (maybe implicitly), describes one session with the system, and can start simple (with only an MSS) but might become quite intricate (because of many ASs, which are not always mutually independent either). Each scenario describes a potential *execution path.*

2.4.2 Core Ingredients of a Use Case

Besides its MSS and ASs, other ingredients for a use case can be distinguished as well, most notably (provided with some explanation):

Use Case Title
The underlying elementary user wish might be a good candidate for the title, e.g., *Register a Student* or *Process a Sale.*

Rationale/Context
Explanation why—and when—this use case is needed. Might be (very) clarifying.
Actually works out the *benefit part* of the underlying user story in more detail

Primary Actor
The role 'calling' the use case. Can be a human being, a sensor, or another system.
The *role* in the underlying user story is the obvious candidate

Preconditions
The (nontrivial) minimal condition(s) to be satisfied before the use case can start. We note that '*less is more*' here: fewer preconditions will imply larger applicability. See mistakes M10 and M11 in Sect. 2.4.5 for counterexamples. Often sufficient is something like:

'*The user is authenticated by the system as a <role>*
and authorised to use this use case'

Here <role> can be the role in the underlying user story. If the role is 'Guest', then there might even be no preconditions. Other potentially unsatisfied conditions can be handled in their 'own' separate ASs (e.g., in case a student number in unknown).

Postconditions
Conditions holding after execution of use case. Consists essentially of two parts:

- A specification of the *state change result*: the new state in terms of the old state
- A specification of the *output*, also for each alternative scenario. For instance: 'No state change' with an 'error' message specific for that AS

Main Success Scenario (MSS)
The normal 'success' path, i.e., the scenario in which everything goes 'well'.

The MSS should satisfy the envisaged postconditions.

Alternative Scenarios (ASs)
Usually—by far—the largest ingredient, since a use case might have many ASs. Each AS describes the alternative sequence of steps for some specific, 'deviating' situation. The ASs and their postconditions should match.

Frequency of Use
How often (roughly) will this use case be used? Might indicate whether the use case plays a central role and whether performance issues might be(come) important.

Some typical values:

- Once a day/week/month/quarter/year
- Five employees several times a day
- Hundreds of people almost continuously worldwide

Open Issues
Questions still left open/unanswered. Can be empty

Miscellaneous
Everything else worth remembering. Can be empty—or left out—if not applicable

The contents of most ingredients should originate from the user organization, but the pre- and postconditions can be formulated by a requirements engineer. The contents of the ingredients *Open Issues* and *Miscellaneous* might (mainly) come from the requirements engineer.

We will now work out an example containing all those ingredients:

Example 2.1: Core Ingredients of a Sample Use Case

Use Case Title	Register a Student
Rationale/Context	Students can register for the university in the period from May 1 to October 1 via the Central Student Administration (CSA). A CSA-employee first does some manual checking before an administrator registers the student
Primary Actor	Administrator of the Central Student Administration

(continued)

Example 2.1 (continued)

Preconditions The user is authenticated as a CSA-administrator and authorized to use this use case

Postconditions

Output

If the registration period is there, the output must be
the generated student number and generated university e-mail address.

If the registration period is over, the output must be
'Unfortunately, the registration period is over' (or so).

If the registration period is not yet there, the output must be something like
'The registration period is from May 1 to October 1'.

State change

If the registration period is not yet there or over, there must be *no* state change.
If the registration period is there, the new state must be the old state plus one student with the given values[(1)] and the generated values for student number and university e-mail address.

[(1)]for name, address, birth date, phone number, gender, and social security number

Main Success Scenario (see Sect. 2.1)

1. The CSA-administrator asks the system to Register a Student with a given name, address, birth date, phone number, gender, and social security number (SSN).
2. The system generates a new *student number* and *university e-mail address* based on the name of the student.
3. The system registers the student with the name, address, birth date, phone number, gender, social security number, and the generated student number and university e-mail address.
4. The system informs the CSA-administrator about the generated student number and e-mail address.

Alternative Scenarios (written in so-called *casual format*)

AS1. If the registration period is over, the user will be informed about it, and nothing else happens.
AS2. If the registration period is not yet there, the user will be informed about the proper registration period, and nothing else happens.

(continued)

Example 2.1 (continued)

AS3. The system will (try to) check whether the student is already registered —e.g., searching for the SSN—and, if so, informs the user about it and asks what should happen next.

Frequency of Use

Roughly 5000 times between May 1 and October 1 (during working days)

Open Issues

1. Doesn't a student register for a particular *study*?
2. Shouldn't this use case be available only from May 1 to October 1?
3. Between October 1 and May 1, the previous registration period is over, and the next one isn't there yet. When should we go over from the 'too late' message to the 'too early' message?
4. Related to Alternative Scenario AS3: Are SSNs really unique (if filled in)? Or could students from different countries accidentally have the same SSN?

Miscellaneous

The university seriously considers the possibility to start a study in February as well, initially for only some studies. The consequences for this use case are not clear yet.

Some additional remarks

The answer of the university to the first open issue might be that a student first has to register for the university and only then (s)he can register for a particular study, but that the student can do that second step him/herself. So, this suggests that there should come another use case as well: *Register me for a study*, with the student as the primary actor.

The answer to the second open issue might be that the *head* of the CSA-department is allowed to register a student outside that period too, because of special circumstances, e.g., because the university itself made a mistake.

2.4.3 Other Potential Ingredients of a Use Case

Additional ingredients for a use case might be distinguished as well. Several authors/ companies distinguish various other ingredients too; see https://templatelab.com/use-case-templates, for instance. Examples of such other ingredients are discussed below.

Use Case ID

Useful for referential purposes, especially when there are many use cases. When there are very many use cases or different development teams, a Use Case ID could even be (sub)structured, e.g., 'UC3.5', indicating Use Case 5 within 'sub-area' 3

Scope
Usually the 'system under consideration'.

Becomes relevant if there are several 'systems under consideration'

Level
For instance:

- *User-goal*: a use case to be started by a user
- *Subfunction*: a use case called within another use case, e.g., a payment-UC

However, a use case can occur on both 'levels'. For instance, the use case *Register as a customer* ('user-goal') can also be an optional subfunction within the use case *Place an order*.

Trigger
The action that starts the use case. So, in principle, it is the first step in the use case. It may be a time(r) event, so a trigger by 'the clock'.

Secondary Actors
Actors involved in the use case besides the primary actor and the system (if any). Might be human beings, sensors, actuators, and/or other systems

Stakeholders and Interests
Who care about this use case and why (their interests). The *primary actor* is one of them, likely with the *benefit*-part of the underlying user story as a concrete interest. Typical examples of stakeholders might be members of the company's executive board, regulatory bodies, and tax authorities, even though they might not directly interact with the system themselves.

This UC-ingredient might also trigger hints for further specific requirements for the use case, e.g., a confirmation toward the customer or another stakeholder to be informed or even new use cases, e.g., potential stakeholder wishes.

Special Requirements
Usually 'non-functional' (i.e., quality) requirements worth remembering.

Could alternatively be a subparagraph of *Miscellaneous*. Can be empty

Technology List
For example, I/O methods worth remembering.

Could alternatively be a subparagraph of *Miscellaneous*. Can be empty

Data Variations List
For example, data formats worth remembering.

Could alternatively be a subparagraph of *Miscellaneous*. Can be empty

Various authors/companies distinguish even more ingredients for a use case, e.g., ingredients relevant for management or ingredients which can appear in later stages.

Some examples are as follows: priority (among all other use cases to be developed), development status, due date, responsible (main) developer, development team, relevant business rules, performance constraints/expectations, and all kinds of other quality requirements such as user interface requirements, (non-)concurrency requirements, security requirements, privacy requirements, etc.

2.4.4 Some Guidelines for Writing Use Cases (Do's)

Now we mention some guidelines for writing good use cases, the so-called *dos*. Some of them were already (implicitly) mentioned earlier. Section 2.4.5 contains several *don'ts*.

G1. Try to be as clear as possible, all the time! Although this sounds like an open door, it is maybe the most important—and difficult—guideline of them all, but also a challenging one, because your insight increases all the time.

G2. A good candidate for the use case title might be the underlying user wish, for instance, *Register a Student*. A user wish might have the form:

<(action) verb> **a** <noun (phrase)>

The action verb in the user wish might already indicate what should be done; see also Sect. 2.2.1 (*Elementary user wishes*). The action verb should indicate *what* should be done (i.e., the intent), not *how* it should be done. So, for example, use *Enter* instead of *Type in* or *Scan* (or *Speak in*). The way the data is entered might change over time, but the intent probably stays the same.

G3. Try to write *UI-independent*, i.e., avoid to presuppose or to describe some UI (user interface). So, avoid expressions like '*... presses the button*', '*... tics the box*', etc., but use '*... enters ...*' or '*... confirms*' or so.

G4. Be aware of homonyms and synonyms, e.g., '*Last week, professor Zhang gave two exams and now she has 150 exams to grade*'. So, how many exams were there? 2? 150? 152? Or are there different notions of 'exam' perhaps?

G5. Use the terminology as used in the application domain. For instance, if you are working for/in a ferry company, learn to use *Trip*, *Journey*, *Departure*, *Return*, *Crossing*, *Round trip*, *Passage*, *Voyage*, etc. correctly. There might be synonyms among them, but there might also be homonyms or, even worse, combinations. Anyway, it might be useful to create and keep a *Glossary of terms*.

G6. A use case should represent one 'session' with the system. In other words, it must be possible to execute a UC in one 'go'. See mistake M30 in Sect. 2.4.5.

G7. Use an *active* sentence form, not a passive sentence form.
For instance, use '*The user gives ...*' instead of '*... is given*'.
In the latter case, the actor is missing. See mistake M5.

G8. Use cases should preferably be written by the user (organization), although someone else, say a business analyst, might help them apply these (and other) guidelines, to spot—and solve—potential misunderstandings and to correct mistakes, e.g., like those in Sect. 2.4.5.

G9. The UC-step should describe an *action*, not a situation. See mistake M6.

G10. A precondition and a postcondition should describe a *situation*, not an action. See mistakes M7 and M8.

2.4.5 Common Mistakes in Use Cases (Don'ts)

Now we present some *don'ts*. Over the years, we have seen many mistakes/misunderstandings/misuses in use cases. We collected them and present more than 30 common ones here. Some of the following examples refer to a (virtual) university registration system—concerning students, courses, exams, grades, lecturers, study programs, admissions, enrolments, etc.—but they do illustrate general issues. Try to avoid these mistakes/misunderstandings/misuses in your own use cases.

M1. Wrong or misleading verb/naming: '*Select* ...' instead of '*Enter* ...' when something is added, or '*Enter* ...' instead of '*Select* ...' in case of retrieval. Keep CRUDA in mind: Create, Retrieve, Update, Delete, Archive.
M2. Or '*Calculate* ...' while the system returns only the *ingredients* for the calculation ('Do-it-yourself'?). Shouldn't the system itself do the calculation?
M3. No indication that the system does anything, e.g., check, create, update, or delete.
M4. Unclear whether the system is checking constraints, and which ones.
M5. No indication of who/what is executing the UC-step concerned, e.g., '*... is given*' instead of, e.g., '*The system gives ...*'. See Guideline G7: Use an *active* sentence form, not a passive sentence form.
M6. The UC-step consists of a *statement* instead of describing an *action*, e.g.: '*... has been done*'. See Guideline G9.
M7. Conversely, the precondition describes an *action* instead of a *situation*, e.g.: '*The user logs in*' instead of '*The user is logged in*'. See Guideline G10.
M8. Similarly, the postcondition describes an *action* instead of a *situation*, e.g.: '*The system sends ...*'. See Guideline G10. Shouldn't this send-action be a (last) step *within* the use case?
M9. The system doesn't inform the primary actor about the (end) result, i.e., no feedback to the actor.
M10. Unnecessary preconditions, e.g. '*The student did at least one exam*' as a precondition for '*Send progress update to a student*'. The progress update might simply reflect that that student had no results. (Or should that student not get a progress update?)
M11. *Constraints* are treated as preconditions: However, usually the constraints should be checked *during* the use case—by the system—and not *beforehand*, i.e., before the use case could be applied at all.
M12. Missing precondition(s) while they are silently used in the use case.

M13. The system executes the *first* step ... Out of its own? Usually the actor executes the first step, which subsequently acts as a trigger for the system. Isn't the first step of the actor hidden in the preconditions somewhere?
M14. When writing, for instance, '*a* course': any course or '*the* course under consideration'?
M15. Vice versa: talking about '*the* course' while at that moment there is not one particular course (yet).
M16. Be very careful with plural or singular: the course*s* or the course under consideration? For example, it makes a difference whether it is *before* or *within* a loop.
But also: 'Enter *a* grade' while actually *a set of* grades should be entered.
M17. A save/update (of everything) **after** a loop instead of a (singular) save/update **within** a loop? It might be the intention (i.e., 'all or nothing'), but are you sure?
M18. In general, in case of loops: What should be **within** the loop, **before** the loop, and **after** the loop? For example, '*Send progress update*' after a loop over several students: The *same* progress update to each student?
M19. Writing only 'percentage' instead of 'percentage *of* ...'
M20. Counting the number of *failed* courses while one wants to determine the number of study points *earned*
M21. '*The system computes* ...': What happens with the result?
(Unclear whether it is a retrieval or an update/addition)
M22. '*The system does* ... and *the user does* ...':
split it into two steps (or why not?).
M23. '*Review a personal study program*': Just Review or Review *and (dis)approve*?
M24. No indication of what happens in case of disapproval
(e.g., partly or completely rejected?)
M25. In general, '*If* <condition> *then the system/actor does* <action>': And else?
M26. '*The system/actor does not confirm*': Doing nothing?
How—and when—will the other party become aware of that?
Probably something like '*The system/actor refuses/denies*' is meant.
M27. '*An overview of all courses is given*': Really, ALL courses in the world?
Or all courses of that university, that faculty, or that study program, for instance? In other words: What is the scope here?
M28. '*Report about* ...': There is no indication whatsoever of what the contents of the report/overview has to be. Usually this needs a lot of further elicitation and specification.
M29. '*The system returns the total number of study points of all students*':
This suggests only one number as the complete end result.
Probably the total number of study points *per student* is meant, the end result being a *list* of students, each with his/her total number of study points

M30. Fragment taken from a use case, and the related mistake:

6. Actor asks <other person> to solve <encountered problem>. 7. <other person> solves <problem>. 8. Actor <continues>.	These steps are usually not in one 'go'/session. So then they should not be in the same UC! Split it into separate use cases. See Guideline G6

Another example that typically will not be in one 'go' (i.e., in one session) is '*System sends questionnaire. Actor processes received questionnaire*': You cannot expect an answer 'by return' or that the actor already sits and waits for incoming questionnaires when the system sends a questionnaire. See the FinSys-discussion in Sect. 3.3 (*Communicating with other actors*) and also the discussion in Sect. 10.9 (about *asynchronous feedback*)

M31. '*The actor views the information*', as the last step in a retrieval-UC: Not strictly needed as part of the use case.

M32. Referring to an old step-number but, after changing the use case, it became a different step-number...

M33. Frequency of Use: We often see a wording which actually boils down to '*Each time this use case is used*'. But that does not contain any info...

So, be careful and, moreover, try to be as clear as possible!

2.5 System Sequence Descriptions

Our next step is to depict the results schematically and to **integrate** the MSS and the ASs of a use case. For those purposes, we introduce *system sequence descriptions*. A **system sequence description** (SSD) schematically depicts the interactions between the primary actor (user), the system (as a black box), and other actors (if any), including the messages (with their parameters) between them. An SSD is a kind of stylized use case, making the prospective inputs, checks, state changes, and outputs more explicit, heading toward formalization. We will introduce the notion of ***textual* SSD** (tSSD) for that purpose.

First we present a very simple example of a textual SSD, for the removal of a student. Besides the MSS, the textual SSD incorporates one alternative scenario, namely, the scenario that the student number is not known to the system:

User ➡ System: Remove student x ;
System ➡ System: check whether student x is known ;
if student x is not known
  then System ➡ User: 'Student number is not known'
  else System ➡ System: remove the info of student x ;
     System ➡ User: 'Done'
end

Further examples, possibilities, and explanations will follow in Sect. 2.5.1.

2.5.1 A Grammar for Textual SSDs

How can textual SSDs look like? To answer that question, we introduce a small but powerful grammar to define the possibilities for a textual SSD.

We express our grammar for **textual SSDs** in so-called **Backus-Naur Form**: The rewriting rules in the grammar contain *nonterminals*, written in plain text, and *terminals*, written in **bold**. In the rules, the symbol '::=' expresses that the nonterminal on the left can be replaced by an expression on the right. The vertical bar '|' can be read as 'or'. The pair '[' and ']' indicates that the expression between them is optional, i.e., could be left out. The pair '{' and '}' indicates that the expression between them can be repeated zero or more times. So, a rule set such as

X ::= [**nice**] A|B {**or** B}|X **;** X

expresses that the nonterminal X can be (1) replaced by the nonterminal A optionally preceded by the word '**nice**' or (2) replaced by the nonterminal B, zero or more times followed by the word '**or**' in combination with the nonterminal B or (3) replaced by two occurrences of the nonterminal X separated by a semicolon ('**;**').

Rewriting rules can be applied *repeatedly*. For more background on Backus-Naur Form, see, e.g., https://en.wikipedia.org/wiki/Backus%E2%80%93Naur_form.

In our grammar for textual SSDs, the nonterminal A stands for *atomic instruction* or *basic step*, P for *actor* or *participant*, M for *message*, S for *instruction* or *SSD*, C for *condition*, B for *basic condition*, N for *instruction name*, and D for *definition*:

A ::= P ➡ P**:** M
P ::= **System** | **User** | …
S ::= A | S **;** S | **begin** S **end**
| **if** C **then** S [**else** S] **end**
| **while** C **do** S **end** | **repeat** S **until** C
| **for each** <element in a given set> **do** S **end**
| S **,** S | **maybe** S **end** | **either** S {**or** S} **end** /* *Introducing non-determinism*
| **perform** N /* *(Procedure) Call* or '*Include*'
D ::= **define** N **as** S **end** /* *Introducing an abbreviation*
N ::= <name> | <name>**(**<parameter list>**)** /* *Abbreviations can be parameterized*
C ::= B | **true** | false | not C | (C **and** C) | (C **or** C) /* *The usual Boolean operators*

Informal explanation

- An atomic instruction of the form 'x ➡ y**:** z' must be read as:
  'x sends z to y' when y ≠ x and as 'x does (executes) z' when y = x.
  Here, z can be some information, a request/instruction, or an action.
  You might simply write '→' instead of '➡'.

- The terminal **System** represents the *system under consideration*, and **User** represents the *primary actor*. Other participants are application dependent ('domain specific') and will naturally appear during development. Other participants can be other *persons* or other *systems*, because it is (very) likely that the system under consideration must interact with other systems as well.
- The expression 's1**;** s2' means 'first do s1, then do s2'. This is also known as *sequential composition*.
- The expression '**begin** s1 **end**' just means 'do s1'. We note that '**begin**' and '**end**' can be used as 'brackets'; see our notes on binding rules on the next page.
- The expression '**if** c1 **then** s1 **end**' means 'do s1 only if c1 holds'.
- The expression '**if** c1 **then** s1 **else** s2 **end**' means 'do s1 if c1 holds; else do s2'.
- The expression '**while** c1 **do** s1 **end**' means 'do s1 as long as c1 holds': first check c1, and then do s1 if c1 is 'true'.
- The expression '**repeat** s1 **until** c1' means 'do s1 until c1 holds': first do s1, and then check c1. So s1 is done at least once.
- Sometimes you want to express that something similar has to be done for each member in a given set, independently from each other and without the need for a specific order. We express that with the **for each** grammar rule, which expresses iteration over all members in a given set. As a side remark, we note that this also allows parallel execution when it comes to implementation. Practical examples can be found in, e.g., Chap. 10 (cf. Sect. 10.6); for instance:

  for each airco x in this room which is in state 'Off' **do** ... **end**

  We emphasize that the *scope* of the **for each** should always be limited and clearly expressed (i.e., which set?). So, for instance, do not write '**for each** airco x which is in state "Off"' (or do you really mean all aircos in the world?)

- The expression 's1**,** s2' means 'do s1 and s2 in any order' indicating the freedom to choose any order. We note that this is not equivalent to parallelism or so.
- The expression '**maybe** s1 **end**' means 'do s1 or do nothing'.
- The expression '**either** s_1 **or** s_2 **or** ... **or** s_n **end**' means 'choose one of s_1, s_2, ... s_n and do it'.
- The expressions '**define** n1 **as** s1 **end**' and '**define** n2(p_1, ..., p_k) **as** s2 **end**' introduce the names n1 and n2 as abbreviations, where the second one is parameterized. Some general parameterized examples are HandleForm(F) at the end of Sect. 2.6.1, HandleList(L) in Sect. 2.6.2, and BrowseFor(C) in Sect. 3.5.2. HandleCodedItem(item-ID [; q]) in Sect. 9.1 has two parameters, where 'q' is an optional parameter.
- The expression '**perform** n' means 'execute the SSD where abbreviation n stands for'. This expression represents a *(Procedure) Call* or *Include*.
- For conditions we introduce the usual constructs (such as the 'inclusive or').

Table 2.5 Rewriting expressions which mention the checking actor

if a1: c1 **then** s1 [**else** s2] **end**	a1 ➡ a1: check c1; **if** c1 **then** s1 [**else** s2] **end**
while a1: c1 **do** s1 **end**	a1 ➡ a1: check c1; **while** c1 **do** s1**;** a1 ➡ a1: check c1 **end**
repeat s1 **until** a1: c1	**repeat** s1**;** a1 ➡ a1: check c1 **until** c1

Binding rule

We use the binding rule that '**,**' binds stronger than '**;**' in order to avoid ambiguity. Therefore, you have to read 's1**,** s2**;** s3' as '(s1**,** s2)**;** s3', which means 'do s1 and do s2 in arbitrary order, and then do s3'. To get the reading 's1**,** (s2**;** s3)', you can use the 'brackets' **begin** and **end** and write 's1**, begin** s2**;** s3 **end**'.

For the formal semantics of these expressions, see our paper Declarative Semantics of Actions and Instructions [Bro2].

For practical reasons, we consider our keywords to be case-*in*sensitive. Then we could, for instance, use **begin** ... **end** when those two related keywords are close to each other, **Begin** ... **End** when they further apart, and **BEGIN** ... **END** when the distance between the two keywords is very large. We applied this in Sect. 9.1, for instance, most notably in the definition of HandleCodedItem.

We also note that the values (i.e., terminals) for the nonterminals M, N, B, and P (other than **System** and **User**) are application dependent ('domain specific'). They will appear during the development of the specific application.

Because usually more than one actor is active in a use case and an SSD, namely, at least the system and the primary actor, (very) occasionally, it might not be clear in case of a condition which actor has to check it. For that purpose, we will extend our grammar with the option to indicate for a condition which actor has to check it. This changes three grammar rules, where the option '[A:]' has now been added:

S ::= **if** [A:] C **then** S [**else** S] **end**
  | **while** [A:] C **do** S **end**
  | **repeat** S **until** [A:] C

We will apply this, for instance, in HandleCodedItem in Sect. 9.1. Since the expression 'a1: c1' indicates the action of actor a1 to check condition c1, we obtain the equivalences in Table 2.5. They can be used as rewriting rules.

We note that, as the grammar does prescribe, the usual Boolean operators (such as **not**, **and**, and **or**) can be applied to only the condition-part, not to the expression 'a1: c1' as a whole.

Section 2.4.1 on the MSS and ASs of a use case mentioned some useful sentence forms. We can translate them to basic steps in a textual SSD in a straightforward manner:

S1. The User asks the System to <pUW>	**User → System:** <pUW>
S2. The System checks <condition(s)>	**System → System:** check <condition(s)>
S3. The System asks the User for <extra info>	**System → User:** <extra info>?
S4. The User does <own action>	**User → User:** <own action>
S5. The User sends back <requested info>	**User → System:** <requested info>
S6. The System does <subsequent action(s)>	**System → System:** <subsequent action(s)>
S7. The System sends <result/request> to <secondary actor>	**System →** <secondary actor>**:** <result/request>
S8. The System sends <result> to the User	**System → User:** <result>

Example 2.2: A Textual SSD

As an illustration we give a tSSD-example based on the use case *Process a Sale* from Larman [Lar]. We take the MSS of the use case as described in his Sect. 6.8. The primary actor here is **Cashier**, the word which we will use in our textual SSD as well (instead of our usual '**User**'). We will inherit Larman's step numbers. Some of his steps consist of more than one step in the textual SSD, e.g., his Step 4. Such additional steps are then shortly indicated by 'Step 4 too', etc.

The two parts of Step 4 in the use case can be done in any order. The three parts of Step 8 can also be done in any order. Remember the binding rule that '**,**' binds stronger than '**;**'. The two parts of steps 6 and 7 cannot be done in any order.

Customer → Customer: arrive at checkout with items to purchase;	/* Step 1
Cashier → System: StartNewSale;	/* Step 2
repeat **Cashier → System:** EnterItem(item-ID);	/* Step 3
System → System: RecordSaleLine ,	/* Step 4
System → Cashier: description, price, and running total	/* Step 4 too
until cashier indicates done;	/*
Cashier → System: EndSale;	/*
System → Cashier: total with taxes;	/* Step 5
Cashier → Customer: total;	/* Step 6
Cashier → Customer: request for payment;	/* Step 6 too
Customer → System: process payment;	/* Step 7
System → System: handle payment;	/* Step 7 too
System → System: log completed sale ,	/* Step 8
System → AccSys: sale and payment info ,	/* Accounting system. Step 8 too
System → InvSys: sale and payment info;	/* Inventory system. Step 8 too
System → Cashier: receipt;	/* Step 9
Customer → Customer: leave with receipt and goods	/* Step 10

Note that the MSS uses only basic steps, sequential composition ('**;**'), arbitrary order ('**,**'), and a **repeat**-loop.

For another illustration of our textual SSDs, we refer back to Sect. 2.1, where we worked out the textual SSD for our student registration example containing the MSS plus one AS, namely, the AS in case the registration period might be over.

2.5.2 Distinct Types of Basic Steps

We can distinguish four types of basic steps (with Actor ≠ **System**):

BS1. Actor → **System:** m1 elucidates the *inputs* the system can expect
BS2. **System**→ **System:** m2 elucidates the *checks* and *transitions* by the system
BS3. Actor → Actor: m3 elucidates what happens *outside the system*
BS4. **System**→ Actor: m4 elucidates the *outputs* the system should produce

Basic step BS1 is called an *input step*, BS2 an *internal step*, BS3 an *external step*, and BS4 an *output step*. So, an *external* step is a step not involving **System**. An external step expresses an action outside the system and might be relevant to understand the SSD, but an external step is not directly relevant for the required functionality of the system itself.

A quite common, very simple basic pattern is

input step, followed by an *internal step*, and then followed by an *output step*.

Message m1 is a request to the system to do something. It could have the form

ActionName(<parameter list>) E.g.: *RegisterStudent(<name>, <address>, . . .)*

Message m2 typically expresses what the system has to do. It could have the form

ActionName(<parameter list>) or Check <condition>

e.g.: *Check whether the course is known*

Message m3 might concern one actor doing something or concern two different actors. If the same actor is mentioned twice, the step indicates what that actor him/her/itself has to do. Otherwise, it could, for instance, express a request or exchange of anything between two actors, e.g., information, documents, goods, or money.

Message m4 could be the info asked for by the user, say in case of retrieval, or a question to the user; say for further information, or a notice to the user; say 'Done', or a message to another system; say containing information or a request.

In the tSSD in Sect. 2.5.1, you can easily see that S1 and S5 are *input* steps, S2 and S6 are *internal* steps, S4 is an *external* step, and S3, S7, and S8 are *output* steps.

Exercise 2.1
Classify the basic steps in Example 2.2 (as input steps, internal steps, external steps, or output steps).

If we neglect the external steps in an SSD, which are not directly relevant for the required system functionality, an SSD typically starts with an *input* step and typically ends with an *output* step.

2.5.3 Structuring Textual SSDs

It is very useful to structure large use cases and SSDs. That is where *definitions* are handy: You can give a textual SSD a name—by means of the construction '**define** <name> **as** <textual SSD> **end**'—and use that name instead of the complete textual SSD by means of '**perform** <name>'. As explained, this can also be parameterized.

The idea of abbreviations/definitions is ubiquitous: Programming languages have *procedures* and *sub-procedures/sub-routines*—which can be defined and called upon—and UML has its *Include* relationship. Also science uses definitions and even in everyday life we do. The definition mechanism is useful to:

1. Give a textual SSD a name and use/call it several times.
2. Factor out common parts of various textual SSDs and give that common part a name as well, e.g., *HandlePayment*.
3. Make changes in a textual SSD in only one place and use (call) the changed version several times, e.g., when the payment procedure changes or gets more options: Say first only cash, then also with a check, then also with a credit card, etc.; see the *HandlePayment* example below.
4. Initially introduce only the name (**perform** <name>) while deferring the details (**define** <name> **as** ... **end** and possible parameters) to a later moment.
5. Use the definition mechanism in a nested way, i.e., to make substructures too (as in the next example).

We give an example, *HandlePayment*, which supports factoring out and illustrates some useful sub-structuring, where the underlined names constitute clickable links:

define HandlePayment **as**
  either perform HandleCashPayment
      or perform HandleCheckPayment
      or perform HandleCreditPayment
  end
end;

define HandleCashPayment **as** ... **end;**

define HandleCheckPayment **as** ... **end;**

define HandleCreditPayment **as** ... **end**

The (sub)structuring of scenarios can become quite extensive and complex in practice. That also holds for scenario integration (Sect. 2.7). To clearly illustrate how it works, Chap. 9 contains a large 'feasibility study' of such (sub)structuring and integration. The example is based on Larman's use case *Process a Sale* [Lar].

2.6 The Conceptual Notion of a *Form*

In order to indicate a bunch of parameters and their values clearly and in one 'go', we introduce the conceptual notion of a *form*. The conceptual notion of a form does not always need to be a paper form or digital form, as Example 2.3 nicely illustrates. Moreover, as explained in Sect. 2.6.3, forms can be 'dynamic'. We subsequently introduce and explain *input forms*, *input lists*, *dynamic aspects*, and *search forms*.

2.6.1 Input Forms

A **form** essentially consists of 'parameter fields', and in each such 'field', the user might fill in a parameter value.

If a value is *required* for a field, this could be indicated by a '*' after or (probably clearer) in front of that field.

If a field represents a *date*, the user might get the opportunity to select the date from a calendar, maybe indicated by an icon, such as . Sometimes the user should be able/forced to choose between only specific dates, as in the case of booking a hotel room or a flight.

If a field represents a *time* and the user has to select the time from a limited list—for instance, for a reservation for a particular theatre performance—this could also be indicated by an icon, say by .

In general, if a field has a limited list of possible values, the system might force the user to select the value from that limited list. In practice, this possibility is often indicated by the sign '▼' after that field.

In general, you can ignore the layout in the sample forms we present. In the sample form hereafter, a value is *required* for the fields P_1, P_2, P_5, and P_7 and is *optional* for P_3, P_4, and P_6. The values for the fields P_1 and P_4 can be chosen 'freely'. As indicated, the values for P_2 and P_3 should be chosen from a specific list of possibilities. For P_5, a date has to be selected from a calendar, and for P_6 a time might be selected from a limited list. Finally, P_7 must be answered by 'Yes' or 'No'.

A sample form

* P_1	__________		
* P_2	__________	▼	*List of possible values for P2*
P_3	__________	▼	*List of possible values for P3*
P_4	__________		
* P_5	__________	(calendar)	
P_6	__________	(clock)	
* P_7	__________	▼	*'Yes' or 'No'*

Examples of fields with a limited list of possible values are Boolean fields ('Yes/No-fields'), a field like *gender*, and fields with limited lists of candidates, such as the list of current courses or the list of current course registrations of a student. Such a limited list should be produced by the system. This can be a fixed list (such as for a Yes/No-field or for *gender*) or a 'dynamic' list, to be determined 'at run-time' (such as the list of current course registrations of a student).

Example 2.3: A 'Form' Used by a Telephone System
The conceptual notion of a *form* does not always need to be a paper form or a digital form. For example: When you phone a large organization for some question, it might be that their 'phone system' first asks you to type in your customer number "*and press pound*"; then says "*Press '1' if you call for . . ., press '2' if you call for . . .*", etc.; and finally asks you to clearly pronounce the concrete topic you are phoning for, but "*if you don't mention any topic, you will be put through automatically*" (say after 5 s). In fact you 'filled in' a 'form' with three parameters: one parameter by typing in your customer number, one parameter by choosing from a limited list, and one optional 'free format' parameter by pronouncing the topic you are phoning for. Then the system is probably able to forward you to the right department and to provide the employee on duty already with your customer data and topic. The corresponding conceptual 'form' might be as follows, where the system might check the format of the customer number:

A corresponding telephone 'form'

* Customer number	__________		*(Format check)*
* Option	__________	▼	*Limited list of pairs* (1)
Topic	__________		

(1)Each pair consists of a digit (to be 'pressed') and a corresponding option

Given a parameterized user wish, a suitable structure for an *input form* for that user wish can be deduced, i.e., a form that can be used to request to execute the parameterized user wish concerned. Such a 'user wish form' consists of the fields to be filled in by the user and contains for every such field an entry to fill in a value. The input form for the user wish *Register a Student* from Sect. 2.2.2—with three required and three optional parameters—would then become:

```
Register a Student
 * name                    ____________
 * address                 ____________
 * birth date              ____________ ▦
   phone number            ____________
   gender                  ____________ ▼
   social security number  ____________
```

For handling a form, we introduce a general definition called *HandleForm*:

```
DEFINE HandleForm(F) AS                    /* For any form F
   System ➡ User: 'Please fill in the following form: ' ;
   System ➡ User: Form F (to be filled in by the user) ;
   User ➡ User:    Fill in form F ;
   User ➡ System: Filled-in form F
END
```

2.6.2 *Input Lists*

Sometimes, it is necessary—or simply convenient—to register a *set* of instances of a concept 'in one go', say all the order lines of an order or, at initialization time, all instances of a generic concept, say a concept such as *Allowable Status* or *Allowable Unit of Measure* (see the example after Table 2.6).

In that case, the user could use an input list or an enhanced input list. An *enhanced* input list is an input list with indications such as '*', '▼', '▦', and '⏱', as shown in Table 2.6. An (enhanced) **input list** represents a set of similar forms. The enhanced input list in Table 2.6 corresponds to the sample form in Sect. 2.6.1 but now with the form entries 'twisted', so to say.

Table 2.6 An enhanced input list

*P_1	*P_2▼	P_3▼	P_4	*P_5 📅	P_6 ⏱	*P_7▼

The following input list *Allowable Unit of Measure* is a concrete example, one which might be entered at 'initialization time' (here with the *Type of Measure* to be chosen from a limited list):

Allowable Unit of Measure

*Abbreviation	*Description	*Type of Measure▼
kg	kilogram	Continuous
m	meter	Continuous
L	litre	Continuous
pcs	pieces	Discrete
m3	1,000 L	Continuous
lbs	0.4536 kg	Continuous
dozen	12 pcs	Discrete

For handling an input list, we introduce a general definition called *HandleList*, similar to the definition of HandleForm:

DEFINE HandleList(L) **AS** /* For any input list L
System ➡ User: 'Please complete the following input list: ' ;
System ➡ User: Input list L (to be completed by the user) ;
User ➡ User: Complete input list L ;
User ➡ System: Completed input list L
END

As an illustration, we present the definition of a textual SSD called *CreateOrder*, followed by the used input form called *Order header* and the used input list called *Order lines*, for an order and its order lines, respectively.

In the textual SSD *CreateOrder*, S stands for System and U for User:

DEFINE CreateOrder **AS**
perform HandleForm(Order header) ;
S ➡ S: Generate order ID ;
S ➡ S: Create order with that ID and the info from the Order header form ;
perform HandleList(Order lines) ;
S ➡ S: Create that set of order lines for that order, each extended with
a (locally) unique line number and the computed price per order line(1) ;
S ➡ S: Compute the total price for the order;
S ➡ S: Add the total price for the order;
S ➡ U: 'New order created: ' ;
S ➡ U: The new order (order header with order ID, total price, and all extended order lines)
END

(1)We suppose that each article has a unit price that is known to the system. Therefore, that price per order line is derivable *at that moment*, but those unit prices might change later on

In the following *Order header* form, the default order date is 'today':

Order header
* Order type ____________ ▼ /* '*Commercial*' or '*Internal*'
* Client ____________ /*
* Order date <today>________ /* Default: <today>
/* Or choose a date from the calendar

The input list *Order lines*, used in the textual SSD *CreateOrder*, is as follows:

Order lines

*Article ▼	*Quantity	*Unit ▼

Article ▼: To choose from the list of articles, which all contain a unit price
Unit ▼: To choose from the list of allowable units (such as kilogram, liter, meter, # pieces)

We want to emphasize that textual SSDs are very suitable for analysis purposes. For example, when turning back to the textual SSD *CreateOrder* just defined, one might look again at the two steps that are *between* the two occurrences of **perform** and consider to put them *after* the second **perform**. The reason for reconsidering is that the second **perform** might not end well ('give an error') while the order has already been created at that moment... So, looking again at the textual SSD, it becomes clear that it might be better to put those two steps *after* the second **perform**.

2.6.3 Dynamic Aspects

Forms can be 'dynamic' in several ways. For instance, based on the chosen value (s) for earlier parameter(s), the set of potential values of a parameter can become more restricted. This is illustrated in the form *Individual grade*, used to *Enter a Grade*:

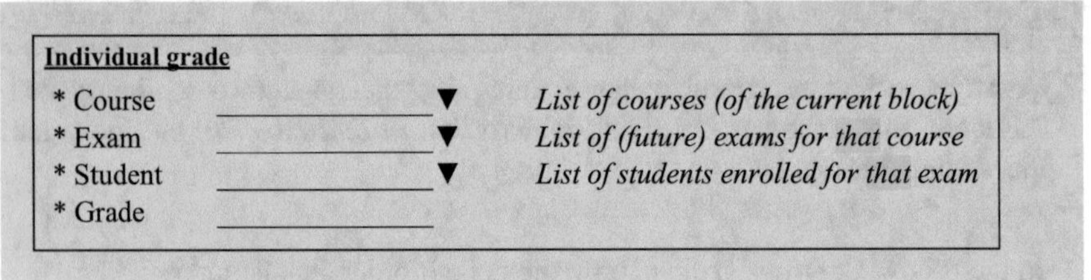

Individual grade

* Course	________ ▼	*List of courses (of the current block)*
* Exam	________ ▼	*List of (future) exams for that course*
* Student	________ ▼	*List of students enrolled for that exam*
* Grade	________	

Strictly speaking, the structure of this form did not change; only the set of potential values changed while the form was filled in step by step. However, it might be that depending on a value filled in, other fields might 'pop up', as you might have experienced in daily life. A typical example might be a tax form: whether or not you have a partner, a house, a second house, an own company, etc., it might lead to 'popping up' extra fields that must be filled in.

The order header form in Sect. 2.6.2 might become another example: If the order type is '*Commercial*', something like a *contract section* might pop up.

2.6.4 Search Forms

Conceptually, 'forms' are also used frequently for searching, e.g., by the website of a shop where a customer can indicate the item she/he is looking for, plus maybe indicating some additionally properties she/he requires, or by the internal system of an organization, say when an employee is looking for the orders of that customer who didn't know his/her customer ID but knows his/her birth date, for instance.

For that purpose, we introduce the notion of a **search form** for a concept C, i.e., a form to search for all instances of concept C that satisfy the criteria expressed in the form. Such a *search form* contains for every relevant property P one or two entries with the possibility to fill in a value as a search criterion. The possibilities and meaning of the search criterion depend on the kind of *data type* of the property. In case of a *text-valued* property P, there can be a search entry which might have the following meaning (although there exist other options as well):

P: [ ] Meaning: The P-value contains that value as a *substring* (if filled in)

In case of a *numeric* or *date* property—in general: a *totally ordered* data type—there are two options:

(a) P: [ ] Meaning: The value of P equals that value (if filled in)

(b) P: from [ ] Meaning: The value of P is at least this value (if filled in)

until [ ] Meaning: The value of P is at most this value (if filled in)

Option (b) contains two criteria, each of which might be left empty. If the first one is filled in, it means *from that value on*. If the second one is filled in, it means *up to and including that value*. Note that Option (b) formally includes Option (a), namely, when both values are filled in and are the same. Hence, strictly speaking, Option (a) is superfluous.

In general, the final search criterion expressed by a (partly) completed search form is the *conjunction* of all search criteria that were filled in, i.e., searching for all objects that satisfy *all* those search criteria.

As an illustration, suppose that you want to search for all sales to customer Smit (or was it 'Smith'?) of at least 10,000 euro in the first quarter of 2022, and there is a search form *Search for Sales* with the structure as shown below. Then you can fill in the form with the values as indicated in italics:

Search for Sales						
Sale ID	________					
Customer name	*Smit*					
Sales employee	________	▼				
Total price	from	*10,000*	euro	until	________	euro
Selling date	from	*01/01/22*	📅	until	*31/03/22*	📅
Delivery date	from	________	📅	until	________	📅

In our example, the result could also contain customers like *Smithson* and *Blacksmith*. Hence, an ordering according to *Customer name* might be useful in this case. So, our search form could be extended with another entry (and filled in) as follows, choosing from the limited list of *Sales properties* and choosing between *ascending* and *descending* order:

Ordered by *Customer name* ▼ *Ascending* ▼

So, in general, because a search form might deliver many 'hits', it might be useful that the preferred ordering of the results could also be indicated according to some selectable criterion, as we just illustrated and as you often need in practice.

We note that one more refinement step would be that the preferred ordering of the results could be further refined as follows, where the pair '{' and '}' indicates that the expression between the curly brackets might occur zero or more times:

Ordered by ________▼ *Ascending/Descending*▼
{ and subsequently by ________▼ *Ascending/Descending*▼ }

A practical application in case of our *Search for Sales* would be:

Ordered by *Customer name* ▼ *Ascending* ▼
and subsequently by *Total price* ▼ *Descending* ▼

2.7 The Scenario Integration Problem

Basic steps, sequential composition (';'), and maybe a few **repeat**-loops are often sufficient for an individual scenario, though arbitrary order (',') might be used too. But you must also be able to do proper **scenario integration**, i.e., the integration of all the individual scenarios *for a given use case*. However, proper scenario integration is often neglected.

In order to be able to integrate all the scenarios of a given use case, you also need constructs like conditionals (**if-then**), alternatives (**if-then-else**), options (**maybe**), and choices (**either-or**), as Example 2.4 illustrates.

Example 2.4: Scenario Integration
As an abstract illustration of scenario integration, suppose we got a use case with an MSS and four alternative scenarios, which were brought in separately:

MSS: The MSS consists of four consecutive steps: A; B; C; D.
AS1: Do B2 instead of B if condition H1 holds.
AS2: The user can choose to do E1 and E2 just after D (in arbitrary order, but both E1 and E2 or none).
AS3: The user is free to choose between C, C2, and C3.
AS4: Do A2 immediately after step A if condition H2 holds at that moment.

(continued)

Example 2.4 (continued)

Integration leads to the next result, if the ASs were independent from each other:

```
A;
if H2 then A2 end;            /* Follows from AS4
if H1 then B2 else B end;     /* Follows from AS1
either C or C2 or C3 end;     /* Follows from AS3
D;
maybe E1, E2 end              /* Follows from AS2
```

Exercise 2.2

How many execution paths are possible in Example 2.4?

In practice, the (sub)structuring and integration of the scenarios of a use case can become quite numerous and complex. However, a use case is not just an MSS plus a set of separate, independent ASs. The requirements analysis should not stop here, because the ASs might not be independent, e.g., when two ASs start at the same point in the MSS and are not mutually exclusive. For instance, suppose a fifth alternative scenario turns up for our earlier example, Example 2.4:

AS5: do B3 instead of B if condition H3 holds

But what if both H1 and H3 hold? The requirements analyst should then find out the answer to this question, e.g., by asking the user organization. In general, it is up to the requirements analyst to work out the (sub)structuring and integration of the scenarios of a use case clearly, after consulting the user organization.

Consider the following 'exercise': Write out the integration result if you know that H1 and H3 are mutually exclusive.

Core of the possible answer: Replace the third line by

```
if H1 then B2 else
  if H3 then B3 else B end
end;
```

This could also be the solution when H1 and H3 are not mutually exclusive but H1 is considered to be 'dominant over' H3.

Exercise 2.3

What if H3 would be 'dominant over' H1? What is your underlying case-analysis?

2.8 Validation of Textual SSDs

After all restructuring and integration of all the scenarios of a use case, the result should be validated with the customer. In order to do **validation**, i.e., checking whether a resulting textual SSD (still) captures the requirements of the user organization, we could translate the resulting textual SSD (back) to *natural language*. The user organization then has to comment on it. In principle, the users must be able to understand and confirm this description in natural language or correct it in case of incompleteness, ambiguity, or defect detection. Section 2.8.1 presents rules to translate textual SSDs to natural language.

Some people are used to—and comfortable with—*graphical* representations of processes. A *graphical SSD* (gSSD) can give a quick, visual overview, e.g., of the actors involved. They might support and ease *validation* as well. Section 2.8.2 explains how to systematically *generate* graphical SSDs from our textual SSDs.

2.8.1 Generating Natural Language from Textual SSDs

Section 2.5.1 introduced a grammar to define textual SSDs. It also showed how to use textual SSDs to integrate the various scenarios of a use case and to structure large ones, using definitions. After you have done all that, it would be useful to validate the integration result with the user organization. For that purpose, we give rules to translate textual SSDs stepwise to natural language (NL), in this case to English. We are able to do that because we have a clear grammar for textual SSDs.

We define the translation *inductively*, i.e., by assigning to each textual SSD an expression in English in terms of its direct constituents. The function F defined hereafter does the job, i.e., for each rule in our grammar for textual SSDs, function F assigns an expression in English in terms of its direct constituents.

Mapping rules 4 and 5 suggest a newline. Moreover, mapping rule 4 replaces '**;**' by '**.**', and mapping rule 5 replaces '**,**' by ' **and**'. Mapping rules 6–13 are straightforward, i.e., they leave the language constructs intact, except rule 9, where '**repeat**' will be followed a '**:**'. Mapping rules 7, 8, and 9 include the added option to mention which actor has to check the condition; see the addition in Section 2.5.1.

1.	F(actor1 → **System:** γ)	≝	**the** F(actor1) **asks the System to** F(γ)
2.	F(actor1 → actor1**:** γ)	≝	**the** F(actor1) **does** F(γ)
3.	F(actor1 → actor2**:** γ)	≝	**the** F(actor1) **sends** F(γ) **to** F(actor2)
4.	F(e1**;** e2)	≝	F(e1)**.** <newline> F(e2)
5.	F(e1**,** e2)	≝	F(e1) **and** <newline> F(e2)
6.	F(**begin** e **end**)	≝	**begin** F(e) **end**
7.	F(**if** [a:] c **then** e1 [**else** e2] **end**)	≝	**if** [F(a)**:**] F(c) **then** F(e1) [**else** F(e2)] **end**
8.	F(**while** [a:] c **do** e **end**)	≝	**while** [F(a)**:**] F(c) **do** F(e) **end**
9.	F(**repeat** e **until** [a:] c)	≝	**repeat:** F(e) **until** [F(a)**:**] F(c)
10.	F(**for each** m **do** e **end**)	≝	**for each** F(m) **do** F(e) **end**
11.	F(**maybe** e **end**)	≝	**maybe** F(e) **end**
12.	F(**either** e_1 **or** e_2 **or** … **or** e_n **end**)	≝	**either** F(e_1) **or** F(e_2) **or** … **or** F(e_n) **end**
13.	F(**perform** n)	≝	**perform** F(n)
14.	F(**define** n **as** e **end**)	≝	F(n) **means:** F(e) **end**

Ad 1: Applies if actor1 ≠ **System**. Here, the actor often is the primary actor. But it could also be another actor (a human being or external system). Anyway, it is an *input* step. Usually, γ is of the form <do something>, but γ might be of the form <info>; in that case, '**the** F(actor) **sends** F(γ) **to the System**' would be a more suitable, alternative translation.

Ad 2: Applies if the same actor is mentioned twice. In that case, the step indicates what that actor has to do. Often, the actor is **System**, in which case it is an *internal* step. Otherwise, it is an *external* step. Essentially, γ is of the form <do something>.

Ad 3: Applies if actor1 ≠ actor2 and actor2 ≠ **System**.
(a) If actor1 = **System**, it is an *output* step. Then γ could be the info asked for by the user, some feedback to the user (e.g., 'Done'), a question to the user, or request to the user (in which case '**asks**' is more suitable than '**sends**'), or a message to another system.
(b) If actor1 ≠ **System**, it is an *external* step, between different actors. Then γ could be an exchange of anything, e.g., information, request, documents, goods, or money. In some of those cases, '**gives**' might be a more suitable verb than '**sends**'.

Ad 4: Sequential order is indicated by a dot.

Ad 5: Arbitrary order is indicated by **and**.

Ad 8: Instead of **while**, we could use, e.g., **as long as**.

Ad 14: We could have put a '**.**' after **end** to clearly indicate the end of the definition (since *defines* might be long).

If the actor name (in rules 1–3), message (in rules 1–3), or instruction name (in rules 13 and 14) was well chosen, its 'translation' could simply be that actor name, message, or instruction name itself. Something similar holds for the conditions (in rules 7–9) and member descriptions (in rule 10). So, formally, F(x) = x in those cases. If those expressions were coming from the user organization itself, it is likely that they will understand them.

Essentially, the translation rules then boil down to the following: Replace the basic steps by the sentences indicated, replace '**;**' by '**.**', replace '**,**' by ' **and**', replace '**repeat**' by '**repeat:**', and replace '**define** n **as**' by 'F(n) **means:**'.

You could leave out the occurrences of the word '**the**' in rules 1–3, rules that are used very frequently. It leads to a kind of telegram style.

As a finishing touch, some translations must officially start with a capital letter: the occurrence of F(e2) after the dot in Rule 4, the occurrence of F(e) after '**repeat:**' and '**means:**' in rules 9 and 13, and the first sentence of the complete translation.

To clearly illustrate how the generation of natural language texts from textual SSDs works, Sect. 9.2 contains a large example, based on the textual SSD from Sect. 9.1.

The end result of translating the textual SSD back to natural language might be more structured and may be even clearer than the original description.

As a small illustration, we consider *HandleForm* as defined in Sect. 2.6.1:

```
DEFINE HandleForm(F) AS                    /* For any form F
  System ➡ User: 'Please fill in the following form: ' ;
  System ➡ User: Form F (to be filled in by the user) ;
  User ➡ User:   Fill in form F ;
  User ➡ System: Filled-in form F
END
```

We give the translation for *HandleForm* and also indicate the rules we applied:

```
HandleForm(F) means:                                                    (R14)
  the System sends 'Please fill in the following form: ' to User.       (R3a)
  the System sends Form F (to be filled in by the user) to User.        (R3a)
  the User does Fill in form F.                                         (R2)
  the User sends Filled-in form F to the System                         (R1)
END
```

As you can see, we didn't yet apply the mentioned 'finishing touch' to start some translations with a capital letter. For Rule 1 we used its alternative translation.

Exercise 2.4
Make translation rules towards your own native language (if that is not English).

2.8.2 Generating Graphical SSDs from Textual SSDs

Some people are used to—and comfortable with—*graphical* representations of SSDs, also known as (*system*) *sequence diagrams*, for instance, those in the visual modelling language UML [UML]. A **graphical SSD** (gSSD) is a *graphical* representation of an SSD and can provide a quick overview, especially of the actors involved. Graphical SSDs might support and ease validation as well. We now explain how you can systematically *generate* graphical SSDs from our textual SSDs, instead of drawing them yourselves.

We happily (mis)use the open-source drawing tool *Plantuml* for that—[Pla], https://plantuml.com/, in particular https://Plantuml.com/sequence-diagram—since its textual specification language closely resembles our textual specification language. Actually, Plantuml is a *drawing generation* tool: It generates drawings from text (Plantuml-code). So, you don't have to drag arrows, rectangles, circles, etc. yourself, an important—and big—difference! All in all, our mapping scheme is

textual SSD → Plantuml-code → graphical SSD

Table A.1 in the Appendix (*Our Plantuml Tutorial*) contains inductive rules to map a textual SSD step by step to Plantuml-code. This is possible because we have a well-defined grammar for textual SSDs. We define the mapping from a textual SSD to Plantuml-code *inductively*, by assigning to each textual SSD its corresponding Plantuml-code in terms of its direct constituents.

Table 2.7 shows the resulting graphical SSDs when Plantuml is applied. For each textual SSD X, we express its diagram *D*(X) inductively in terms of the diagrams of its direct constituents, which are indicated by yellow rectangles. We note that inductive rules to generate graphical representations are rare.

For each actor involved, including **System**, a graphical SSD contains a vertical dotted line below that actor, a.k.a. a *lifeline*. A message is displayed above a horizontal arrow going from the lifeline of the sending actor to the lifeline of the receiving actor.

We start with the diagram structures for *SSDs*, followed by the diagram structure for a *definition*. For clarity, we have put the diagram structure for a definition in a frame. For the basic steps, we distinguish three cases. For the **either**-construct, we showed only one **or**. The extension to more than one **or** will be obvious; see Fig. 2.4, for instance.

In the mappings, A_i is the first mentioned (i.e., leftmost) actor of SSD S, A_j is its last mentioned (i.e., rightmost) actor, A_{i1} is the leftmost actor of S1, A_{j1} is its rightmost actor, A_{i2} is the leftmost actor of S2, and A_{j2} is its rightmost actor.

Table 2.7 Mapping textual SSDs to graphical SSDs

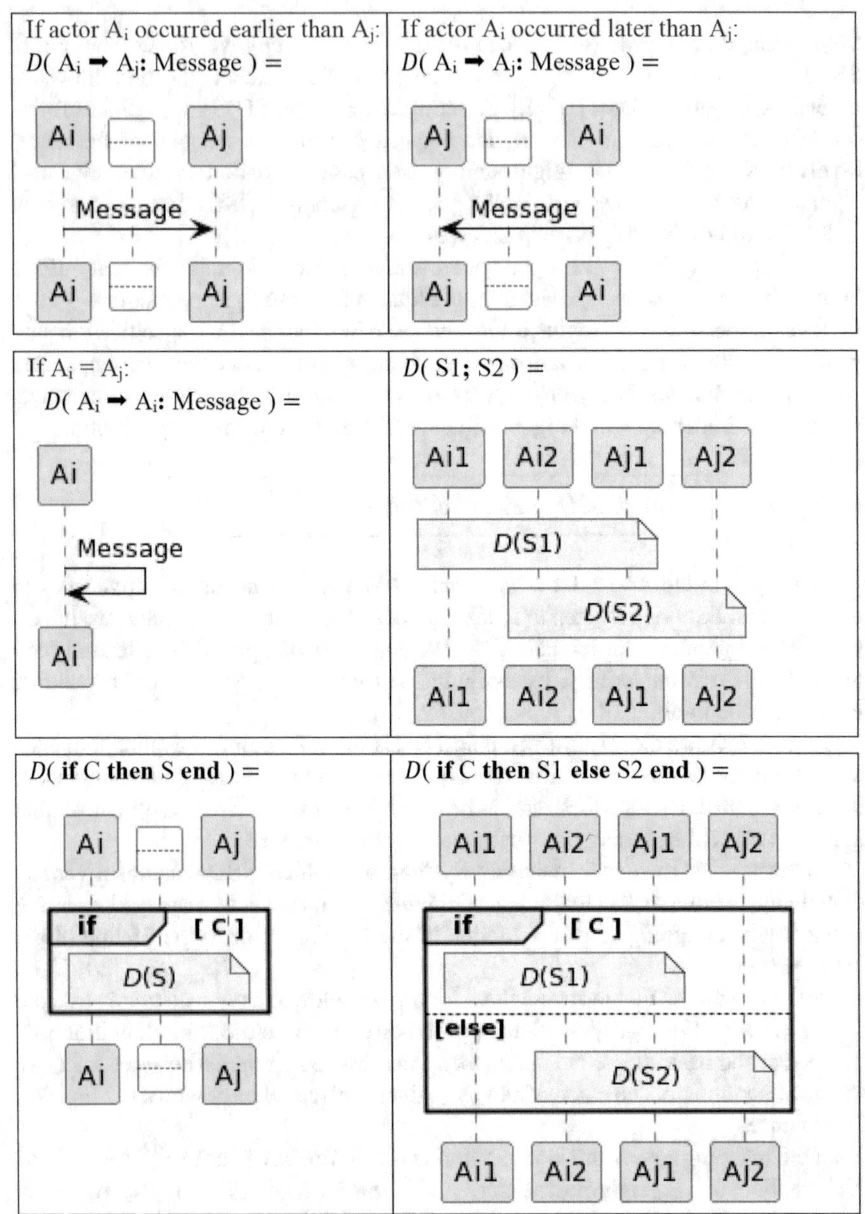

(continued)

Table 2.7 (continued)

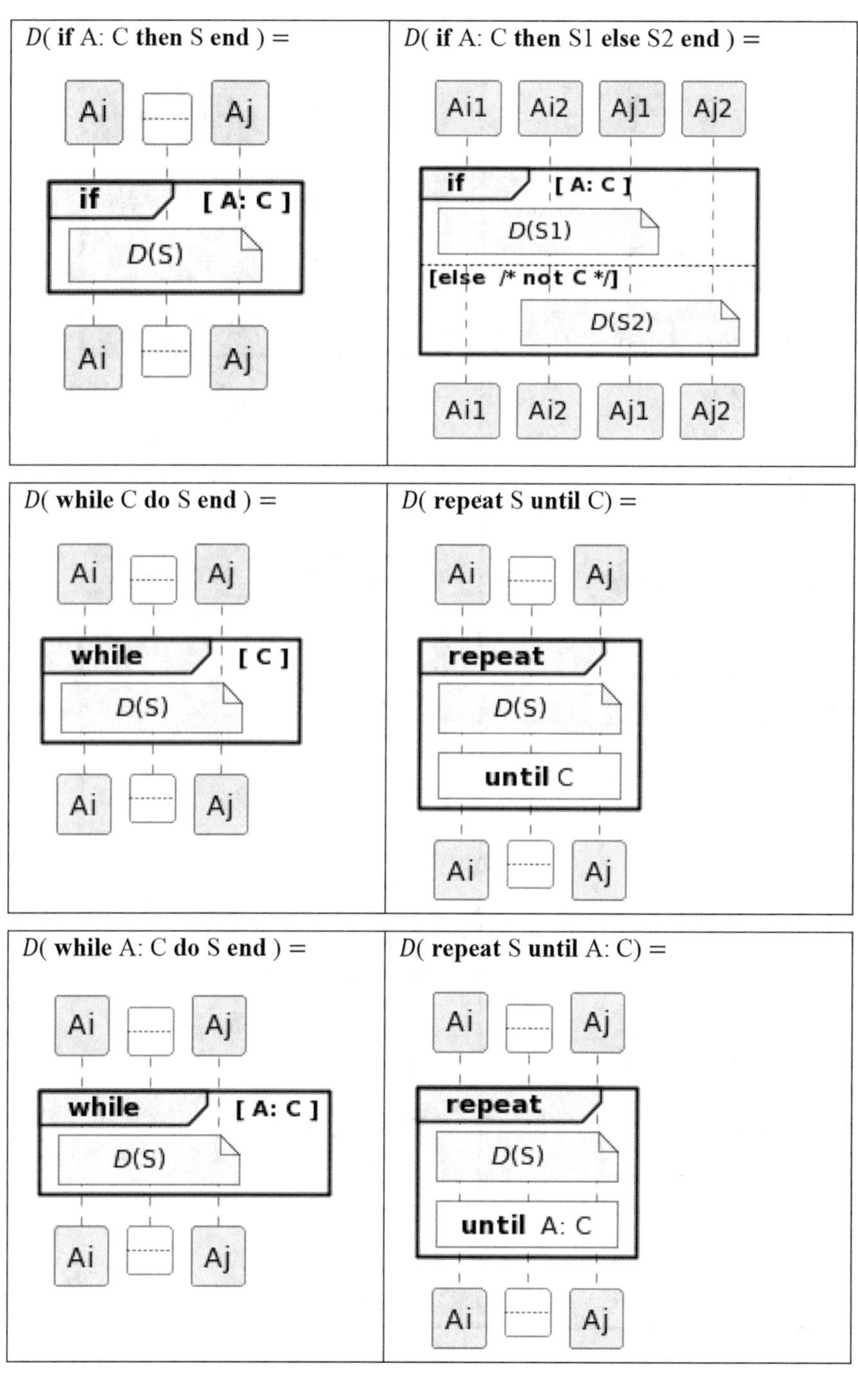

(continued)

Table 2.7 (continued)

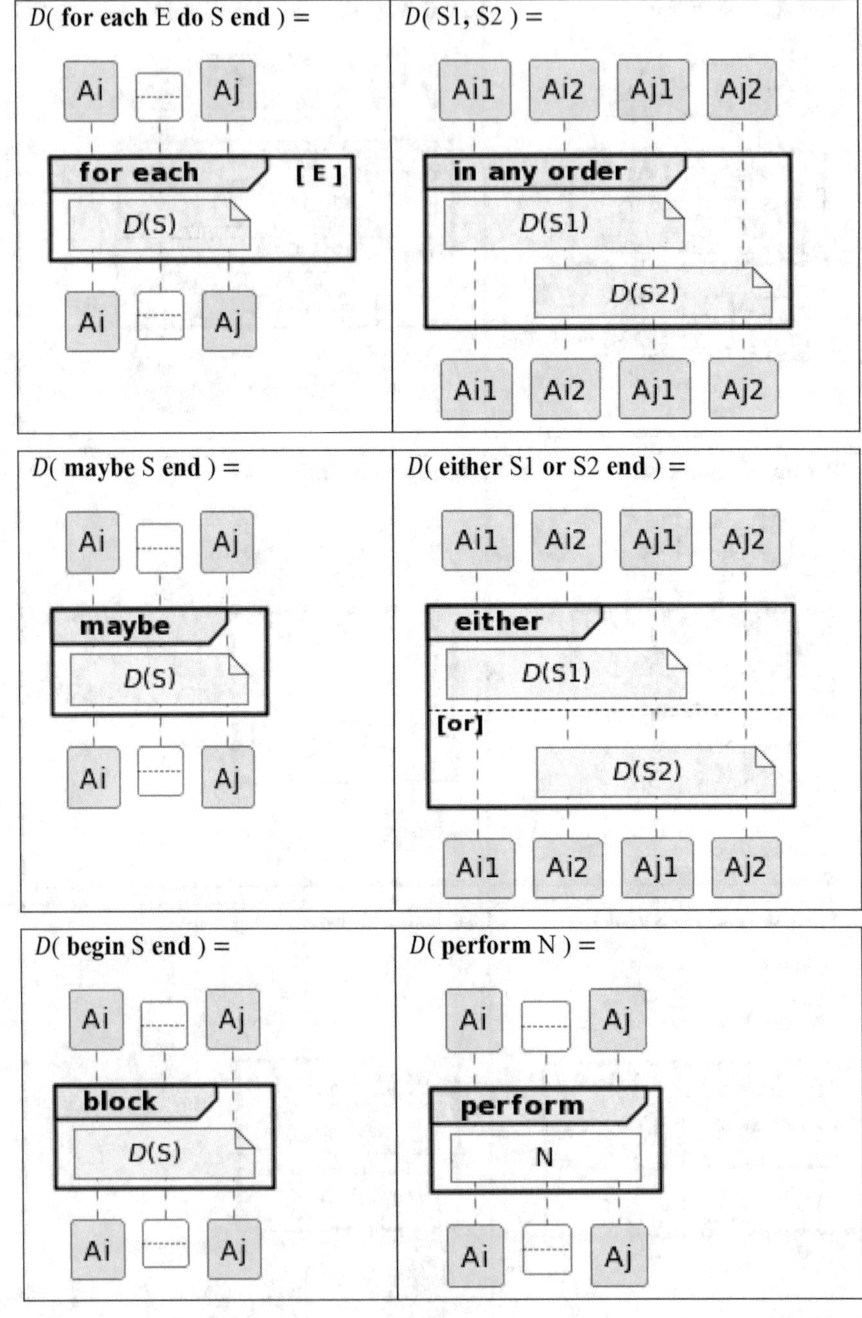

(continued)

Table 2.7 (continued)

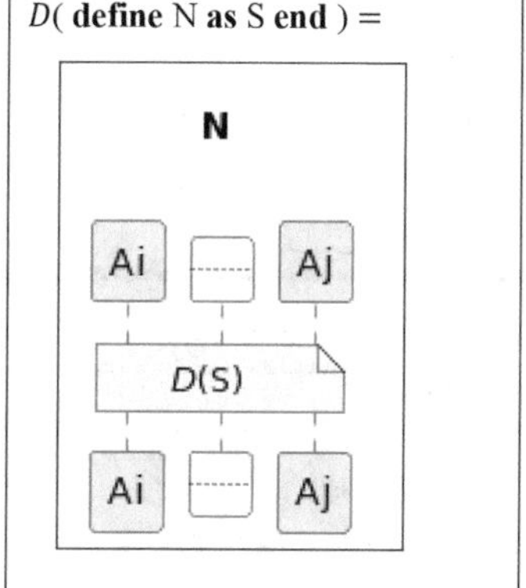

As a concrete example, we generate the graphical SSD from the textual SSD *Process a Sale* from Example 2.2 (although we added two newlines to fit the page). Fitting the page is often a problem with graphical SSDs. See Fig. 2.3, for instance.

As an abstract textual SSD, we take the integration example from Sect. 2.7, including the subsequent adaption:

A;
if H2 **then** A2 **end;**
if H1 **then** B2 **else**
  if H3 **then** B3 **else** B **end**
end;
either C **or** C2 **or** C3 **end;**
D;
maybe E1**,** E2 **end**

Suppose that it is an interplay between only the user and the system. Then the structure of the corresponding graphical SSD will look as in Fig. 2.4.

To clearly illustrate how the generation of graphical SSDs from textual SSDs works, also in larger situations, Sect. 9.3 contains a substantial example, based on the textual SSD from Sect. 9.1.

Some Problems with Graphical SSDs

We now emphasize some problems with *graphical* SSDs as mentioned by Cockburn in *Writing Effective Use Cases* [Coc] and observed by others as well, and we compare our *textual* SSDs with *graphical* SSDs (such as in the visual modelling language UML, https://www.uml.org):

- Graphical SSDs take up much space. Our textual SSDs clearly take up much less space.
- In graphical SSDs, it is often difficult to impossible to fit the needed amount of text on the arrows between the actors. However, in our textual SSDs, there is ample space for the message-text because the basic steps have the form

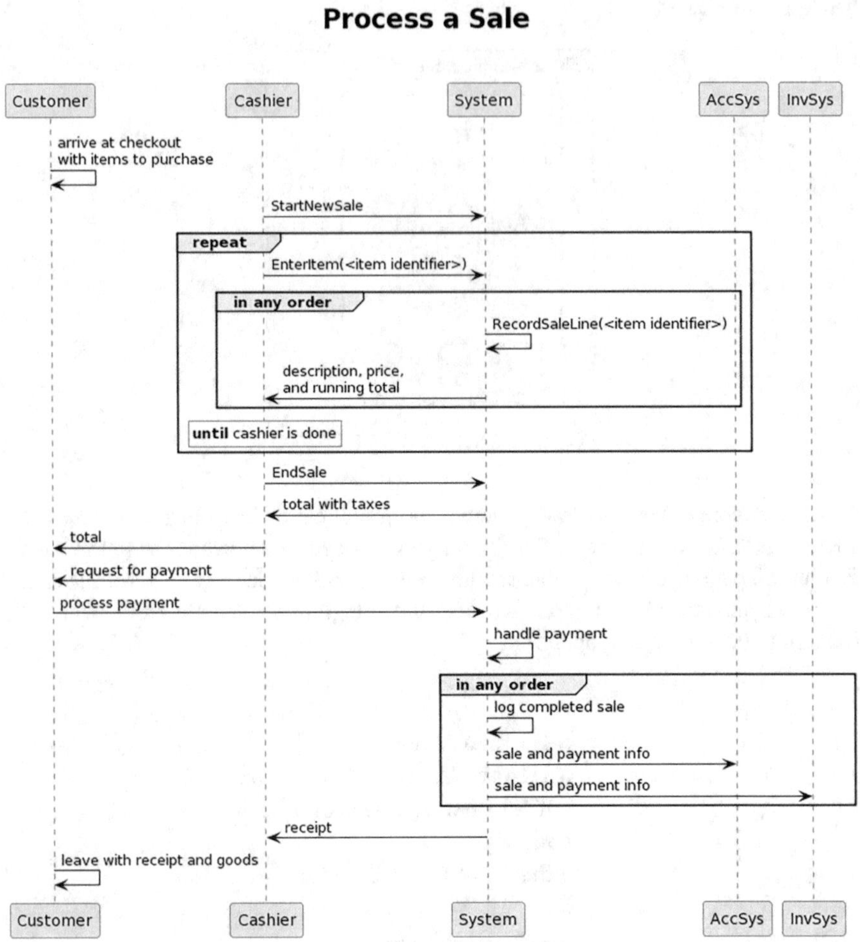

Fig. 2.3 Graphical SSD for *Process a Sale*

Actor ➡ Actor : message-text

- It turns out that graphical SSDs are much harder to read for the sponsor or users because, after all, graphical SSDs constitute a specialized notation and those readers are usually not trained in these visual notations. Our textual SSDs are written in a stylized version of plain English, making our language a 'pseudo natural language'. Moreover, Sect. 2.8.1 presents systematic translation rules from our textual SSDs to plain English.
- Graphical SSDs as used in practice often do not show the internal responsibilities of the system. However, our textual SSDs do, by using steps of the form **System ➡ System**. With our mappings *from* textual SSDs *to* graphical SSDs, the internal responsibilities of the system will naturally appear in the graphical SSDs as well.

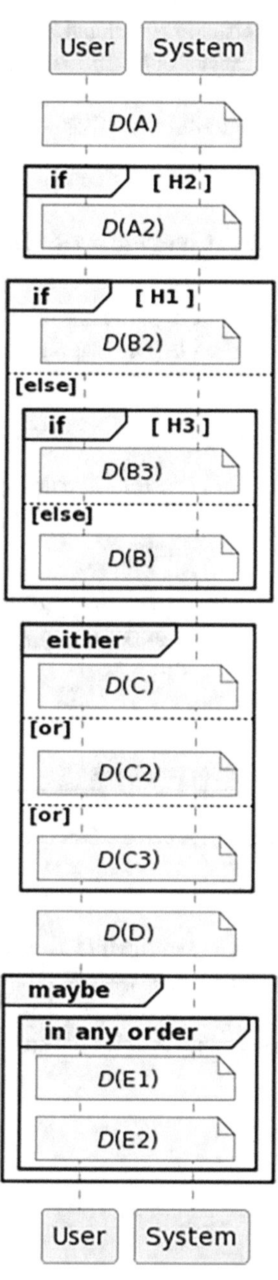

Fig. 2.4 An abstract graphical SSD

- Graphical SSDs are hard to maintain. Our textual SSDs are easier to produce and also easier to change than graphical SSDs. See, for instance, Chap. 10.
- A textual SSD is closer to a programming language than a graphical SSD, while a programming language is usually the next target. A programming language is typically textual and not graphical.

- Usually, graphical SSDs do not have a well-defined grammar or formal semantics, as opposed to our textual SSDs (as defined in our paper [Bro2]).
- In textual SSDs, the task-name in a Call/Include can constitute a hyperlink to the definition itself, as we applied in this book.

2.9 Overview of Our Approach to Develop a User Wish

Figure 2.5 summarizes the wholistic development path for a user wish as we sketched it. The mapping to (software) procedures will be treated in Chap. 6.

eUW	elementary User Wish
pUW ≡ eUW + input parameters	parameterized User Wish
US ≡ UW + actor [+ benefit(s)]	User Story
MSS	Main Success Scenario
AS*	Alternative Scenarios
UC ≡ MSS + AS*	Use Case
tSSD ≡ schematic UC (MSS ⊕ AS*, *integrated*)	textual SSD
↙ ↓ ↘	
NL-text ↓ gSSD *(for validation purposes)*	text in Natural Language / graphical SSD
↓	
↓	
SW-procedure(s)	*See Chapter 6*

Fig. 2.5 A development path for a user wish

It is worthwhile to sketch a complete example of a development path for a concrete user wish. See Fig. 2.6. The mapping to software procedures will be treated in Chap. 6, but you can already see that the structure of the resulting software procedure follows the structure of the textual SSD.

eUW Register a student

pUW Register a student *with a given name, address, country, birth date, ...*

US As an administrator, I want to <eUW> [because .....]

MSS

1. The user asks the system to <pUW>
2. The system fulfils <pUW>
3. The system sends result to the user *(e.g., registered data including the generated student nr.)*

AS*

AS1: If (s)he is a foreigner then ...
AS2: If (s)he was a student before then ...
AS3: ...
⋮

UC

MSS + AS1 + AS2 + AS3 + ...
(But what if the foreigner was a student before?)

tSSD

User ➞ System: <pUW> ;
if student is a foreigner
  then ..... *(this applies even if the foreigner was a student before, as the customer told us)*
  else **if** (s)he was not a student before
    then System ➞ System: generate new student number ;
      System ➞ System: fulfil <pUW + new student number>
    else .....
   end
end ;
System ➞ User: result *(e.g., registered data including the generated student number or an 'error' message)*

software-procedure(s)

E.g., a *stored procedure* in SQL (see Section 6.4):

In the procedure, the variable @out is declared as a return parameter.
Let's suppose here that student number is declared as a so-called `AUTO-INCREMENT` primary key field, explained at the end of Section 6.4.

```
CREATE PROCEDURE RegisterStudent  @n VARCHAR(50), @a VARCHAR,
                 @c VARCHAR(20), ...., @out VARCHAR OUTPUT
AS
BEGIN
 IF @c <> 'NL'          -- if the student is a foreigner
 THEN .....             -- AS1
 ELSE IF .....          -- if (s)he was not a student before
      THEN BEGIN INSERT INTO Student(name, address, ...)
                        VALUES(@n, @a, ...)
                 SELECT @out = 'Done. New student nr. is '+ <...>
           END
      ELSE .....        -- AS2
END
```

Fig. 2.6 Example of a development path for a user wish

Now we show the generated *text in Natural Language* and the generated *graphical SSD* (Fig. 2.7), both generated from our textual SSD and both with all scenarios integrated.

The User **asks the System to** <pUW>**.**
If student is a foreigner
then .....
else if (s)he was not a student before
then the System **does** generate new student number**.**
The System **does** fulfil <pUW + new student number>
else .....
end
end.
The System sends result **to** User

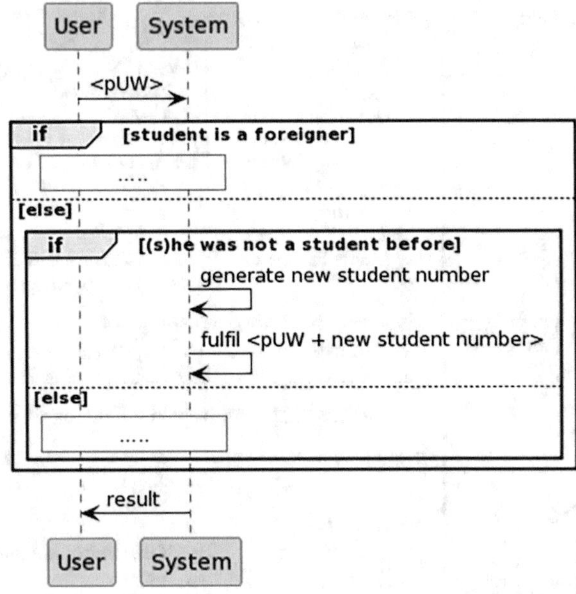

Fig. 2.7 Graphical SSD generated from the textual SSD in Fig. 2.6

When a new user wish pops up, then you can 'walk the line' we just sketched, i.e., follow the aligned development path for the new user wish, completely from *initial user wish* all down to a *specification for implementation*, say, in Java or SQL. The development path for a user wish also includes *validation*.

All in all, it brings us to a development method as described hereafter. It starts with a 'prelude', followed by the development steps for the Main Success Scenario. The development of a subsequent alternative scenario is almost the same, but it has an additional integration step, which is indicated in yellow.

The 'prelude':

eUW	An elementary user wish comes in.
pUW	Which parameters should it have?
US	Which benefit(s) does it have? (Mention at least one)
US	Which actor(s)/role(s)?

The development of a Main Success Scenario:

MSS	Write out the Main Success Scenario.
tSSD	Convert it to a textual SSD.
NL-text	Generate the corresponding NL-text.
gSSD	Generate the corresponding graphical SSD (if desirable).
Validate	Let the customer validate the generated NL-text and/or gSSD.
SW-proc.	Convert the (maybe adapted) tSSD to a software procedure.

For each subsequent alternative scenario there is an extra integration step:

AS	Write out the Alternative Scenario
tSSD	Convert it to a (local) textual SSD
MSS ⊕ AS*	Integrate it into the already existing textual SSD
NL-text	Generate the corresponding NL-text
gSSD	Generate the corresponding graphical SSD (if desirable)
Validate	Let the customer validate the generated NL-text and/or gSSD
SW-proc.	Convert the (maybe adapted) tSSD to a new software procedure

Note that each development cycle results in a concrete software procedure.

The development of a scenario might seem quite *linear*, but in practice, it is usually *iterative*, i.e., where the scenario is refined through successive adaptions. A typical example is *Registering*—e.g., of a student—where the initial list of properties to be registered may 'grow' during the development of the system. The successive incorporation of new alternative scenarios makes the development of a user wish *incremental*. See Sect. 7.2.5 for a further explanation of *iterative* and *incremental* development.

We can write this all out as a business process, in particular an *IS-development* business process. See Fig. 2.8.

So, in other words, this chapter is about *IS development business agility* and *business process alignment*.

2.10 Summary

This chapter treated the development of an *individual* user wish. It started with a preliminary overview and then delved deeper into the topics of user wish, user story, use case, main success scenario, alternative scenario, (textual) SSD, form, scenario integration, and validation, respectively. For example, we worked out how to map *textual* SSDs to natural language and to *graphical* SSDs in a systematic way. This is useful for validation, for explanation, and for customer-friendly documentation. This chapter ended with a complete overview of our approach to the development of a user wish, where the approach was written out as an *IS development* business process.

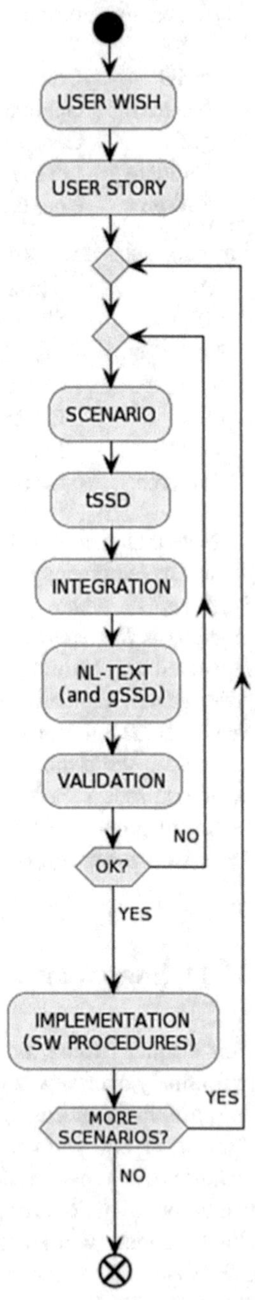

Fig. 2.8 Iterative & incremental development of a user wish with possibly several scenarios

The subsequent notions of user wish, user story, use case, and textual SSD offer *stepwise clarification*, *stepwise refinement*, and *stepwise specification*. Textual SSDs are suitable to integrate the Main Success Scenario (MSS) and the alternative scenarios (ASs) of a use case.

Extending [Cohn3], we note that with their components, user wishes, user stories, and use cases subsequently answer some of the questions *what*, *who*, *why*, and *how*, as schematically depicted in Table 2.8.

Table 2.8 Which notions treat which questions where?

	User wish	**User Story**	**Use Case**
What	user wish	user wish	use case title
Who	–	role	primary actor
Why	–	[benefit]	rationale/context
How	–	–	MSS + AS*

Chapter 3
Development Patterns

Abstract When you have worked out many cases, you may recognize certain *development patterns*. This chapter explicates some of those patterns. Patterns are common in various other areas as well.

The chapter starts with a general development pattern, and from there it subsequently discusses some refinements, such as indicating the elementary user wish and the parameters separately in Sect. 3.2, communicating with other actors—with synchronous or asynchronous feedback—in Sect. 3.3, personalization in Sect. 3.4, and CRUD(A)-patterns in Sect. 3.5.

3.1 Outline of a General Development Pattern

We start with a general development pattern. But first we recall the main notions from the previous chapter.

(1) An (**elementary**) **user wish** often has the form:

<(action) verb> **a** <noun (phrase)>

for instance, *Register* ***a*** *Student*, *Process* ***a*** *Sale*, or *Delete* ***a*** *Room Reservation*.

(2) A **parameterized user wish** (pUW) can have the form:

<user wish> **with a given** <parameter list>

e.g., *Register a Student* ***with a given*** *name, address, phone number, and birth date*, or *Delete a Room Reservation* ***with a given*** *reservation number*. The user wish *Process a Sale* of Larman [Lar] does not have any parameters upfront; cf. our Chap. 9.

(3) A **user story** (US) consists of the user wish plus the intended user role and optionally a benefit part. The most popular template for a user story is the *Connextra template* (see Sect. 2.1):

As a <role>**, I want to** <user wish> [**so that** <benefit>]

B. de Brock, *Developing Information Systems Accurately*,
https://doi.org/10.1007/978-3-031-16862-8_3

for instance, ***As a*** *Planner,* ***I want to*** *Delete a Room Reservation* ***so that*** *the room is available for bookings again*. As just indicated, the <user wish> might be of the following form: <(action) verb> **a** <noun (phrase)>, as in this example. The *benefit*-part indicates an interest of <role> in the user wish.

(4) The subsequent **use case** (UC) will have the <role> in the user story as its *primary actor*—e.g., *Planner*—and might have the elementary user wish as its *title*, e.g., *Register a Student*, *Process a Sale*, or *Delete a Room Reservation*.

Our first pattern is a general basic use case pattern, consisting of three *phases*. Step 1 represents the *input phase*, Step 2 the *execution phase*, and Step 3 the *output phase*:

1. **The** <role>**/user asks the system to** <user wish> **with a given** <parameter list>
2. **The system tries to** <user wish> **with that given** <parameter list>
3. **The system informs the** <role>**/user about the result**

Note that the system *tries to* execute the user wish, because that is not always possible, due to violations of pre-suppositions and/or constraints, such as '*Unknown reservation number*', etc. The result in the output phase might consist of:

- The information asked for, in case of successful retrieval
- 'Done' (plus some relevant info, e.g., the system generated values), in case of a successful state change
- The reason(s) why the user wish could not be executed

All ingredients of the use case can be taken directly from the previous development steps, in particular from the parameterized user wish and user story. For example:

1. **The** Planner **asks the system to** Delete a Room Reservation **with a given** reservation number.
2. **The system tries to** Delete a Room Reservation **with that given** reservation number.
3. **The system informs the** Planner **about the result.**

We recall that a **textual system sequence description** (tSSD) is a kind of stylized use case, already heading toward formalization. A textual SSD is making the prospective inputs, checks, state changes, and outputs more explicit. The general textual SSD for our general development pattern might have the form:

1. **User ➡ System:** <ActionName>**(**<parameter list>**)** ; /* *input* phase
2. **System ➡ System: try to** α **a** β **with a given** <par.list> ; /* *execution* phase
3. **System ➡ User:** result /* *output* phase

where for traceability reasons <ActionName> could be chosen as the concatenation of the (action) verb α and the noun (phrase) β from the original user wish.

Table 3.1 Summary of the relationship between the subsequent grammatical forms

eUW	α **a** β
pUW	α **a** β **with a given** <parameter list>
US	**As a** γ**, I want to** α **a** β [**so that** <benefit>]
UC	1. **The** γ **(User) asks the system to** α **a** β **with a given** <parameter list>
	2. **The system tries to** α **a** β **with that given** <parameter list>
	3. **The system informs the** γ **(User) about the result**
tSSD	1. **User → System:** $\alpha\beta$(<parameter list>) **;**
	2. **System → System: try to** α **a** β **with a given** <parameter list> **;**
	3. **System → User:** result

For the previous example, this would then lead to:

1. **User → System:** DeleteRoomReservation**(**<reservation number>**);**
2. **System → System: try to** Delete **a** Room Reservation **with a given** <reservation number> **;**
3. **System → User:** result

We prefer to use the general word **User** in the textual SSD instead of a specific role—such as *Planner*—because later a user wish might turn out to be relevant for more than just one role. In that case we don't have to adapt the textual SSD. The applicable role(s) can be denoted separately. For instance:

The **User** can be a *Planner* or a *Course Coordinator*.

Table 3.1 summarizes the subsequent related grammatical forms we discussed so far, where α denotes the action verb and β the noun phrase in the original elementary user wish and γ the role in the user story. Step 1 represents the *input* phase, Step 2 the *execution* phase, and Step 3 the *output* phase again.

Note the transparency and the bi-directional *traceability* of it all: from the elementary user wish α **a** β to the 'procedure' $\alpha\beta$ and back.

3.2 Indicating the eUW and the Parameters Separately

It might be sensible that the user first indicates which elementary user wish she/he wants to execute—e.g., *Enter a Grade*—without mentioning the parameter values yet. After that step, the system can present the relevant parameters, maybe provided with a list of their potential values, after which the user can indicate the intended parameter values, e.g., for *which course*. And maybe, based on the chosen value (s) for earlier parameter(s), the set of potential values of the next parameter can become even more restricted, as in the next form (*Individual Grade*), used in Example 3.1:

Individual grade

* Course	______ ▼	*List of courses (of that lecturer)*
* Exam	______ ▼	*List of (recent/future) exams for that course*
* Student	______ ▼	*List of students enrolled for that exam*
* Grade	______	

Before the system can present the potential values for a parameter, it must *retrieve* the values first. In case of the form *Individual Grade*, the system can retrieve the list of courses of the requesting lecturer beforehand but might retrieve the list of exams for that course after the course is filled in. Similar for the list of students for the chosen exam.

We derive our second general development pattern from the textual SSD in Table 3.1, but now starting with only an elementary user wish W, such as *Enter a Grade*, and followed by a step handling the associated parameters:

1. **User ➡ System:** W ; /* *input* part 1
2. **perform** HandleForm(<parameter form for W>) ; /* *input* part 2
3. **System ➡ System: try to** W **with the given** <par. values>; /* *execution* phase
4. **System ➡ User:** result /* *output* phase

For convenience we recall the definition of HandleForm from Sect. 2.6.1, which in itself constitutes a general pattern as well, just as HandleList from Sect. 2.6.2, and the general *browse pattern* BrowseFor(C) to be presented in Sect. 3.5.2:

```
DEFINE HandleForm(F) AS                    /* For any form F
   System ➡ User: 'Please fill in the following form: ' ;
   System ➡ User: Form F (to be filled in by the user) ;
   User ➡ User:   Fill in form F ;
   User ➡ System: Filled-in form F
END
```

A more detailed example will illustrate all this:

Example 3.1 Indicating the Parameters Separately

Consider the following parameterized user wish of a lecturer:

Enter a Grade
of a given student for a given exam of a given course

Probably the set of potential courses is the most limiting option, especially when it can be restricted to the courses that the lecturer is responsible for. The set of potential exams—i.e., those in the near future or recent past—of the

(continued)

Example 3.1 (continued)
chosen course is probably very small and the set of students enrolled for that exam is probably large(r) but also limited. This brings us to the following use case, where the input phase consists of the steps 1–3:

Use Case:

1. *A lecturer asks the system to Enter a Grade.*
2. *The system asks the lecturer to fill in the sent form for entering a grade.*
3. *The lecturer fills in the form for entering a grade and sends it back.*
4. *The system tries to:*
   Enter that grade of that student for that exam of that course.
5. *The system informs the lecturer about the result.*

Steps 2 and 3 together boil down to *handling the form* for entering a grade. So, working out the general development pattern for this case leads to the next textual SSD, using the form Individual grade just presented:

1. **User ➡ System:** Enter a Grade ; /* *input* part 1
2. **perform** HandleForm(Individual grade) ; /* *input* part 2
3. **System ➡ System: try to** Enter a Grade **with the given** /* *execution* phase
   parameter values from the form Individual grade ; /*
4. **System ➡ User:** result /* *output* phase

Given how this concrete textual SSD works, the following constraints are satisfied 'on the fly':

- The course exists, and that lecturer is responsible for it.
- The exam exists.
- The exam is an exam of that course.
- The students exists.
- The student is enrolled for that exam.

So, due to the working of the general textual SSD—in particular, retrieving only existing potential values for each parameter—the chosen values for the parameters are in principle 'correct', that is, they exist and satisfy (most) constraints. See, for instance, the observations in the last part of Example 3.1.

3.3 Communicating with Other Actors

In general, communication with other systems is important. Nowadays, hardly any system operates in isolation. Therefore, usually, a system should communicate/interact/interface with other systems as well. So, during execution of the UC/tSSD, the system might need to communicate with other actors too, e.g., to *send* a command or information (i.e., uni-directional) or *ask for* information (bidirectional). In case of *sending*, the textual SSD might contain a step like:

System ➡ <other actor>**:** <information>

For example **System** ➡ Flashing light 1**:** Switch on
or **System** ➡ **Operator:** Switch Flashing light 1 on

In case the system *asks for* information, that other actor, a.k.a. a *supporting actor*, also has to send the answer back (so, bidirectional). Then the textual SSD might contain the next two subsequent steps:

(a) **System** ➡ <other actor>**:** <question> **;**
(b) <other actor> ➡ **System:** <answer>

This is the situation in which <other actor> sends back the answer immediately ('by return'), a.k.a. *synchronous feedback*. If you are not sure whether <other actor> will send back the answer immediately ('by return'), then the use case—and hence the SSD—should be split, since a use case should represent one session with the system. In other words, it must be possible to execute a use case 'in one go'. In those cases, the original UC/tSSD might end with Step (a) and could be called something like *Send a request for* .... Step (b) should become the first step of a new UC/tSSD, say *Handle incoming answer* ..., having <other actor> as the primary actor.

As an illustration, let us have a look at the elementary user wish *Remove a Student*, in particular the parameterized user wish *Remove a Student with a given student number*. In our sample university, a student can be removed only if she/he paid all her/his debts to the university. This can be checked in FinSys, a separate, automated financial system of the university. For privacy reasons, FinSys is not allowed to mention the size of the debts, but FinSys is allowed to say 'Yes' or 'No' to our system. Suppose that we obtained the following—relatively clear—description from our customer:

Use case *Remove a Student*

> *An authorized university employee asks the system to remove a student with a given number (but our customer does not know yet who should be authorized). The system checks whether the student number is known in the system. If so, then the system asks FinSys whether that student has any debts to the university; otherwise, the system informs the user that the student number is not known, and the use case ends. FinSys gives the answer 'Yes' or 'No' for that student to the system. If the answer is 'No', then the system removes the info of that student; otherwise, the system informs the user that the student still has debts, and the use case ends. As the last step, the system informs the user that it removed the info of that student.*

We had to do some additional requirements elicitation, and we did some reshuffling and restructuring: Because each of the two alternative scenarios is short and the use case then immediately stops, you can replace the first formulation below by the second formulation, which might be handier:

(1) **if** presupposition holds
then <next MSS-steps> **else** <alternative scenario> **end**

(2) **if** presupposition does not hold
then <alternative scenario> **else** <next MSS-steps> **end**

After applying this reshuffling twice, you will arrive at the following tSSD-structure, where HasDebts?(<student number>) is a request from System to FinSys expecting a Yes/No-answer:

Textual SSD: *Remove a Student*

User ➡ System: RemoveStudent**(**<student number>**);**
System ➡ System: check whether <student number> is known**;**
if <student number> is not known
then System ➡ User: 'Student number is not known'
else System ➡ FinSys**:** HasDebts?**(**<student number>**);**
FinSys **➡ System:** <answer> **;**
if <answer> is 'Yes'
then System ➡ User: 'No removal because the student still has debts'
else System ➡ System: remove the info* of student with <stud. nr.>**;**
System ➡ User: 'Done'
end
end

*: Unclear yet which info exactly

If FinSys might not send back the answer immediately ('by return'), then you have to split the use case and textual SSD into two, say into ***Request*** *a Student Removal* and into ***Finalize*** *a Student Removal*. We will work out the two textual SSDs:

Textual SSD: *Request a Student Removal*

User ➡ System: RemoveStudent**(**<student number>**);**
System ➡ System: check whether <student number> is known**;**
if <student number> is not known
then System ➡ User: 'Student number is not known'
else System ➡ FinSys**:** HasDebts?**(**<student number>**)**
end

FinSys will come back to it, but later on (a.k.a. *asynchronous feedback*). So, FinSys has to refer to the 'old' request, one way or the other. We will do it via the student number. Alternatively, this might have been done via a request number, generated by our system or by FinSys. Meanwhile, our system might need to keep track of a 'status of the removal request'. We will ignore this for the moment.

In the following textual SSD, HasDebts(<student number>, <answer>) is a message from FinSys to System answering the Yes/No-question whether or not the student with <student number> has debts.

Textual SSD: *Finalize a Student Removal*

define *Finalize a Student Removal* **as**
  FinSys ➡ **System:** HasDebts(<student number>, <answer>);
  if <answer> is 'Yes'
    then System ➡ User: 'No removal because the student still has debts'
    else System ➡ System: remove the info of student with <student number>;
      /* Which info exactly?
      System ➡ User: 'Done'
  end
end

A remaining open issue in this example was who should be authorized to use this use case. But since we use the word **User** in the textual SSD, this question can be solved later on.

Another open issue in this example is the question which student info should be removed, for instance, also all student's enrolments/participations in courses and exams and so on? Likely some further requirements elicitation has to be done...

We just pointed out that it might be necessary to split a use case into two use cases in case of **asynchronous feedback**, i.e., when the other system might not react 'by return' but only 'later on', and the system under consideration does not wait for the other system. It can also work the other way around: When that other system becomes able to react 'by return', the two use cases can simply be merged. In other words, it is easy to go back from the *asynchronous* to the **synchronous feedback** use case situation—i.e., when the other system can react 'by return' and the system under consideration waits for it—because here you can simply call *Finalize a Student Removal* within the original textual SSD. See Sect. 10.9 as well.

3.4 Personalization ('*Me, Myself, and I*')

Increasingly people are allowed/forced to maintain their own data in a system ('Do-it-yourself'), often on a site called something like *MyXXX.com* (or *MijnXXX.nl* in The Netherlands), where XXX often is the name of the organization. For example, besides—or instead of—the user wish *Enrol a Student for a Course*, i.e., done by someone else, we have the 'personalized' user wish *Enrol* ***myself*** *for a Course*, so done by the student him/herself. The personalized user wish is (much) more limited than the general user wish, because with the personalized user wish, you can enrol only yourself, but with the general user wish, one can enrol 'any' student.

Table 3.2 Summary in case of personalization

eUW	α **myself**
pUW	α **myself with a given** <shorter parameter list>
US	**As a γ, I want to α myself [so that** <benefit>]
UC	1. **The γ asks the system: α me with a given** <shorter parameter list>
	2. ***The system identifies the user as a particular γ***
	3. **The system tries to α that γ with that given** <shorter parameter list>
	4. **The system informs the γ about the result**
tSSD	1. **User ➡ System:** α**Me(**<shorter parameter list>**) ;**
	2. ***System ➡ System: y := the γ represented by the user ;***
	3. **System ➡ System: try to α y with a given** <parameter list> **;**
	4. **System ➡ User:** result

With <parameter list> consisting of the parameter **y** plus <shorter parameter list>

What does such personalization generally mean for the user wishes, user stories, use cases, and textual SSDs? In a sense, the personalized user wish is a *special case* of the more general user wish but leading to one less parameter because the (known) user represents a 'hidden' parameter. The basic idea is here that the user was already authenticated (so 'known') by the system and that the system must reconstruct the 'object' that user represents. Therefore, the use case and corresponding SSD must contain an extra 'reconstruction' step, in which the system identifies the user as a certain <role>. In the next pattern, presented in Table 3.2, we wrote the additional reconstruction step in italics. In that table, α denotes the action verb in the original user wish and γ the role in the user story. Step 1 represents the *input* phase, Steps 2 and 3 represent the *execution* phase, and Step 4 represents the *output* phase.

Let's apply this scheme, for example, to the elementary user wish *Enrol a Student*, in particular to the parameterized user wish *Enrol a Student for a given course*. For the student him/herself, they become *Enrol **myself*** and *Enrol **myself** for a given course*, respectively. So, α becomes 'Enrol', γ becomes 'student', <shorter parameter list> becomes <course>, and <parameter list> consists of the combination of the parameters **y** and <course>.

eUW	Enrol **myself**
pUW	Enrol **myself with a given** <course>
US	**As a** student, **I want to** Enrol **myself so that** I can follow the course
UC	1. **The** student **asks the system:** Enrol **me with a given** <course> *2.* ***The system identifies the user as a particular*** *student* 3. **The system tries to** Enrol **that** student **with that given** <course> 4. **The system informs the** student **about the result**
tSSD	1. **User → System:** Enrol**Me(**<course>**) ;** *2.* ***System → System: y :=*** *the student* ***represented by the user ;*** 3. **System → System: try to** Enrol **y with a given** <parameter list> **;** 4. **System → User:** result

The only (small) thing is that the general ‘with’ should be ‘for’ in this case.

3.5 CRUDA-Patterns

We recall the CRUDA functions from Sect. 2.2.1. They are basic functions generally applicable to data in a system:

- Create: add data to the system
- Read: only look at data in the system
- Update: change data in the system
- Delete: remove data from the system
- Archive: archive data in the system

Table 3.3 recalls some alternative action verbs that might be used.

We will now zoom in on each of the CRUDA functions. In principle, CRUDA-patterns are special cases of the patterns sketched earlier in this chapter.

Table 3.3 Some alternatively used CRUDA verbs

CRUDA	Some alternatively used action verbs
Create	Register, Enter, Add, Insert, Store
Read	Retrieve, View, See, Search, Select, Get
Update	Refresh, Change, Modify, Edit, Alter, Adapt, Replace, Rename
Delete	Remove, Erase, Destroy
Archive	File (away)

3.5.1 Create

An *elementary user wish* of the form

Create/Register/Enter/Add/Insert/Store a <noun (phrase)>

probably indicates a Create of an individual object. For instance, for a university system, the noun (phrase) could be

> Student, Student Assistant, Lecturer, Study, Course, (Course) Enrolment, Exam (Enrolment), Exam Grade, etc.

Then, the *parameterized user wish* should contain the relevant parameters (properties) for the object, except the system-generated ones such as *student number* and *university e-mail address* in our example *Register a Student* in Sect. 2.1.

We recall that a *postcondition* essentially consists of two parts: a description of the *state change result* and a description of the *output*. The postcondition for a *Create use case* will probably be that:

- The *new state* is the old state plus the individual object *or* the state stayed the same
- The *output* could be 'Done' (plus, e.g., the added information), in case of a successful state change, *or* the reason(s) why the user wish could not be executed

3.5.2 Read

A *elementary user wish* of the form

Read/Retrieve/View/See/Search/Select/Get a <noun (phrase)>

probably indicates a Read (retrieval). The noun (phrase) can refer to an *individual object* (e.g., Student, Lecturer, Course, etc.), but the noun (phrase) could as well indicate something *complex*, e.g., a 'report', 'overview', 'summary', 'schedule', or so.

With such open terms, (much) *extra requirements elicitation* has yet to be done: Which information should be in that report? And in which detail? And how to 'summarize' information exactly? Summations or averages? And over what exactly?

Example 3.2 The Desirable Content of a Report (Elicitation example)
As a small elicitation example, we shortly present our discussion with the university about their elementary user wish *Retrieve a Personal Progress Report.*

(continued)

Example 3.2 (continued)

After some elicitation, it turned out to be for first-year students, where the report consists of a grades overview of the student and the number of points/ credits she/he earned. Each course stands for a number of points, usually 5 per course.

Clear? No, not yet. For example, what exactly should be in the overview? Well, Course ID, Course Name, Year, Number of Credits, Grade, and Date.

Year of what? Year of the course in the program (1, 2, or 3). And which date? Not the date when the grade was determined/given but the date of the exam.

And for only first-year students, as we understood it? Well, no, not exactly: Actually, our interest is in the credits earned for first year *courses*, so usually for first-year students, but it might apply to second-year students as well, for instance.

And one more thing, they told us: For the number of points earned, only the courses *within the program* followed by the student should be counted. The rationale behind all this was to determine whether the student might need a (negative) Binding Study Advice, an important advice, with legal consequences.

Wouldn't it be useful then—for substantiation reasons—to indicate in the overview whether or not the course is within the student's program, we asked. Good suggestion, they said.

So, all in all, if we understood correctly, we said, the *Personal Progress Report (over the first year)* of student x consists of:

1. A gradings overview of student x, for each grading consisting of Course ID, Course Name, Year of the course in the program, Indication whether or not the course is within the student's program, Number of Credits, Grade, and Date of the exam
2. In summary, the total number of points earned by student x for *first year* courses *within his/her program*

'Correct. But could you also add the *average* of the points earned by that student for his/her first-year courses within the program?' they replied…

In general, the postcondition for a *retrieval use case* will likely be that:

- The state stayed the same
- The output is the information asked for
  or the reason(s) why the wish could not be executed successfully

A frequently occurring form of retrieval is what we call *browsing*, for instance, when looking around for 'suitable' *products* on the website of a shop, for 'certain sorts' of *clients* in the company's system, or for 'interesting' *courses* on the website of a university. In general, when you are looking for interesting instances of a concept C (such as *products*, *clients*, or *courses* in the mentioned cases) but you don't know exactly the most suitable search criteria (yet).

This brings us to a general *browse pattern* which delivers a subset of all C-instances in the system. It uses the notion of *search form* as introduced in Sect. 2.6.4. It could work as follows:

Use Case: **Browse for Cs**

1. *The User asks the System to browse for Cs*
2. *The System sends the User an 'empty' search form for Cs; no search fields filled in yet*
3. *The User fills in some search fields, indicating which search conditions to apply*
4. *The User sends the System the filled-in search form*
5. *The System sends the User all Cs satisfying all conditions expressed in the search form*
6. *If the User is not satisfied with the result, steps 3–5 will be repeated*

The corresponding textual SSD, where U stands for User and S for System:

DEFINE BrowseFor(C) **AS**
  U ➡ S: Browse for Cs;
  S ➡ U: 'empty' search form for Cs;
  repeat
    U ➡ U: Add/Adapt some search fields, indicating which search conditions to apply;
    U ➡ S: Filled-in search form (indicating which search conditions to apply);
    S ➡ U: All Cs satisfying all the conditions expressed in the search form
  until the User is satisfied with the result
END

Postconditions
The *output* consists of a subset of all Cs, namely, all Cs satisfying all the conditions expressed in the search form as finally filled-in. The *state* stayed the same.

3.5.3 Update

A *user wish* starting with an action verb like

Update/Refresh/Change/Modify/Edit/Alter/Adapt/Replace/Rename/ Increase/Decrease

probably indicates an Update. An Update is subtle because an update must indicate *which* objects have to updated, and *which* of their components, and in *which* way. It could have the form

Update/Refresh/Change/Modify/Edit/Alter/Adapt/Replace/Rename/Increase/Decrease
<*specific components* in a *specific way* for each *object with a given property*>

For example, a Dean of a faculty might want to

Increase *the number of expected students by 10%* and *the allocated workload by 5%* for each *master course for academic year 22/23*

The ingredients in this example are as follows:

The specific components: *the number of expected students* and *the allocated workload*
The specific ways: *by 10%* and *by 5%*, respectively
Objects with a given property: *master course for academic year 22/23*

Frequently, only one object should be updated, '*the object with a given ID value*', e.g., '*the student with a given student number*'; or only one component should be updated, e.g., '*the address*' or '*the allocated workload*'; or, in particular, only one component of only one object, e.g., *Update Student Address*.

The postcondition for an *Update use case* might be that:

- The *new state* consists of the old state minus all 'old' objects that were updated plus all 'new' updated objects, *or* the state stayed the same
- The *output* could be 'Done' (plus, e.g., the *number* of updated objects), *or* the reason(s) why the user wish could not be executed

As just formulated, it is an 'all-or-nothing' update. However, the desirable postcondition could be that each object that could have been updated successfully indeed *has been* updated successfully. In that case, the output should probably also indicate which objects have and which have not been updated successfully.

3.5.4 Delete

An *elementary user wish* of the form

Delete/Remove/Erase/Destroy <expression>

probably indicates a Delete. Here <expression> is often of the form '*each object with a given property*', for instance '*each course of last year*'. Often, only one object should be removed: '*the object with a given ID value*', e.g., '*the student with a given student number*' or '*the department with a given name*'.

The postcondition for a *Delete use case* might be that:

- The *new state* consists of the old state minus all objects satisfying <expression> *or* the state stayed the same
- The *output* could be 'Done' (plus, e.g., the number of deleted objects), in case of successful deletes, *or* the reason(s) why the wish could not be executed

As just formulated, it is an 'all-or-nothing' delete, which should often be the case. However, the desirable postcondition could be that each object that could have been deleted successfully indeed *has been* deleted successfully. In that case, the output should probably also indicate which objects have and have not been deleted successfully.

Sometimes, a *delete* should be a *cascading* delete, suggesting that other data should be deleted as well. For instance, maybe the deletion of a student should also entail the deletion of all his/her enrolments that are still in force. Probably, some extra requirements elicitation has to be done in such cases to determine which other data should be deleted as well.

3.5.5 Archive

When a product is no longer sold by a company, when someone is no longer a client of an organization (e.g., of Social Services), when a course will no longer be given, or a student leaves the university, the corresponding data can be deleted, it seems...

However, that data might be needed again later, e.g., for particular questions about that former product, client, course, or student or for some (monthly or yearly) reporting. Therefore, instead of *deleting* certain data, it might be needed to *archive* that data. That is, the data is still in the system—as opposed to *deleting* data—but somehow 'marked' as being archived.

Archiving might also be needed—and even be obligatory—due to legal retention periods, e.g., in governmental situations. In other words, maybe the system should retain the *history* of the certain data. Therefore, we added a fifth basic function, extending the acronym CRUD to CRUDA:

- archive data in the system (Archive)

When data must be archived, several elicitation questions might come up:

- Which data must be retained? Maybe name, birth date, and social security number, but also phone number, (latest) address, or (latest) marital status?
- But is it allowed to retain that data? Maybe it isn't, due to privacy legislation, especially when it regards personal data.
- And for how long? For example, regarding specifications of former products, probably quite long for expensive products, say cars, and quite short for cheap products, e.g., screws.
- All the details, or only on an aggregate level? Maybe all the details for a year, and after 1 year on a more aggregate level, after 5 years on an even more aggregate level, and deleted after 10 years.
- When does a retention period formally start (or end)? This might be an important issue, from a legal point of view. Moreover, the length of the prescribed retention period might differ per type of data.

- That starting date, or better the end date, of the retention period should also be in the system, or reconstructable by the system. And once the system 'knows' the end date, the system might delete that data 'automatically'.

All in all, archiving might need its own separate requirements analysis, maybe with separate domain experts, although that might come in a later stage. The *purpose* of that archiving plays an important role and should be leading during the requirements analysis.

3.6 Summary

This chapter discussed some *development patterns*. It started with a general development pattern (Sect. 3.1), and from there on, it subsequently worked out some refinements and variants, such as indicating the parameters separately (Sect. 3.2), communicating with other actors (Sect. 3.3), personalization (Sect. 3.4), and CRUDA patterns (Sect. 3.5), including browsing (in Sect. 3.5.2). Other general patterns are *HandleForm* and *HandleList*, defined in Sect. 2.6.

Chapter 4
Domain Modelling

Abstract In the beginning of a development project, it is hard to uncover/pinpoint the potentially relevant concepts and how they are related to each other. A *domain model* might be helpful in that stage. A domain model constitutes a visual, rather informal, usually incomplete, and suggestive description.

Section 4.1 explains the notion of a *domain model*. Section 4.2 discusses how to find potentially relevant candidate *concepts*, their *properties*, and their *associations*, the main ingredients of a domain model. Section 4.3 treats various special cases.

Although a domain model can be a communication vehicle, especially initially, in a later stage, you need a precise, full-fledged *conceptual data model*, the topic of Chap. 5. We note that a domain model is not strictly necessary: you can start to construct a conceptual data model directly. But making a domain model first, might help you to get a first impression of the relevant concepts and their relationships.

4.1 Domain Models

A **domain model** is a visual representation of the concepts, their associations, and maybe—some of—their properties that *might* be relevant for the application to be developed. A domain model can have the following ingredients:

- **Concepts**, a.k.a. *conceptual classes*
- Their relevant **properties**, a.k.a. their *attributes*
- Their mutual **associations**, a.k.a. their *relationships*

A domain model is usually represented by an undirected graph—so, consisting of nodes and lines—with the ingredients as indicated in the following overview:

Overview of the Ingredients of a Domain Model
A **node** represents a *Concept* or a *Concept* with *Properties*:

(continued)

B. de Brock, *Developing Information Systems Accurately*,
https://doi.org/10.1007/978-3-031-16862-8_4

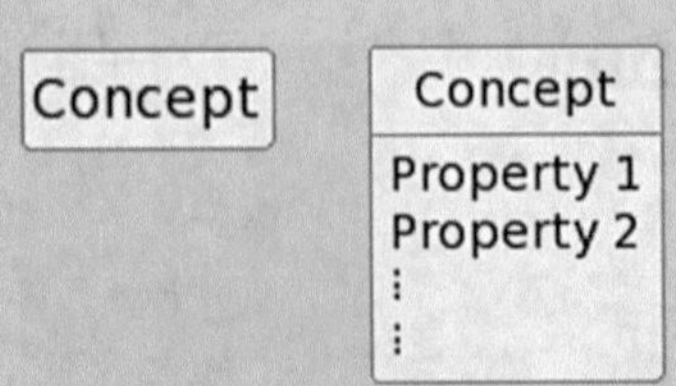

A **line** represents an *Association* between two concepts:

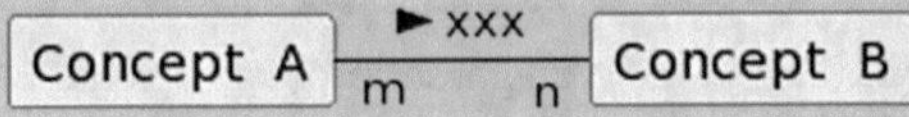

(1) m and n are so-called **multiplicities**.
Usually ‘1’, ‘0..1’ (at most 1), or ‘*’ (0 or more, a.k.a. ‘many’);
sometimes you may also encounter ‘+’ (1 or more), but we will hardly use it.

(2) The phrase xxx (often a verb phrase or preposition) ‘describes’ the *association*.

(3) The symbol ▶ indicates the **reading direction** for the attached phrase xxx (▶ or ◀ for horizontal lines, and ▲ or ▼ for vertical lines).

The reading direction applies to the phrase xxx that is actually used, but it is not intrinsic to the association: Often, the reading direction could be turned around by using another expression instead of xxx. For instance, when xxx is a verb in active voice, you could change it into a passive voice:

Concept A ▶ xxx (m … n) Concept B   Concept A ◀ is xxx-ed by (m … n) Concept B

So, in a domain model, the following ingredients can be distinguished: *concepts*, their *properties*, *association lines*, *multiplicities, association ‘descriptions’* (usually verb phrases or prepositions), and their *reading directions*. However, not all ingredients need to be present in a domain model: In particular, the *properties* and *multiplicities* might not be clear in the beginning and could be left out. Another reason to leave out the properties is when a domain model becomes very large, i.e., consisting of many nodes and lines. Then it might be clearer to leave the properties out.

An association with on both sides a ‘*’ or a ‘+’ is called a **many-to-many association** or a *many-to-many relationship*, such as ‘enrols for’ in Example 4.1:

Example 4.1: A Tiny Domain Model
An example of a (very) small domain model with all these ingredients, which you might come across:

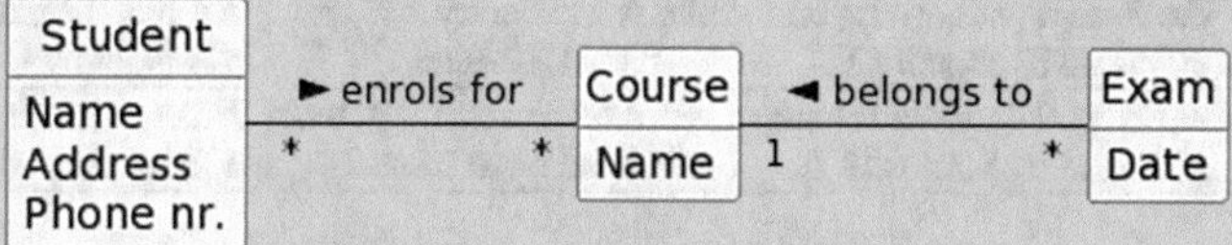

We note that '◄belongs to' could be changed into 'has►'.
The graph above expresses the following:

- Student, Course, and Exam seem to be relevant concepts.
- Name, Address, and Phone no. seem to be relevant properties of Student.
- Name seems to be a relevant property of the concept Course.
- Date seems to be a relevant property of the concept Exam.
- An exam belongs to exactly 1 course.
- A course has 0 or more exams (i.e., exams belonging to it).
- A student enrols for 0 or more courses.
- For a course, 0 or more students enrol for it.

The graph represents a kind of minimum knowledge ('*what we understood until now*'). We note that the graph does *not* express:

- That Student, Course, and Exam are *the only* relevant concepts
- That Name, Address, and Phone no. are *the only* relevant properties of the concept Student, etc.

In daily practice, the verb phrase used to describe the association might be an *action verb* (e.g., 'enrols for') or a *state verb* (e.g., 'is enrolled for'). A verb describing a state might actually be better than an action verb, because a domain model should express possible *states* (i.e., statics, not dynamics).

In general, an association of the form, with 'xs' representing a verb,

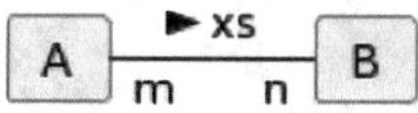

expresses two statements, namely, one for each side. Each statement depends on the **multiplicity** involved (with 'xs' pronounced as 'ikses' and 'xd' as 'iksed'):

Table 4.1 The statements expressed by the multiplicities in 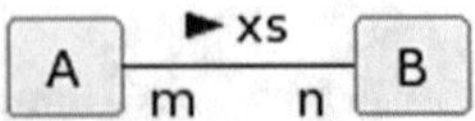

	n = '*'	n = '1'	n = '0..1'
m = '*'	An A xs 0 or more Bs and a B is xd by 0 or more As	An A xs exactly 1 B and a B is xd by 0 or more As	An A xs at most 1 B and a B is xd by 0 or more As
m = '1'	An A xs 0 or more Bs and a B is xd by exactly 1 A	An A xs exactly 1 B and a B is xd by exactly 1 A	An A xs at most 1 B and a B is xd by exactly 1 A
m = '0..1'	An A xs 0 or more Bs and a B is xd by at most 1 A	An A xs exactly 1 B and a B is xd by at most 1 A	An A xs at most 1 B and a B is xd by at most 1 A

(a) for n = '*': An A xs 0 or more Bs
for n = '1': An A xs exactly 1 B
for n = '0..1': An A xs at most 1 B
for n = '+': An A xs 1 or more Bs

(b) for m = '*': A B is xd by 0 or more As
for m = '1': A B is xd by exactly 1 A
for m = '0..1': A B is xd by at most 1 A
for m = '+': A B is xd by 1 or more As

Table 4.1 works out most combinations.

Intermezzo: Multiplicities in Mathematical Terms

For those interested in it: The multiplicities can be expressed in terms of the mathematical notions of *relation*, *function*, and *injection* as well:

A —▶xs— B (m, n) indicates a relation R ⊆ A × B.

We introduce and use the following suitable definitions and notations:

- R is a **relation** ⇔ R is a set of ordered pairs
- **dom(R)** is the set of all first coordinates in R
- **rng(R)** is the set of all second coordinates in R
- R^{-1} = { (b;a) | (a;b) ∈ R }, called the *inverse of R*
- R is a **function** ⇔ R is a relation and for each a ∈ dom(R) there is exactly one b with (a;b) ∈ R
- R is an **injection** ⇔ R and R^{-1} are functions

For a **relation** R, we define:

- R is **out of** A ⇔ dom(R) ⊆ A
- R is **from** A ⇔ dom(R) = A
- R is **into** B ⇔ rng(R) ⊆ B
- R is **onto** B ⇔ rng(R) = B

(continued)

This terminology applies to functions and injections as well, because they are also relations.

What do the multiplicities say in terms of relations, functions, and injections? See Table 4.2.

After this intermezzo, we continue with an example without multiplicities mentioned yet. It illustrates how you can construct a 'questionnaire' to determine/discuss the multiplicities with the customer.

Example 4.2: A Small Domain Model Without Multiplicities
We give an example without multiplicities and with properties of only one of the concepts (Book). The example concerns a library with several branches. In this example, the relevant properties of a book are ISBN, Title, Author, Branch (the book is in), Book ID (as used in that branch), Publisher, and Physical Condition:

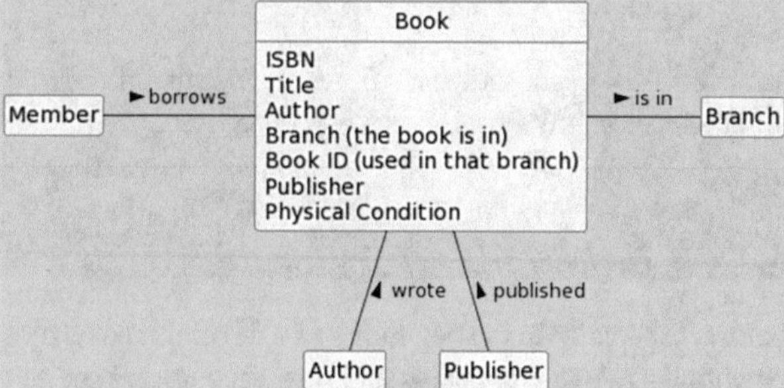

For determining the multiplicities, you have to check/discuss a kind of questionnaire with a 'multiple-choice' statement for each side of each line. In this case, the following multiple-choice statements have to be checked/discussed with the library:

1a. A member borrows *exactly 1/at most 1/0 or more* book(s).
1b. For each book, *exactly 1/at most 1/0 or more* member(s) borrow(s) that book.

2a. An author wrote *exactly 1/at most 1/0 or more* book(s).
2b. For each book, *exactly 1/at most 1/0 or more* author(s) wrote that book.

3a. A publisher published *exactly 1/at most 1/0 or more* book(s).
3b. For each book, *exactly 1/at most 1/0 or more* publisher(s) published that book.

(continued)

Table 4.2 Multiplicities in terms of relations, functions, and injections

	n = '*'	n = '1'	n = '0..1'
m = '*'	R is a relation out of A into B	R is a function from A into B	R is a function out of A into B
m = '1'	R^{-1} is a function from B into A	R is an injection from A onto B	R is an injection out of A onto B
m = '0..1'	R^{-1} is a function out of B into A	R is an injection from A into B	R is an injection out of A into B

Example 4.2 (continued)

4a. A book is in *exactly 1/at most 1/0 or more* branch(es).

4b. For each branch, *exactly 1/at most 1/0 or more* book(s) is/are in that branch.

Exercise 4.1

(a) Discuss each of the eight multiple choice statements in Example 4.2. (We note that you might encounter some problems here.)

(b) Add the corresponding multiplicities to the domain model in Example 4.2 (Cf. Sect. A.2 of the Appendix to see how you can draw domain models.)

As stated before, especially in the beginning of a development project, it is hard to uncover the potentially relevant concepts and how they are related to each other. A limited domain model might be useful then, because it can:

- Depict your initial impression of the relevant concepts and associations in the application area.
- Show and delimit the intended scope and borders of the system.
- Help reach agreement with the customer on the scope of the system.
- Help understand the terminology used.
- Help create a vocabulary/ontology regarding the relevant concepts, their properties, and their associations.
- Grow steadily when the understanding of the intended application grows, and, hence, new versions of the domain model might come up.

Other benefits of domain modelling are that it can:

- Reveal and eliminate—or at least reduce—misunderstandings
- Lead to standardization of terminology
- Create a common language and vocabulary, also among different parties and departments on the customer-side ☺
- Improve consistency of information

In other words, a domain model can be a communication vehicle, especially in the beginning. In a later stage, you need a precise and full-fledged *conceptual data model*, the topic of Chap. 5.

4.2 Finding/Discovering/Determining Relevant Candidates

Which concepts, properties, and associations are relevant? To get a first impression: visit the organization, not only digitally but also on site; take a good look at their processes during the visit; talk with stakeholders in various roles (roles from high to low); look at the information inputs and outputs—from (order) forms, receipts, and simple retrievals to complex reports—and discuss issues with the domain experts, where you might need different experts for different sub-domains. Existing models and documents might also be interesting, but they might be incomplete or outdated, and maybe do interviews and (requirements) workshops. This will surely reveal, or at least give insight into, their *user wishes*. Those user wishes will already contain hints about relevant concepts and properties. The other way around, there seems to be no reason for concepts or properties that do not appear in—or follow from—a user wish or use case.

The *noun phrase* in the elementary user wish is probably a relevant *concept*: We recall that a user wish can have the basic form

Register / Retrieve / Update / Remove / Archive a <noun (phrase)>

where <noun (phrase)> could, for instance, be *Customer / Product / Sale / Student / Lecturer / Course / Exam* etc.

The *parameters* in a parameterized user wish might indicate *properties* of that concept, in particular in case of Creates. For instance:

Register a Student with a given name, address, birth date, phone number, gender, and social security number.

And also check the other way around: Given a concept with its properties in a domain model, it is useful to check whether they are mentioned in the Create-UW for that concept as well, or why they are not. Since modelling is an ongoing process with corrections and additions, especially in the beginning, new properties might have occurred in the meantime.

Use cases can be helpful as well, by looking at the nouns, verbs, and prepositions they contain. *Nouns* might indicate *concepts* or their *properties*, while *verbs* and *prepositions* might indicate *associations* or their ingredients. So, in a use case, you could emphasize them, e.g., by coloring them or underlining them. It is useful to first write each sentence in a use case on a separate line (if that wasn't done yet).

Example 4.3: Analyzing a Use Case
As an illustration, we look at the use case *Enter a Grade* mentioned in Sect. 3.2. An earlier version of that use case (without 'dynamic forms') ran as follows:

> *A lecturer asks the system to enter a grade. The system presents the potential courses (of that lecturer). The lecturer indicates the intended course. The system presents the potential exams for that course. The lecturer indicates the intended exam. The system presents the students enrolled for that exam. The lecturer indicates the intended student. The lecturer adds the grade. The system tries to enter that grade of that student for that exam of that course. The system informs the lecturer about the result.*

For clarity, first we write each sentence on a separate line. Then we mark:

- The *actors* in the use case, say in yellow or by a dashed line (in this case lecturer and system)
- The *verbs* indicating what the actors do, say in green or by a dotted line (in this case asks, enter, presents, indicates, etc.).

Then we arrive at the remaining, more 'domain specific' parts. Now we mark:

- Relevant *nouns*, say in blue or by a normal line (in this case grade, course(s), lecturer, exam(s), student(s), and result)
- Relevant *prepositions* and *verb phrases*, say in grey or by a double line (in this case of, for, enrolled for, and about).

This leads to the following 'colorful' result:

1. A lecturer asks the system to enter a grade
2. The system presents the potential courses (of that lecturer)
3. The lecturer indicates the intended course
4. The system presents the potential exams for that course
5. The lecturer indicates the intended exam
6. The system presents the students enrolled for that exam
7. The lecturer indicates the intended student
8. The lecturer adds the grade
9. The system tries to enter that grade of that student for that exam of that course
10. The system informs the lecturer about the result

When we start with the associations suggested by the prepositions and verb phrases in lines 2, 4, and 6, we get:

(continued)

Example 4.3 (continued)

The expression '*grade of that student for that exam of that course*' is more subtle and suggests that the grade refers both to the student and to the exam. Note that we already understood that an exam refers to a course. Then we get:

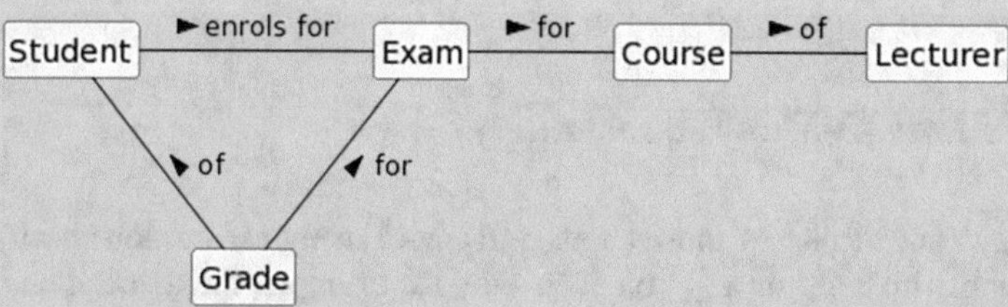

This domain model includes almost all candidate concepts (i.e., the blue nouns), except *result*. That is because *result* is not a basic concept but a *derivable* notion, i.e., derivable from the other information in the domain model. We note that derivable notions could (and should) be skipped in the domain model. They can be introduced—and defined—in a later stage, e.g., as a retrieval specification and result.

The multiplicities are left out since they are not clear yet. We also didn't recognize specific properties of the concepts yet.

We note that this simple domain model covers only one use case (namely, *Enter a Grade*). Other use cases will probably extend this initial domain model.

There are many widespread 'common' concepts, which recur frequently in various applications. General examples are Customer/Client, Supplier, Product/Service, Order, Sale/Purchase, Transaction, Payment, Employee, and Department.

More systematically, different groups of common concepts can be distinguished:

- *Customer*, in other organizations a.k.a. Client, Guest, Member, Student (in universities), Patient (in hospitals), etc.
- *Physical* and/or *organizational* units: Building, Office, Floor, Room, Shop, Warehouse, Branch, Division, Department, Unit, (Project) Team, etc.
- *Products/Services*-related concepts: Product/Item/Good, Service, Catalogue, Supplier, Order (incoming by customers vs. outgoing towards suppliers), Bill of Material, Delivery, Store/Stockroom/Warehouse, etc.
- *Money-related* concepts: Sale, Purchase, Transaction, Invoice, Bill, Credit card, Bonus card, Bank (Account), Payment, Receipt, IOU ('*I owe you*', an official acknowledgement of a debt), etc.
- *Employees*, with subclasses/roles: (Account) Manager, Secretary, Administrator, (Department) Head, Controller, Planner, Coordinator, Lecturer, etc. These roles are relevant for user stories as well.

4.3 Some Noteworthy Cases

This section treats various special cases you might come across in practice. We often introduce them by first mentioning an illustrative example, followed by a treatment of the general situation.

4.3.1 *Many-to-Many Associations*

We always need to know more about a 'many-to-many association' itself, i.e., an association with a '*' or a '+' on each side, for example, the association '*Student enrols for Course*' in Example 4.1 or the association '*Member borrows Book*' in Example 4.2 when it is 'many-to-many' (but also when it would be 'many-to-one'). For example, at least you need to know *which* student enrolled for *which* course and *which* member borrowed *which* book. Additionally, you might also need to know *when* the student enrolled for the course or (until) *when* the member borrowed the book.

In general, a many-to-many association typically represents a 'hidden' concept which you need to know and which you should make explicit: For a many-to-many association between concepts A and B, you at least need to know *which* A-instances are associated with *which* B-instances.

Turning the verb in a many-to-many association into a noun, i.e., *nominalizing* the verb, might give a hint for the concept, e.g., *enrol* ⇒ *enrolment* and *borrow* ⇒ ~~*borrowment*~~ *loan*. You can replace a many-to-many association between two concepts by the formerly hidden concept and two 'many-to-one' associations between the hidden concept and each of those two concepts. The hidden concept is probably a meaningful concept in the user world anyway.

In general, the left association can be replaced by the right one:

A —►xs— * * — B   A — ◄α 1 * — C — ►β * 1 — B

For the two examples we just mentioned:

1. With A = 'Student', xs = 'enrols for', and B = 'Course', you get C = 'Enrolment', α = 'of', and β = 'for':

   Student — ◄of 1 * — Enrolment — ►for * 1 — Course

2. With A = 'Member', xs = 'borrows', and B = 'Book', you get C = 'Loan', α = 'by', and β = 'of':

   Member — ◄by 1 * — Loan — ►of * 1 — Book

In the Entity-Relationship model of Chen [Che], those hidden concepts—such as Enrolment and Loan—are also known as *relationships*, next to *entities* (i.e., concepts), in this case Student, Course, Member, and Book. However, we consider relationships as entities of which you didn't realize it yet... We uniformly treat them all as concepts!

4.3.2 Ternary Associations and Beyond

The associations which we presented until now could be called *binary* associations, because they were associations between *two* concepts. But sometimes you might encounter associations between three or more concepts, for example, *A <u>student</u> rates a <u>lecturer</u> in a <u>course</u>*. How to handle and represent them?

Also a **ternary association**, i.e., an association between three concepts, represents a hidden concept which you need to know explicitly. As stated before, turning the verb into a noun (so, nominalizing the verb) might give a hint for the concept: *rate => rating*. Then you can talk about

The rating *by* a student *of* a lecturer *in* a course

You can handle that ternary association and represent it by three *many-to-one* associations as follows:

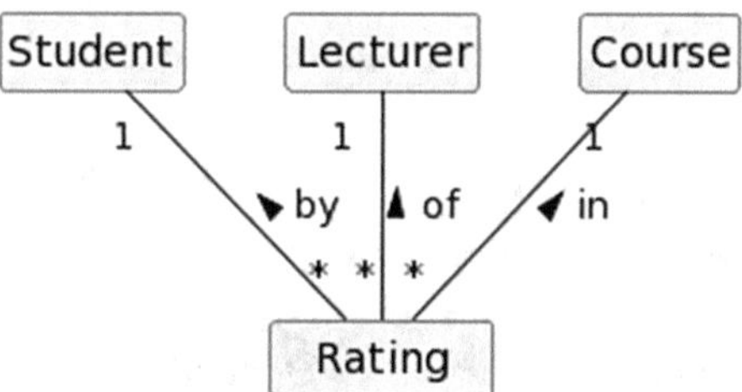

In general, associations usually follow from sentences of the form

A <Concept 0> <verb> <Concept 1> ... <Concept n>

where <Concept 0> is the subject of the sentence and the other concepts are the (in)direct objects of the sentence. Those (in)direct objects might be preceded by a preposition and an indefinite article ('a' or 'an'), as in our example:

A student rates *a* lecturer *in a* course

The association represents a hidden concept which you need to know explicitly. As stated before, turning the verb into a noun (so, nominalizing the verb) might give a hint for the concept.

An ***n*-ary association** is an association between *n* concepts. You can handle an *n*-ary association by replacing it by n + 1 *many-to-one* associations. If α0, α1, ... αn are the (new) association names, then you get

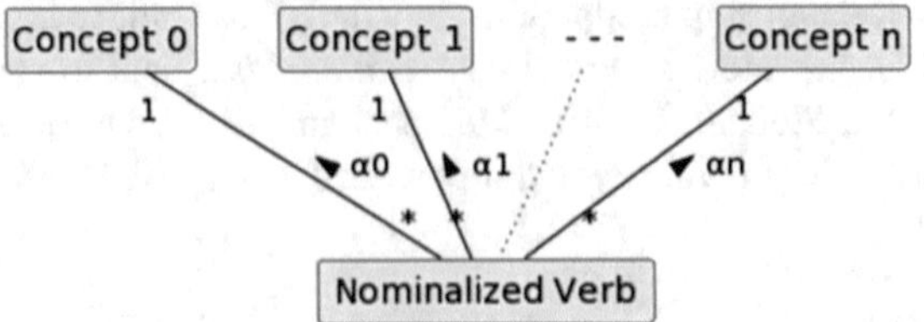

For α0, α1, ... αn, you might use the prepositions in the 'nominalized' sentence. Note that for n = 1, you simply get back the binary situation. We note that n can also be 0, namely, in case of *intransitive* verbs. For example, *A ship arrives*. Applying our nominalization rules would lead to *The arrival of a ship*. And maybe you might need to know more about arrivals too, e.g., the time of arrival. This then leads to:

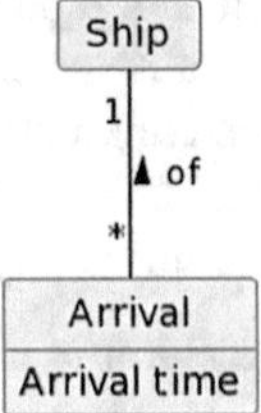

4.3.3 *Individual Items Versus 'Catalogue' Items*

We introduce this topic by a concrete example, followed by a general treatment.

Example 4.4: Individual Items Versus 'Catalogue' Items
We return to Example 4.2, our library example (with books, borrowing members, etc.). Relevant properties of a book were ISBN, Title, Author, Branch (the book is in), Book ID (as used in that branch), Publisher, and (Physical) Condition, for instance. Maybe you encountered some problems with the exercise to discuss the multiple-choice statements over there. Well, indeed, there are some problems, as we will explain now.

The library usually has several copies of popular books (sometimes even 10 book copies). We might distinguish between a (physical) copy of the book and the book 'title', as a librarian calls it. The 'title' can be considered as a kind of 'catalogue item'. And as a further clarification: A book copy might have coffee stains or 'dog-ears', but a book title hasn't. It is possible that a book is in the library's catalogue but that the book isn't in the library physically (e.g., because they recently lent their only copy). Note in the previous sentence that

(continued)

Example 4.4 (continued)
the word 'book' turns out to be a *homonym*, i.e., a word with two or more different meanings: first used as book title and then as book copy in that sentence.

Once you distinguish between book *title* and book *copy*, you have to distribute the original book properties over the two new notions: The properties belonging to 'book title' are ISBN, Title, Author, and Publisher. Those belonging to 'book copy' are Book ID (as used in that branch), Branch (the copy is in), and (Physical) Condition. You also have to reconsider the associations the original book notion was involved in: The associations 'wrote' and 'published' refer to 'book title' and the associations 'borrows' and 'is in' refer to 'book copy'. This all leads to the following new domain model:

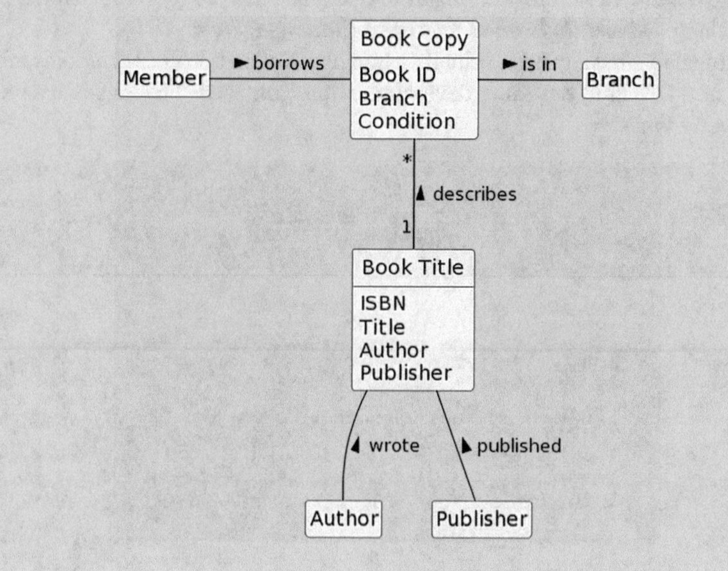

In general, when you have to split a concept like *Item* (e.g., *Item* = Book), say into *Individual Item* and *Catalogue Item*, you have to distribute the original *Item* properties over the two new concepts. You also have to reconsider the associations the original *Item* concept was involved in; you have to distribute them over the two new concepts. The original *Item* concept could be replaced by:

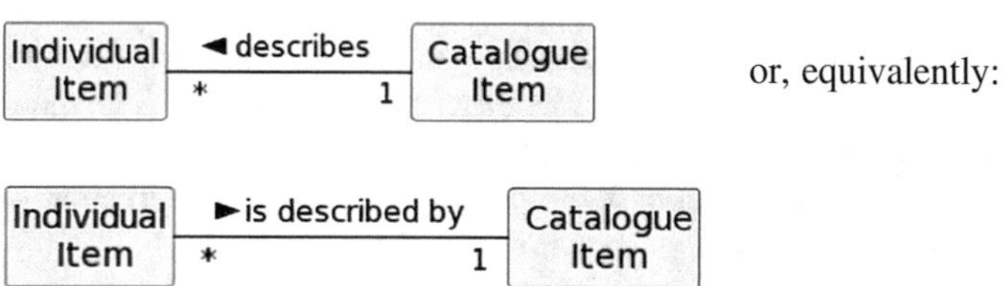

or, equivalently:

In Object-Oriented design, a concept such as *Catalogue Item* is known as a *description class*, e.g., in [Lar] and in Object-Oriented Design of Coad & Yourdon [C&Y].

A **homonym**, simply said, is a word with two or more different meanings. The use of homonyms might lead to ambiguous sentences, although that might not always be clear from the start, unfortunately. This phenomenon of homonyms appears very often in practice, actually almost always. And, surprisingly, especially when it concerns the core notions of the organization! Just to mention a few examples: 'flight' in an airline company, 'bed' in a hospital, 'study' and 'exam' in a university, and 'book' in a library (as you just saw). Consider, for instance, the sentence '*Flights to New York take 8 hours but the flight of last Monday took 10 hours*'. Here, '*the flight of last Monday*' is an individual flight, while '*Flights to New York*' refers to a 'catalogue flight'. The current section gives a hint how this particular homonym confusion regarding flights can be solved, namely, by distinguishing between *Individual flight* and *Catalogue flight*.

Unfortunately, that a word is actually a homonym often becomes clear only after a while, if at all. Within the same development project, such 'challenges' can even occur several times.

Exercise 4.2
Answer the questions in Guideline G4 in Sect. 2.4.4.

Exercise 4.3
(a) Explain the following domain model (making use of Table 4.1):

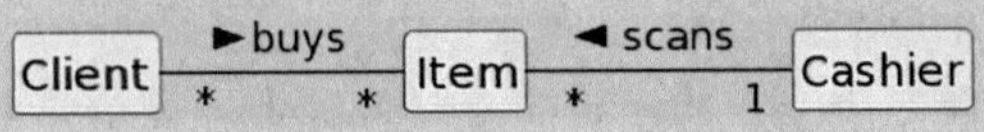

Client —(►buys; * … *)— Item —(◄scans; * … 1)— Cashier

(b) Critically discuss the model.
(c) What is wrong with this model?
(d) Improve it.

4.3.4 *Directed Graphs*

Sometimes you have to represent directed graphs (i.e., consisting of nodes and arrows between them), where a node can have 0 or more incoming arrows and 0 or more outgoing arrows. A flight network between airports is the standard example.

A general directed graph—and a flight network between airports in particular—can be represented in a domain model as shown in Fig. 4.1a, b.

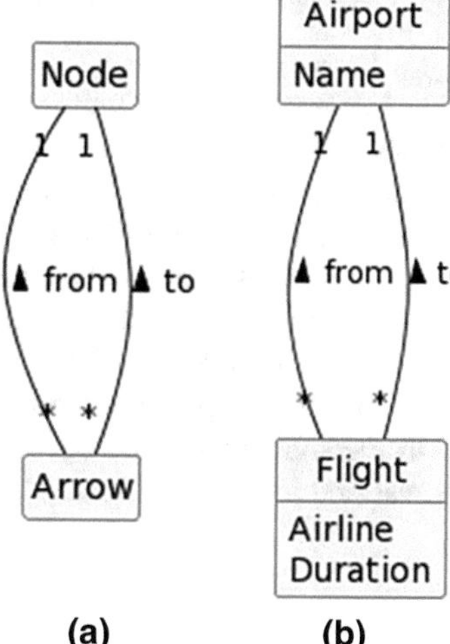

Fig. 4.1 (**a**) Domain model for a general directed graph. (**b**) Modelling a flight network between airports (including durations)

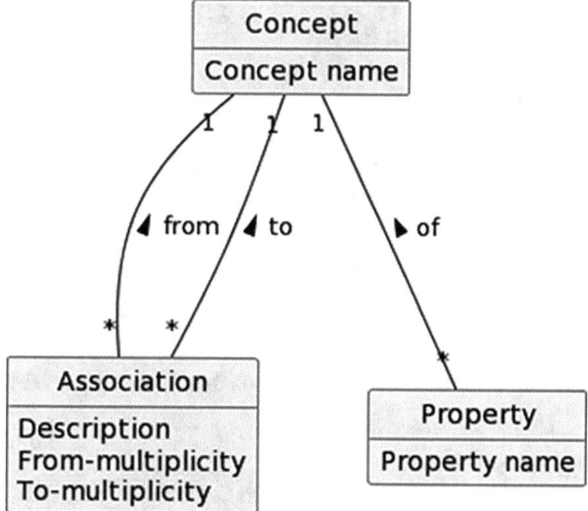

Fig. 4.2 A domain model for domain models

We note that a domain model with *concepts* ('nodes') and only 'many-to-one' *associations* ('arrows') can be represented as a directed graph as well. From Sect. 4.1 we can derive that a domain model with concepts, properties, and associations with descriptions, multiplicities, and reading directions can be modelled as depicted in Fig. 4.2.

4.3.5 *Trees and the Like*

Sometimes you have to represent trees (consisting of nodes and arrows) or, more general, directed graphs where a node can have 0 or more incoming arrows and 0 or 1 outgoing arrow. Folder structures—with subfolders and files—are examples, such as the concrete one shown in Fig. 4.3.

So, in that case, the arrows point from the 'child' to the 'parent'. A node with no incoming arrows is called a **leaf**, and a node with no outgoing arrows is called a **root**. Other examples are organizational hierarchies: departments, sub-departments, and so on, but also employees, their subordinates, etc.

In a domain model, a folder structure (with subfolders) or a general tree can be represented in a domain model by a many-to-0/1 association as shown in Fig. 4.4.

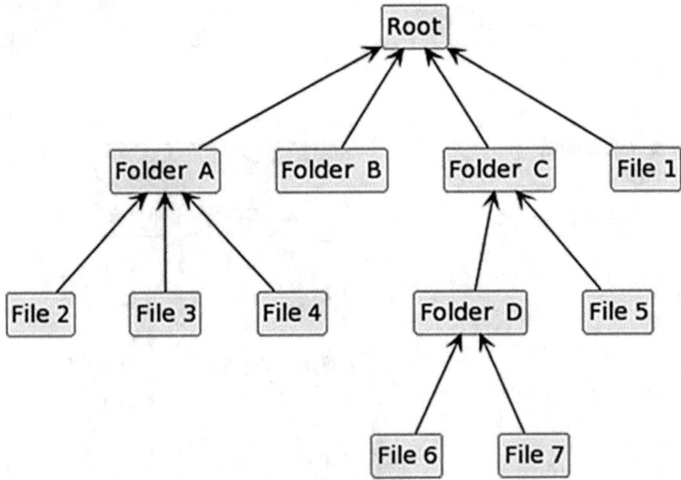

Fig. 4.3 Concrete directory with a root, four folders, and seven files in total

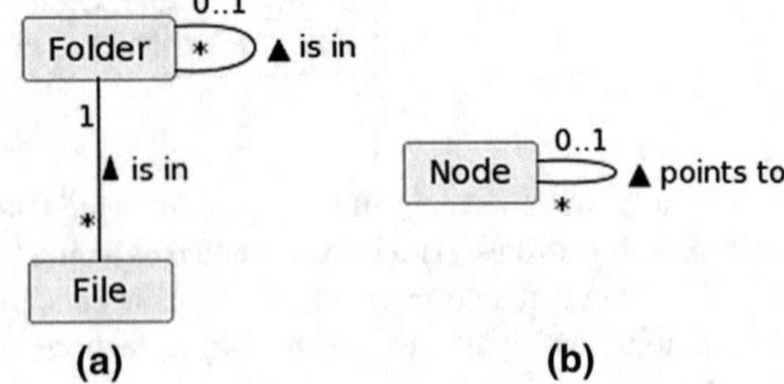

Fig. 4.4 (**a**) General structure for folders with subfolders and files. (**b**) General structure for trees and the like

4.3.6 Other Concepts Related to Themselves

As you just saw, a concept can be related to itself. This occurs not only in case of trees. Other examples are the many-to-many associations *Person once married with Person* and product structures (i.e., products and their direct parts):

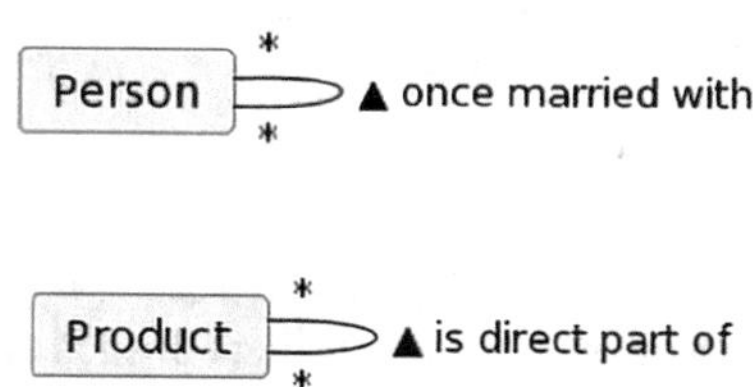

The hidden concepts in these many-to-many associations are 'Marriage' and 'BOM-entry' (as it is called), where BOM stands for *Bill of Material*. So, these many-to-many associations can be transformed into the models shown below. For clarity we added a characteristic property to each hidden concept.

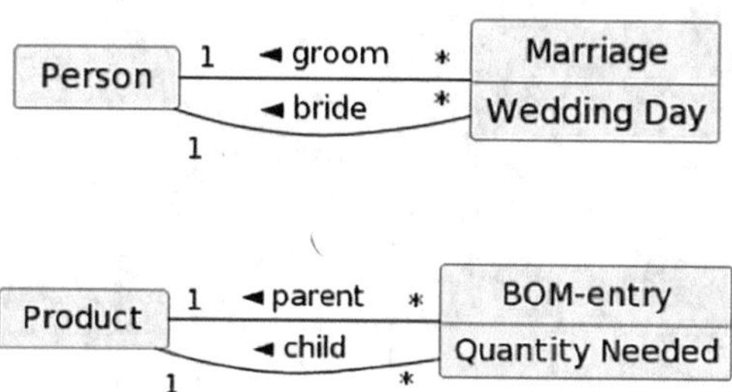

Note that *Product* represents a 'catalogue' item, not an individual product; see our discussion in Sect. 4.3.3.

In general, for a concept C related to itself, you can introduce a 'hidden' concept HC and distinguish two roles, say role A and role B, and replace the left domain model by the right one:

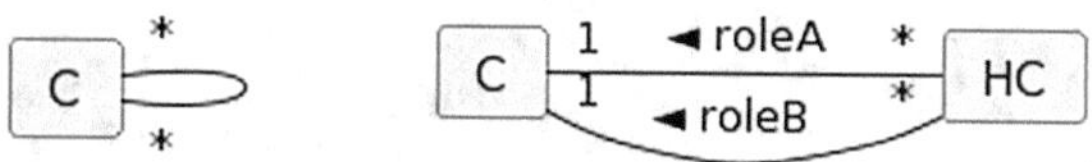

We note, perhaps unnecessarily, that the self-reference is intended on the level of the concept itself, not on the level of the instances of the concept.

4.3.7 Generalization and Specialization

Sometimes a concept has a *sub-concept* which could be distinguished. Classical examples are *Vehicle* with sub-concepts like *Car*, *Boat*, and *Airplane*, where *Car* can

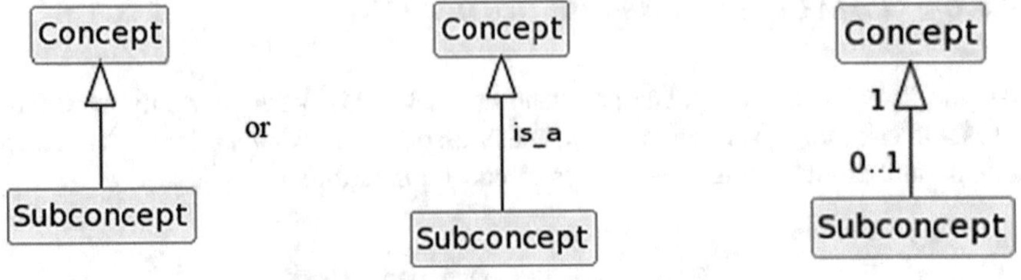

Fig. 4.5 Representation of a concept with a sub-concept

also have sub-concepts again, e.g., *Van* and *Passenger Car*. From a modelling perspective, it is not always necessary to distinguish such sub-concepts.

In general, a concept is a **sub-concept** of another concept if and only if each instance of the sub-concept is an instance of the other, more general concept as well. That a concept is a sub-concept of another concept is usually indicated as shown in the first or second picture in Fig. 4.5. The implicit multiplicities in that case are 0..1 and 1, as the third picture (redundantly) indicates.

Example 4.5: Generalization and Specialization

In our Marriage-example (with 'bride' and 'groom'), the concept *Person* has two relevant sub-concepts we might distinguish, namely, *Man* and *Woman*. Classically, 'bride' can refer to *Woman*, and 'groom' can refer to *Man*, which brings us to the more specific model on the right.

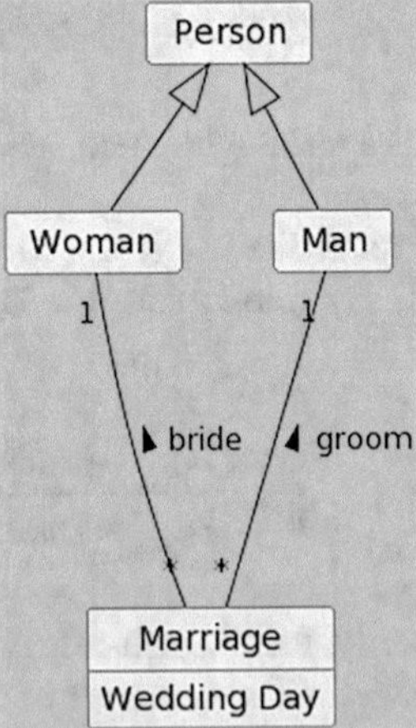

However, as pointed out in Sect. 1.7, things might change in the course of time. When people can marry with people of their own gender, this model becomes too specific. Then we can return to the previous marriage model, the

(continued)

Example 4.5 (continued)
one without the sub-concepts 'man' and 'woman' having the associations 'bride' and 'groom'. We can replace those association names by, say, 'partner1' and 'partner2', as shown in the following picture:

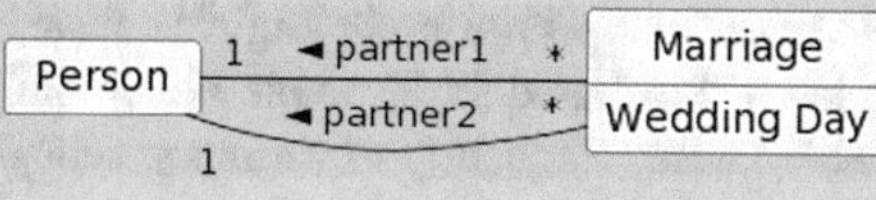

Distinguishing sub-concepts within a concept is known as **specialization**. The other way around, considering two or more concepts (such as *Man* and *Woman*) as sub-concepts of a (new) overarching concept is known as **generalization**.

Properties and associations of the generalized concept apply to the specialized concept as well, but the specialized concept can have additional properties and associations.

4.4 Summary

This chapter introduced the process of *domain modelling* and the resulting *domain models*. A domain model is a *graph* consisting of *concepts* (represented by nodes), their relevant *properties* (included in those nodes), and their mutual *associations* (represented by annotated lines). An association line can be annotated by two *multiplicities,* a *'description'* (usually a verb phrase or a preposition), and a *reading direction*. The *properties* and *multiplicities* could be left out. The minimal version and the maximal version might look as in Fig. 4.6.

When you just start modelling an application, (minimal versions of) domain models might be useful, because in that early stage, many things are not clear yet. In a later stage, you need a full-fledged *conceptual data model*, the topic of the next chapter.

Section 4.2 mentioned several manners to find out which concepts, properties, and associations are relevant for the system to be developed, among others: site visits

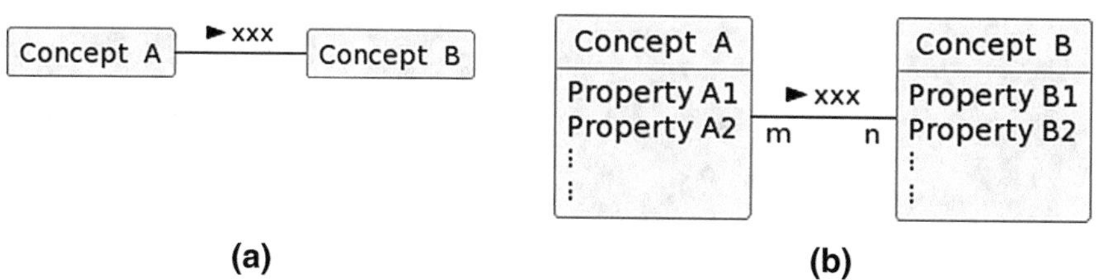

Fig. 4.6 (**a**) Minimal version of an association. (**b**) Maximal version of an association

and watching the processes over there, talks with people in various roles, talks with domain experts, interviews, workshops, and their current information products. Existing models and documents might also be interesting but might be outdated.

And of course, the formulation of *user wishes* is very important to find relevant notions. For example, the noun phrases in user wishes are probably relevant concepts. *Use cases* are helpful too. For example, their *nouns* might indicate *concepts* or their *properties*, while *verbs* and *prepositions* might indicate *associations* or their ingredients. This is clearly illustrated in Example 4.3. Finally, there exist many 'common' concepts which occur frequently in various practical applications.

Section 4.3 worked out various special cases: many-to-many associations; ternary associations and beyond; individual items versus 'catalogue' items; directed graphs; trees and the like; concepts related to themselves; and finally generalization and specialization. We did this by presenting concrete examples as well as treating the general situation.

Chapter 5
Conceptual Data Models

Abstract This chapter is about *conceptual data models*. Where a domain model is usually a rather informal, incomplete, and suggestive description, a conceptual data model is intended to be a precise and fully detailed specification.

The notion of conceptual data model is introduced in Sect. 5.1. By means of an example, Sect. 5.2 sketches how to come from a domain model to a conceptual data model in a stepwise manner. Section 5.3 explains such a stepwise transformation in general. Section 5.4 introduces and explains the different kinds of arrows we use in conceptual data models. Section 5.5 discusses so-called functional dependencies and a few normal forms, which are other types of data modelling constraints to be considered. Similar to Sect. 4.3, Sect. 5.6 works out various special modelling cases, for instance, individual items versus 'catalogue' items; directed graphs, trees, and the like; concepts related to themselves; and generalization and specialization. Section 5.7 presents a way to prepare validation of a conceptual data model by a user organization, namely, by systematically *generating* a description in natural language from the conceptual data model. This 'user-friendly' description might also be useful for explanation, further discussion, and later documentation.

5.1 Introduction

Via the functional requirements, you can determine what the system must *do*, i.e., its *dynamics*. But you must also determine what the system must *know*, i.e., which data the system must contain in order to support all its applications, so, its *statics*. In particular, you must determine the conceptual structure of the persistent data that the system must be able to retain, i.e., its 'state space'. By **persistent data** we mean, simply said, the data the system must retain also when it is not 'at work', or, to put it in other words, data which is also available after fully closing the application. The data the system must retain temporarily only during a session, i.e., when the system is 'at work', might be called **session data**.

By the **conceptual data model** (CDM) of a system, we mean the conceptual structure of the data that the system must be able to retain. Typical ingredients of a conceptual data model are:

B. de Brock, *Developing Information Systems Accurately*,
https://doi.org/10.1007/978-3-031-16862-8_5

- o **Concepts**, ⎤ yes, indeed, also
- o their relevant **properties** and ⎥ ingredients of a
- o their mutual **associations** ⎦ Domain Model
- o the *association details*, i.e., the **references**
- o how instances of a concept can be **uniquely identified**
- o for each property: - its **possible values** and
  - whether a value is **required or optional**
- o if required also some remaining **constraints**, a.k.a. *integrity rules*

So, a domain model is simply not enough. In general, (much) more requirements analysis is needed before you have a conceptual data model, because a domain model is far from complete and insufficiently precise.

A domain model is not strictly necessary: you can start to construct a conceptual data model directly (as the author always does).

5.2 From *Domain Models* to *Conceptual Data Models*: An Example

Based on an example, this section illustrates step by step how to come from a *domain model* to a *conceptual data model*, following Sect. 5.1. Section 5.3 explains it in general.

As a small example, we start with the following *domain model* from Sect. 4.1, which contains three concepts, two associations, and altogether five properties:

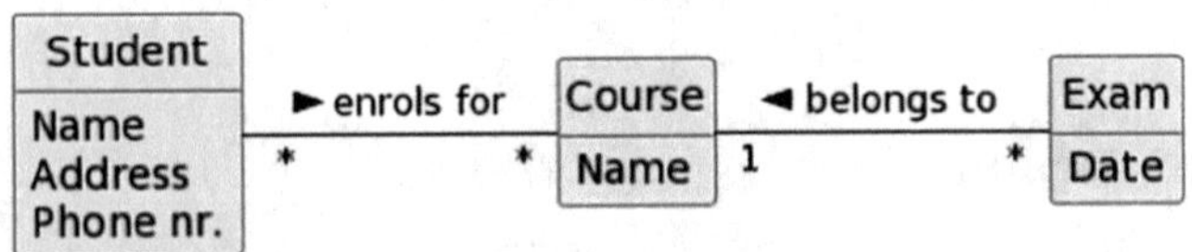

According to Sect. 4.3.1, you can transform each many-to-many association into two 'many-to-one' associations around a newly introduced (and formerly hidden) concept. The many-to-many association '*enrols for*' also represents such a hidden concept. In this case, the concept will be something like '*Enrolment*'. We might also want to know the enrolment date, for example. All in all, this will lead us to the next domain model:

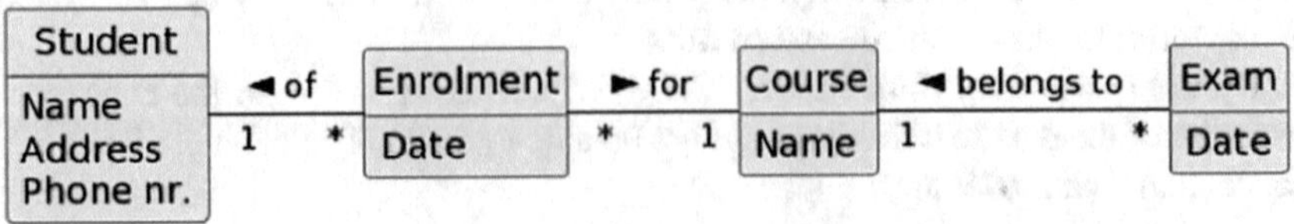

In order to come a conceptual data model, we now consider its other ingredients.

What about the *association details*—i.e., references—to be added? An *enrolment* should refer to the corresponding *student* and to the corresponding *course*, while an *exam* should refer to the corresponding *course*. In general, we extend the concepts with such references and indicate them by '^' in front. We also replace each *many-to-one* association *line* by an *arrow* with a 'crow's foot'. So, altogether:

We don't need the explicit multiplicities anymore because the arrow head indicates that each instance of concept A refers to exactly 1 instance of concept B, while the crow's foot indicates that each B-instance is referred to by 0 or more A-instances. Typically, a new B-instance *starts* with 0 A-instances referring to it. That is also the reason why '+' (1 or more) doesn't apply so often.

Altogether, for our example, this leads to the following directed graph:

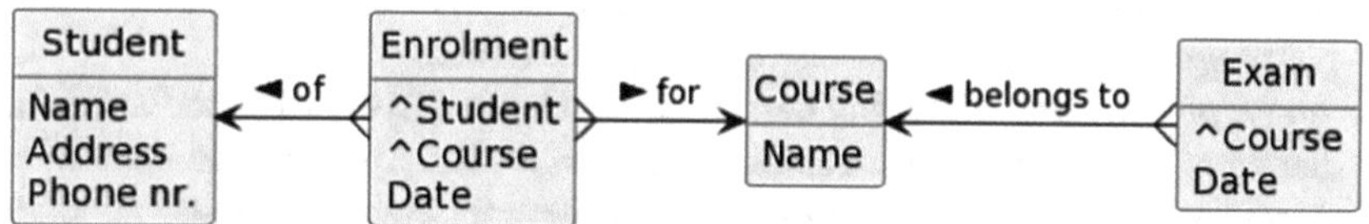

If the reading direction always follows the arrow, as in this example, the indication of the reading direction (►, ◄, ▲, or ▼) could be left out.

Next, for each concept in a conceptual data model, we want to know in which way(s) each instance of that concept can be *uniquely identified* in any state. A property (combination) is **uniquely identifying** (u.i.) within a concept if and only if in any state of the model the same value for that property (combination) cannot occur twice within that concept. A property (combination) which is uniquely identifying within a concept in a conceptual data model is called a **conceptual key** of that concept if and only if it is *minimal*, i.e., no proper subset of that a property combination is uniquely identifying within that concept.

So, this domain model triggers the following *uniqueness* questions, essentially questions meant for the user organization:

1. How can a *student* be uniquely identified? Let's suppose that the answer of the user organization is by *student number* (as in use case *Register a Student* in Sect. 2.1).
2. How can a *course* be uniquely identified? By its name maybe? But some course names might by very popular across faculties (e.g., *System Design* or *Information Systems*). Or must the names be unique per faculty? Or do they have a unique course code as well? Let's suppose that the answer to the last two questions is 'Yes'. So, a course can be uniquely identified in two different ways: by *course code* and by the combination of *course name* plus *faculty*.
3. How can an *exam* be uniquely identified? Probably its date is not enough. The combination of *course* and *date* maybe? Let's suppose that the answer is 'Yes'.

4. How can an *enrolment* be uniquely identified? Maybe the combination of student and course? Or can a student enrol for the same course more than once? '*Yes, a repeater*' might be the answer. Or maybe the combination of *student*, *course*, and *enrolment date*? Let's suppose that the answer is 'Yes'.

- For the moment, we ignore the complication that 'Course' seems to be a homonym: Course in the study program versus (yearly) execution of the Course.

For which properties is a value *optional*? In this example, phone no. is the only property for which a value is optional.

The details of the *possible values* for the properties are not so important at this stage. Nevertheless, the users' answers could be:

1. A *student number* is a (natural) number of 6 digits and divisible by 11 (meant for simple checks).
2. A *student name* and a *student address* can be any string in the Latin alphabet (so, no Cyrillic or Arabic or so).
3. A *phone number* can be a string of at most 20 characters, being a digit, '-', '.', or ' '. But a phone no. is not required. (However, later on, the need for '+' was put forward, because of possible foreign phone numbers.)
4. An *enrolment date* can be any date since September 2010—when the university started to keep track of exam enrolments—but it cannot be a date in the future.
5. A *course name* is a string (in the Latin alphabet), for practical reasons no longer than 50 characters.
6. A *course code* consists of a combination of exactly nine letters and digits.
7. The *faculty* of a course can be chosen from a fixed list with all 10 faculties.
8. An *exam date* can be any date (since ...?) and can be a date in the future.

So, one date might still be determined since the university didn't know yet from when they want to register the exams. But fixing such a first date upfront may not be necessary for the moment. The university stresses the alphabet issue because they also have students from Russia, China, and Arabic countries, for instance, but the university uses only the Latin alphabet.

Finally, there are no additional *integrity rules*, the last potential ingredient of a conceptual data model mentioned in Sect. 5.1.

Now that we discussed all ingredients of the conceptual data model, we are ready to construct the conceptual data model, starting from the domain model:

1. Replace the many-to-many association by the formerly hidden concept plus two 'many-to-one' associations.
2. Extend concepts with the references that follow from the associations—and indicate them by '^' in front—, replace the association *lines* by *arrows*, and leave the *multiplicities* out.
3. Determine the uniqueness constraints per concept, and add the properties following from the uniqueness discussions. We will indicate the uniqueness constraint by a '!' in front of the properties involved. So, within each concept, the value of the property (combination) preceded by '!' is unique. If there is another uniqueness constraint within the concept, we will indicate that uniqueness constraint by a '%' in front of the properties involved; e.g., see 'Course'.

4. Put the properties for which a value is *optional* (i.e., no value is required) between the brackets '[' and ']'.
5. Determine the *possible values* for the individual properties.
6. Add any additional *integrity rules* (but in this case, they were not there).

In summary, we use the following notations:

1. A property can be *optional*, indicated by '[' and ']' around it.
2. A property can be a *primary* property, indicated by '!' or sometimes '%' in front. A **primary property** of a concept C is a property of C that is an element of at least one of the conceptual keys of C.
3. A property can be a *referencing* property, indicated by '^' in front.
4. Additionally, a property can be a *Yes/No*-property, indicated by '?' as its end.

Combined, a property P could even appear as [!^P].

Altogether, this leads to the next graphical overview, followed by a handy, complete enumeration of the (many) details of the possible property values. Since the reading direction always follows the arrow, we can leave the reading direction out.

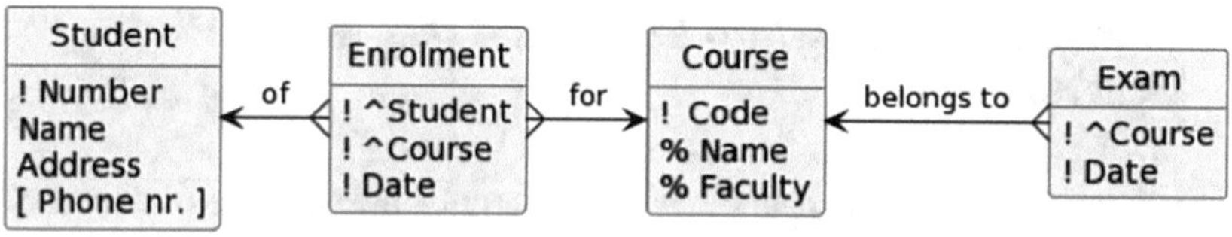

<u>**Student**</u>	/*
! Number	/* a natural number of 6 digits and divisible by 11
Name	/* any string in the Latin alphabet (so, no Cyrillic or so)
Address	/* any string in the Latin alphabet (so, no Cyrillic or so)
[Phone nr.]	/* a string of at most 20 characters (a digit, '+', '-', '.', or ' ')

<u>**Enrolment**</u>	/* <u>Enrolment *of* a Student *for* a Course</u>
! ^Student	/* the Student enrolled
! ^Course	/* the Course enrolled for
! Enrolment date	/* any date since September 2010, but not a date in the future

<u>**Course**</u>	/*
! Code	/* a combination of exactly 9 letters and digits
% Name	/* a string (in the Latin alphabet) of at most 50 characters
% Faculty	/* a member of a short, fixed list of the names of the faculties

Exam	/*
! ^Course	/* the Course the Exam *belongs to*
! Exam date	/* any date (since …? The university doesn't know yet);
	/* the exam date can be a date in the future

Since the above property lists per concept already contain all the info in the preceding directed graph, the graph itself becomes superfluous, in principle. Nevertheless, the graph provides a convenient overview. The directed graph could even be reduced to an overview of only the concepts and their functional relationships, by hiding the properties, e.g., in case the graph is large:

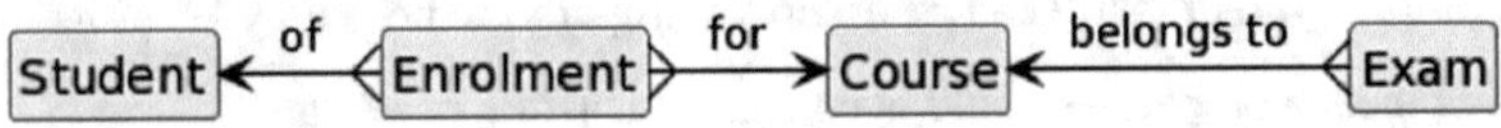

So, the conceptual data model can be completely represented by the annotated property lists per concept, while the directed graph conveniently gives an overview.

5.3 From *Domain Models* to *Conceptual Data Models*: General Case

We recall that the conceptual data model must describe the structure of the set of allowable persistent states. Although you can make a conceptual data model directly, i.e., without having a domain model first, we nevertheless explain how to come from a domain model to a conceptual data model in a stepwise manner, generalizing the concrete example in Sect. 5.2. The subsequent steps are:

1. Replace each *many-to-many association* in the domain model by the 'hidden' concept and two 'many-to-one' associations—as explained in Sect. 4.3.1—and give the new concept a proper name.

   (a) Replace all *many-to-one* association *lines* by *arrows* with a crow's foot, and leave the *multiplicities* out. We note that the multiplicities became superfluous because the arrows implicitly indicate the original *many-to-one* multiplicities. See Sect. 5.4 for other associations than *many-to-one* associations.
   (b) Extend the concepts with the *references* that follow from the associations/arrows in the (new) model. Figure 5.1 shows how this could look like 'around' a concept C in a diagram.

2. Determine, add, and specify the relevant properties, including those that follow from the *uniqueness* discussions with the user organization. During development, usually new relevant properties will also pop up.
3. Determine and 'mark' the properties for which a value is *optional*, according to the user organization.
4. Specify the *possible values* per property, according to the user organization.
5. Add all other remaining *integrity rules* (if they are there).

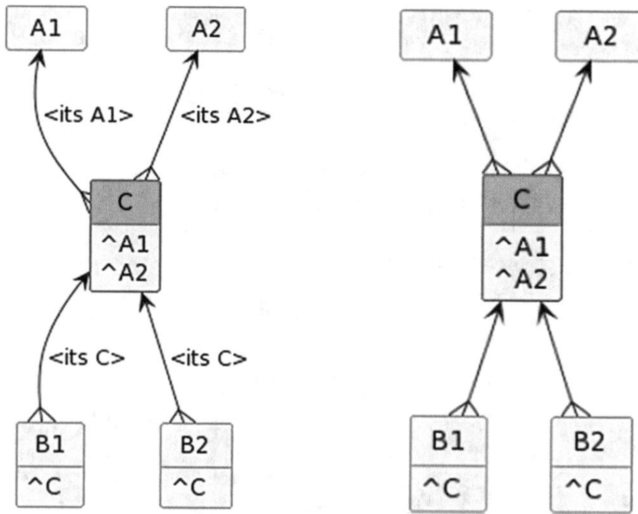

Fig. 5.1 Potential references 'around' a concept C, with and without descriptions near the reference arrows

The first two steps are of a more or less 'mechanical' nature. But as you can see in several steps, especially 3–5, (much) more requirements analysis is needed before you have a conceptual data model, since a domain model is far from complete.

Exercise 5.1
Starting from the domain model in Example 4.4—shown again here—and supposing that a book can be written by only one author, we subsequently ask you to:

(a) Add the (likely) multiplicities
(b) Replace the many-to-many associations (if present)
(c) Replace all association lines by arrows and extend the concepts with the references that follow from the associations (if not present yet)
(d) Add a 'borrowing date' at the proper place
(e) Add uniqueness constraints for the two concepts with known properties
(f) Now suppose that a book can have several contributing authors and adapt the conceptual data model
(g) Transform all reading directions such that they follow the arrow (where still necessary)

(continued)

Exercise 5.1 (continued)

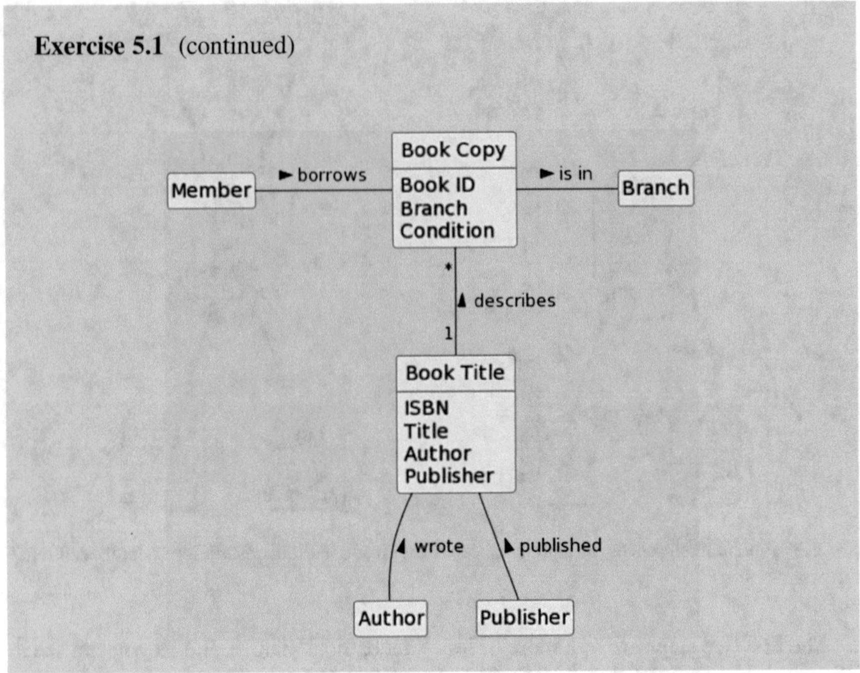

5.4 Using Arrows for Conceptual Data Models

Table 5.1 shows for each multiplicity case how an association in a domain model can be transformed using arrows for a conceptual data model. The association lines are replaced by *arrows*, while the *multiplicities* are *left out* since the arrows implicitly indicate the original multiplicities.

If an association is 1-to-1, the situation is as in the first figure in the 1-to-1 cell, in principle. If going from an A to 'its' B and then going from that B to 'its' A always gives the original A again, then the As and the Bs appear in pairs. In that case, the question arises whether the two concepts shouldn't be merged. If so, the second figure in the 1-to-1 cell applies. However, whether that makes sense will depend on the concrete situation.

There are two alternatives for the '0..1' to '0..1' case, but they both are asymmetric: A [!^B] --> B and A <-- B [!^A]

After the replacement of the *many-to-many* associations, *many-to-one* and *one-to-many* associations are the most common ones in practice.

Table 5.1 Transforming the association A ▶xs B (m, n)

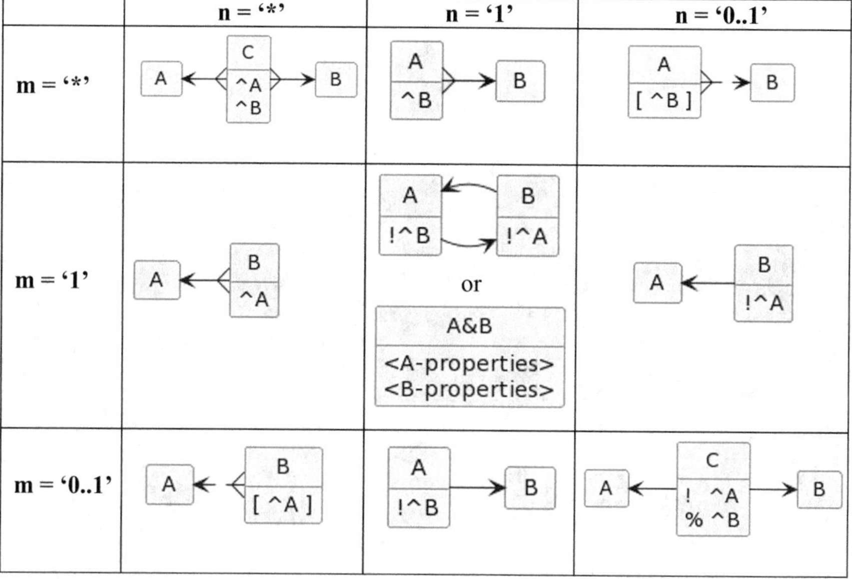

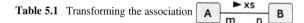

Altogether, i.e., in Table 5.1 and in the alternatives for the '0..1' to '0..1' case, we used four different arrows:

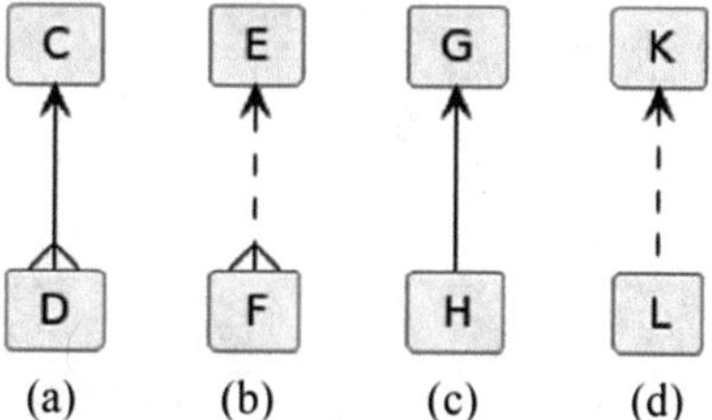

They express the following:

(a) a D refers to exactly 1 C and
a C is referred to by 0 or more Ds

(b) an F refers to at most 1 E and
an E is referred to by 0 or more Fs

(c) an H refers to exactly 1 G and
a G is referred to by at most 1 H

(d) a K refers to at most 1 L and
an L is referred to by at most 1 K

In the graph of a conceptual data model, the arrow in (a) will occur most frequently.

The arrow for the notion of *sub-concept* in the domain model is left unchanged for a conceptual data model. It has the implicit multiplicities 0..1 and 1.

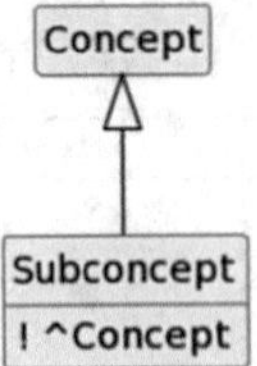

Exercise 5.2
In a certain university, each course must have exactly one employee as its course coordinator. How to model that? We got the following proposals. Discuss them by answering the accompanying questions.

(a) What does the following proposal express? What does it imply for the just mentioned condition? Is the proposal correct? Why (not)? Illustrate the proposal with a graph; use the arrows mentioned in this section.

Course coordinator
! ^Employee
^Course

(b) What does the following proposal express? What does it imply for the just mentioned condition? Is the proposal correct? Why (not)? Illustrate the proposal with a graph; use the arrows mentioned in this section.

Course coordinator
! ^Employee
! ^Course

(c) What does the following proposal express? What does it imply for the just mentioned condition? Is the proposal correct? Why (not)? Illustrate the proposal with a graph; use the arrows mentioned in this section.

Course coordinator
! ^Employee
% ^Course

(d) What does the following proposal express? What does it imply for the just mentioned condition? Is the proposal correct? Why (not)? Illustrate the proposal with a graph; use the arrows mentioned in this section.

Course coordinator
^Employee
! ^Course

(continued)

Exercise 5.2 (continued)

(e) Give a correct proposal in case none of the previous proposals is correct. Illustrate the proposal with a graph; use the arrows mentioned in this section.

(f) Explain for each proper solution how to determine which employees are course coordinators.

5.5 On Functional Dependencies and Normal Forms

A *functional dependency* is another type of constraint to consider. We will introduce it by means of an example. Consider a conceptual data model containing a Citizen-concept with the following properties:

Citizen: ! SSN, name, street, house-nr, postal code, city

where SSN (social security number) is uniquely identifying. In several countries, including the Netherlands, a postal code belongs to only one street and only one city. That means that two citizens having the same postal code live in the same city and street. In that case, *street* and *city* are called *functionally dependent* on postal code (PC) in Citizen. This is usually denoted as follows:

{ PC } ⟶ { street, city } in Citizen

More general, if A and B are sets of properties within a concept C then:

B is called **functionally dependent** on A within C ⇔ in each state, each pair of instances of C that have the same values for A also have the same values for B.

Notation: A ⟶ B in C

Consequently, if A is uniquely identifying within C, then A ⟶ {b} in C for each property b of C.

A concept C in a conceptual data model is in **Boyce-Codd normal form** (BCNF) ⇔ only uniquely identifying subsets uniquely identify 'other' properties, loosely speaking. More formally:

A concept C in a conceptual data model is in **Boyce-Codd normal form** (BCNF) ⇔ for each set A of properties of C and each property b of C with $b \notin A$:
if A ⟶ {b} in C then A is uniquely identifying

Another important normal form is the *third normal form*. Before we can formulate it, we need the notion of a *secondary property* of a concept C:

A **secondary property** of a concept C is a property of C that is not an element of one of the conceptual keys of C.

A concept C in a conceptual data model is said to be in **third normal form** (3NF) $\Leftrightarrow$ for each set A of properties of C and each *secondary* property b $\notin$ A of C:
if A $\longrightarrow$ {b} in C then A is uniquely identifying within C

So, Boyce-Codd normal form implies third normal form.

Yes, there are a *first* normal form (1NF) and a *second* normal form (2NF) as well (and even more), but they are obsolete or unimportant, so we neglect them.

All in all, our Citizen-model is not in Boyce-Codd normal form or third normal form, because the functional dependency {PC} $\longrightarrow$ {street, city} holds in Citizen and *street* and *city* are secondary properties of *Citizen* while {PC} is not uniquely identifying within *Citizen*.

However, we could slightly change the conceptual data model by making *Postal Code* a concept on its own:

Citizen:	<u>SSN</u>, name, PC, house-nr
Postal Code:	<u>PC</u>, street, city

This aligns with the widespread practice, at least in the Netherlands, that upon registration of a person, one has to enter only the postal code, and then the system comes back with the street and city. (On implementation level, the database table or class *Citizen* might have a *street* and *city* though.)

What we just did can be done in general: if A $\longrightarrow$ {b} in C where A is not uniquely identifying within C and b is a secondary property of C while b $\notin$ A—so C is not in third normal form—then (1) we can introduce a new concept with A as its conceptual key when such a concept is yet not present, (2) add b as one of its properties, and (3) remove b as a property from concept C. Note that this does not disturb any conceptual key of C.

You can immediately apply this as soon as you realize that somewhere in your conceptual data model, such a functional dependency should hold. By applying this to all secondary properties, as in the example concerning {PC} $\longrightarrow$ {street, city}, you can make your conceptual data model such that each of its concepts will be in third normal form.

5.6 Some Noteworthy Cases Worked Out

Although the previous, general sections already illustrate and cover all modelling situations in principle, there are some special situations worth to work out explicitly. Though the first two steps in Sect. 5.3—replacing the *many-to-many associations* and adding the *references*—are of a more or less 'mechanical' nature, we work them out for each of the special cases from Sect. 4.3.

5.6.1 *Transforming Many-to-Many Associations*

Applying our two steps from Sect. 5.3 to a many-to-many association and using Sect. 4.3.1, you can transform

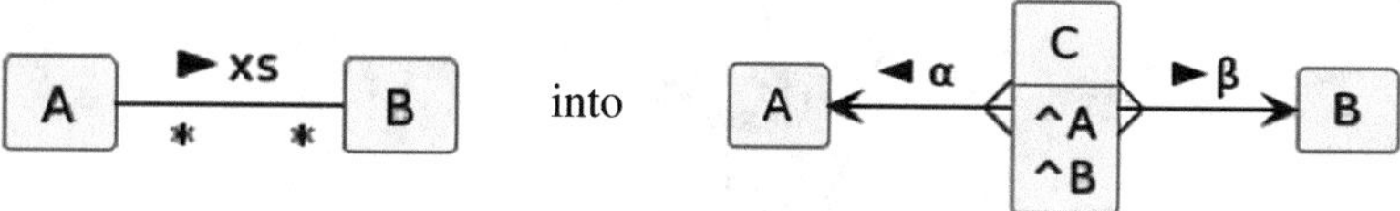

5.6.2 *Treating Associations in General*

We work out how to handle and represent associations between any number of concepts in a conceptual data model. First we recall the introductory example from Sect. 4.3.2:

A student rates a lecturer in a course

The 'hidden' concept about which you need to know more turned out to be *rating*. Then you can talk about

The rating by a student of a lecturer in a course

First we replaced that ternary association by three *many-to-one* associations:

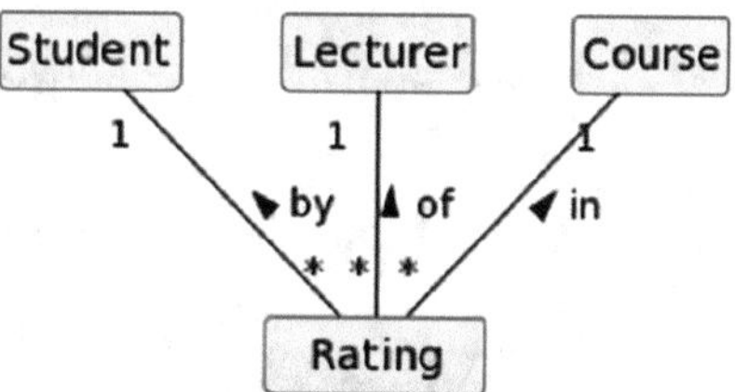

In a conceptual data model, this transforms into a concept *Rating* with three references. You probably also need to know the value of the rating, i.e., a property of Rating. The concept with its properties is then as follows:

Rating: ^Student, ^Lecturer, ^Course, value

Or, in a diagram:

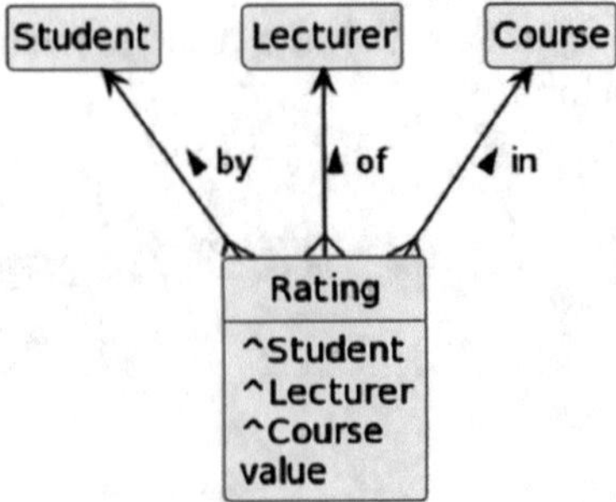

In general, as shown in Sect. 4.3.2, *n*-ary associations can be turned into n *many-to-one* associations and the new, formerly hidden concept. If β1, β2, … βn are the (new) association names, this results in the following domain model:

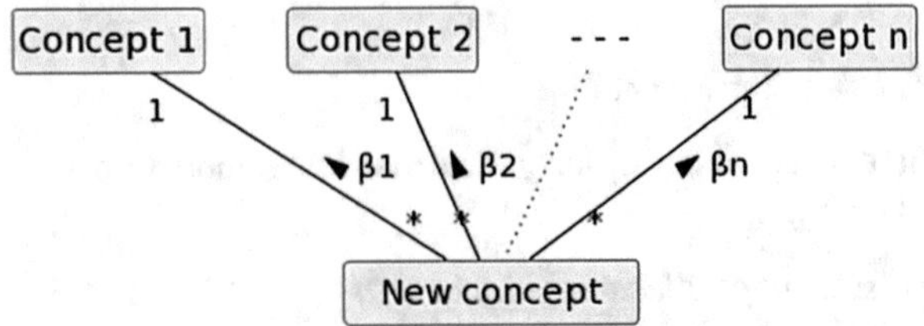

In a conceptual data model, this turns into a concept with *n* references:

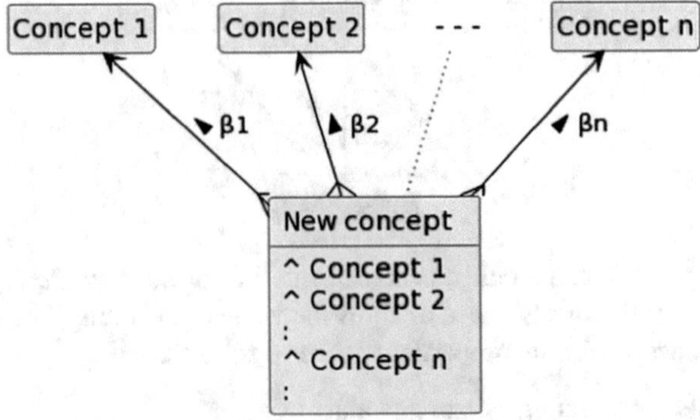

Note that for n = 2, you simply get back the binary situation from Sect. 5.6.1. We recall from Sect. 4.3.2 that n can also be 1, for example, *A ship arrives*. Applying our rules of nominalization would then lead to: *The arrival of a ship*. And if you want to know more about arrivals, e.g., the time of arrival, this leads to:

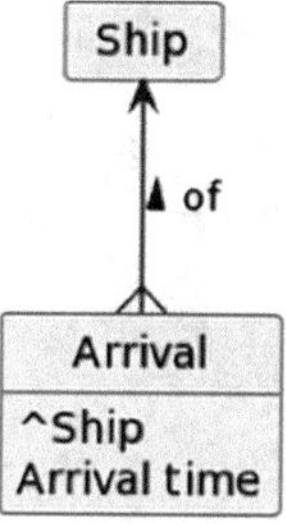

Example 5.1: Discussing Further Refinements of Rating
With the model we have now, all combinations of students, courses, and lecturers are possible. However, not all lecturers teach all courses. The university does have *classes*, where a certain lecturer teaches a certain course. The requirement might come up that a rating can apply to only a class. That leads us to a conceptual data model with the following concepts and properties:

Rating: ^Student, ^Class, value
Class: ^Lecturer, ^Course

Or, depicted in a diagram:

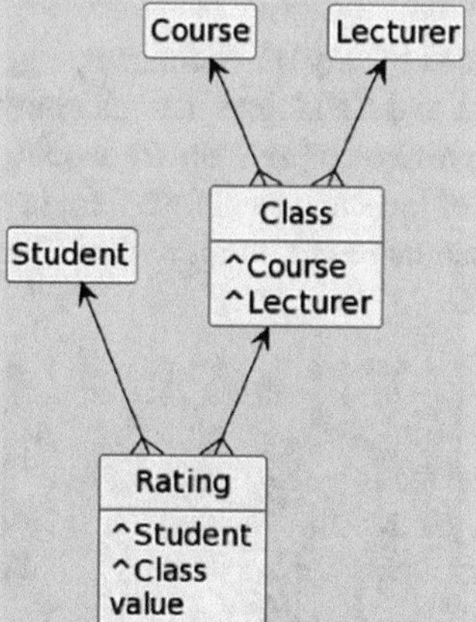

After a (short) while, it turned out that some students rated a class in which they didn't even participate... So, the requirement had to be strengthened: A student can rate only a class in which she/he participated. Turning the verb

(continued)

Example 5.1 (continued)
participate into a noun gives a hint for the concept: *Participation*. That leads us to the conceptual data model with the following concepts and properties:

Rating: ^Participation, value
Participation: ^Student, ^Class
Class: ^Lecturer, ^Course

Exercise 5.3
(a) Explain the new conceptual data model.
(b) Draw the diagram for the new conceptual data model.

5.6.3 *Individual Items Versus 'Catalogue' Items*

As explained in Sect. 4.3.3, you might need to split a concept, say *Item* into *Individual Item* and *Catalogue Item*. If you add the corresponding reference, you get:

Here, *Item* can be replaced by any other concept, e.g., *Product* or *Book*.

Both the Individual Item and Catalogue Item can have an identifier, say *Item ID* and *Catalogue* ID, although *Catalogue Item ID* would be more correct. So, with (say) five individual items of the same catalogue item in store, there could in fact be six different IDs. Even when there are no individual items in store, we happily still have the *Catalogue Item ID*.

Exercise 5.4
(a) Adapt the conceptual data model in this section by including that *Item ID* and *Catalogue Item ID* and indicate the conceptual keys.
(b) Adapt the conceptual data model in this section if items do not have individual Item IDs but you only need to know the quantity—and unit of measure—of each catalogue item.

5.6.4 *Directed Graphs*

Section 4.3.4 showed how to represent directed graphs in domain models. Now we show how to represent them in conceptual data models and work out more details. If there can be at most one arrow *from* any given node N1 *to* any given node N2 in the graph, then that combination should be unique, as indicated in the conceptual data model in Fig. 5.2a.

If there can be more than one arrow from a given node N1 to a given node N2 in the graph, as in the directed graphs in Fig. 5.2 themselves, then the previous uniqueness constraint does not apply. Probably an additional property might be used to uniquely identify the arrow. In mentioned cases, the association name would do. Alternatively, arrows might get a unique Arrow-ID.

Conversely, if a conceptual data model contains a subpart as shown in Fig. 5.2b, then this indicates a directed graph. Reference r1 can be chosen as the 'from'-- reference and r2 as the 'to'-reference, or the other way around.

Exercise 5.5
Try to make a conceptual data model for *labelled graphs*, such as the graphs in Fig. 5.2. Make your assumptions explicit (if any). What would be the contents of the conceptual data model for Fig. 5.2b? And for Fig. 5.2a?

Given the representation of a directed labelled graph in a conceptual data model, a visualization of that graph can easily be generated. Suppose you have a concept called *Arrow* with the properties *From*, *To*, and *Label*; a concrete state could look as in Fig. 5.3a. You can easily generate a visualization of the graph via a drawing generation tool such as Plantuml; see Sect. A.3.1 in the Appendix. It would give a result as in Fig. 5.3b.

Without the **Label**-column, we have a directed unlabelled graph.

A useful application of directed graphs is to represent the *allowed status changes* of, say, orders. Example 5.2 illustrates this. In that way, the set of allowed statuses and allowed status changes can be adapted easily, without the need for structural adaptions or adaptions of any code. Moreover, for a use case such as *Change Order Status*, the system can now easily offer the user only the allowed new statuses, given the current status of the order at hand.

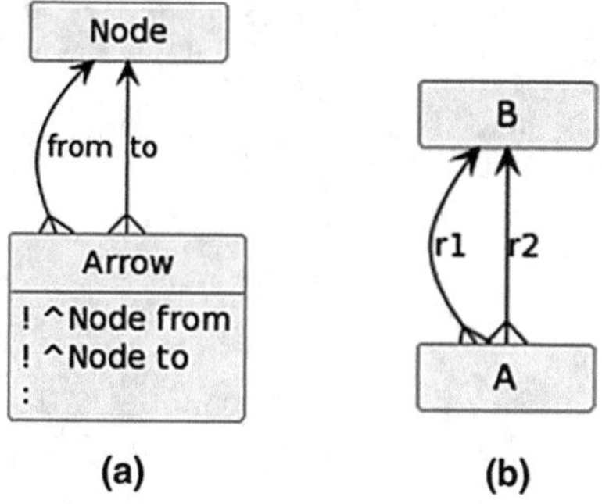

Fig. 5.2 (**a**) Representing a directed graph. (**b**) Indication for a directed graph

Concept: **Arrow**

From	To	Label
A	B	L1
A	B	L2
A	C	L1
C	D	L1
C	A	L4
C	E	L3
B	C	L1
D	F	L5
E	F	L5

(a)

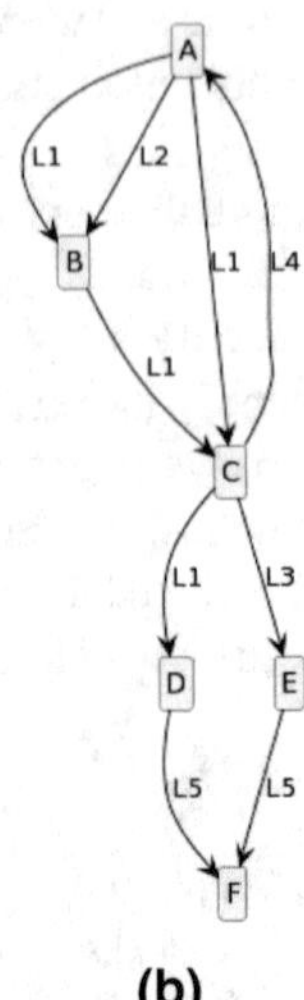

(b)

Fig. 5.3 (**a**) A directed labelled graph between nodes A and F represented in a conceptual data model. (**b**) The generated visualization of that labelled graph

Example 5.2: Representing Allowed Statuses and Allowed Status Changes

Allowed order statuses and allowed order status changes could, for example, be represented as follows, where both statuses within an allowed status change refer to the set of allowed statuses:

Allowed Status

Status
Announced
Confirmed
Open
Suspended
Completed
Checked
Closed

Allowed Status Change

Status before	Status after
Announced	Confirmed
Announced	Open
Announced	Closed
Confirmed	Open
Confirmed	Closed
Open	Suspended
Open	Completed
Suspended	Open
Completed	Checked
Checked	Closed

The (unlabelled) graph generated from **Allowed Status Change** would then be as in Fig. 5.4.

(continued)

Example 5.2 (continued)

An underlying conceptual data model (including a structure for orders) could be as in Fig. 5.5.

Here the property *Remarks* in *Order* might be used to give further explanation, for example, why the particular order has the status 'Suspended'.

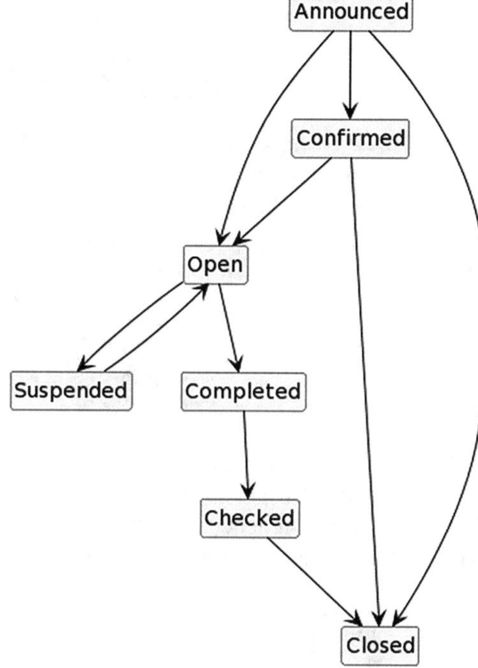

Fig. 5.4 The generated (unlabelled) graph of allowed order status changes

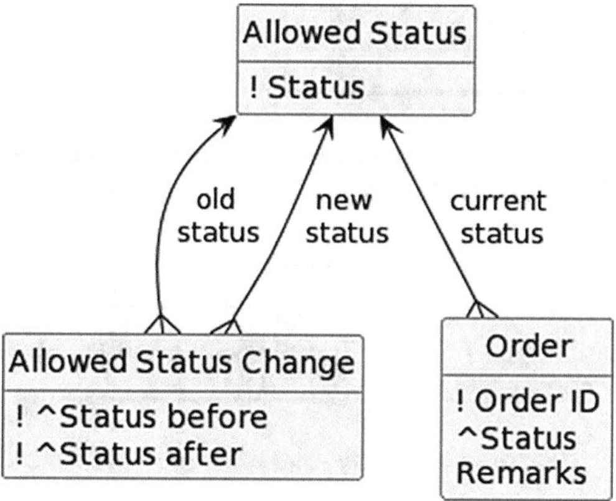

Fig. 5.5 An underlying conceptual data model

5.6.5 Trees and the Like

Section 4.3.5 showed how directed graphs where each node can have 0 or 1 outgoing arrow (such as trees) can be represented in domain models by many-to-0/1 associations. The arrows point from the 'child' to the 'parent' in those cases. Since the outgoing arrow is *optional*, such a directed graph can be represented in a conceptual data model as follows:

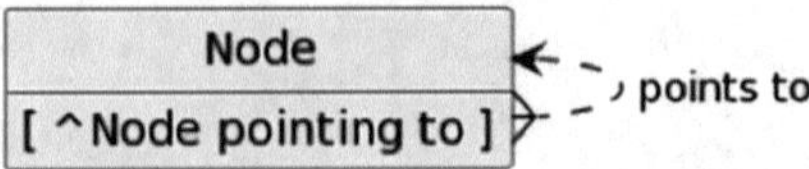

A concrete example of such a concept might be *Employee* in an organization. An employee might have a 'boss', also being an employee of that organization. But not each employee does have a boss, e.g., the highest boss doesn't. In other words, *Boss* is optional. If employees are uniquely identified by *Emp-ID*, this leads to the following conceptual data model:

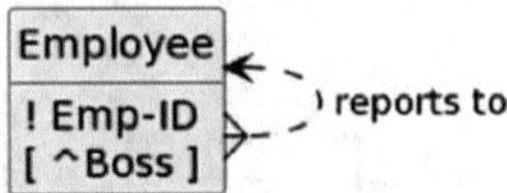

Next, we show a concrete state, and since a tree is a special kind of directed graph, we can also generate a visualization. We left out the first entry in the state. Following Sect. A.3.1 in the Appendix, the graph is generated upside down, as opposed to the normal presentation of such hierarchies.

Emp-ID	Boss
E0	- -
E1	E0
E2	E0
E3	E1
E4	E1
E5	E1
E6	E2
E7	E2

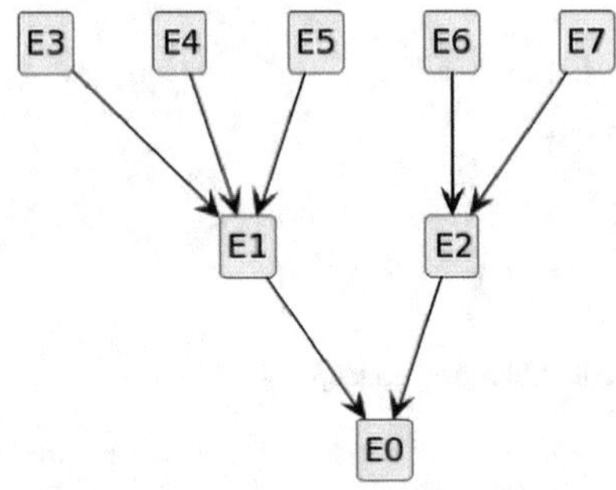

In a matrix organization, an employee can have two bosses, say a functional boss she/he reports to and a project boss she/he works for, for instance. This would lead to:

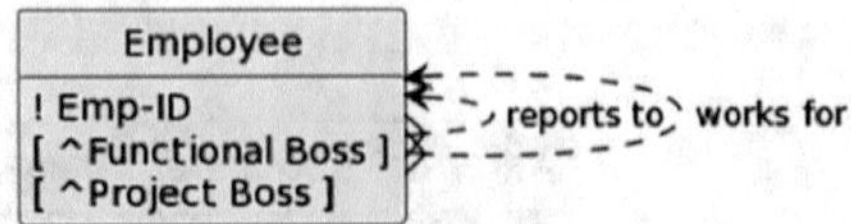

For some other tree-like examples, we refer back to Sect. 4.3.5.

5.6.6 *Other Concepts Related to Themselves*

As pointed out in Sect. 4.3.6, a concept can also be related to itself via a many-to-many association; see the first domain model in Fig. 5.6. Applying our first two steps, i.e., replacing the *many-to-many associations* and adding the *references*, we transform the first domain model into the second domain model in Fig. 5.6. Replacing the association lines by the arrows, we get the third picture in Fig. 5.6, a conceptual data model.

Using a practical example, the left domain model in Fig. 5.7 can be transformed into the right conceptual data model. Here, 'contains' means 'contains as a direct part'. 'Product containing' is called the 'parent', and 'Product contained' is called the 'child'. A 'Containment' is also known as a 'BOM-entry'; see Sect. 4.3.6.

According to the criteria, the right picture in Fig. 5.7 indicates a directed graph, cf. Fig. 5.2b, with products represented as nodes and containments represented as arrows. Table 5.2 contains a concrete example, and Fig. 5.8 shows the generated graph, with the number of direct pieces as labels (plus a legend).

We recall from Sect. 4.3.6 that the self-reference applies to the level of the concept itself, not to the level of the instances of the concept.

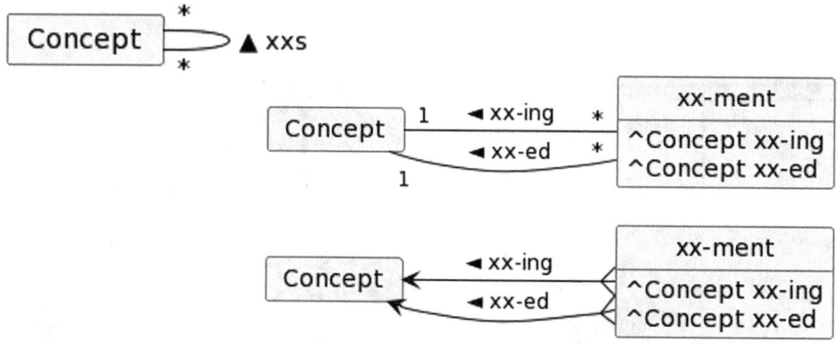

Fig. 5.6 Domain models and a conceptual data model for a concept related to itself

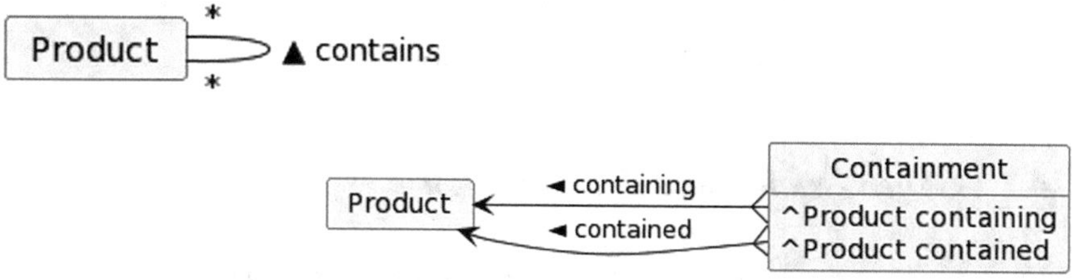

Fig. 5.7 A domain model and a conceptual data model for bills of materials

Table 5.2 Bills of materials including the number of direct pieces

Containing product	Contained product	#pieces
Storage_wall	Normal_drawer	3
Storage_wall	Chest	1
Storage_wall	Supports	16
Storage_wall	Cupboard	2
Storage_wall	Shelf	8
Chest	Normal_drawer	4
Chest	Thumb_screw	16
Chest	Supports	8
Chest	Surround	1
Cupboard	Supports	8
Cupboard	Surround	1
Cupboard	Thumb_screw	16
Cupboard	Shelf	4
Normal_drawer	Bolt_and_nut	6
Normal_drawer	Drawer_board	7
Normal_drawer	Thumb_screw	2
Supports	Thumb_screw	3
Supports	Support_part	2

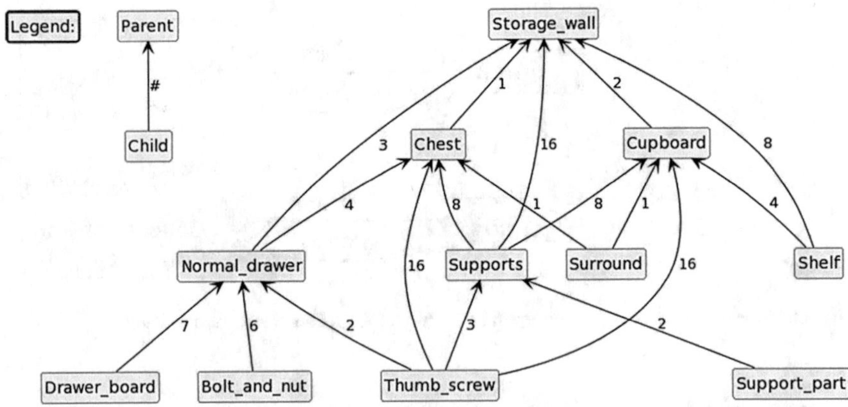

Fig. 5.8 The generated BOM-graph with the number of direct pieces

5.6.7 Generalization and Specialization

Section 4.3.7 showed how a sub-concept of another concept can be indicated in a domain model. When we work it out in a conceptual data model, we will use the same symbol and get:

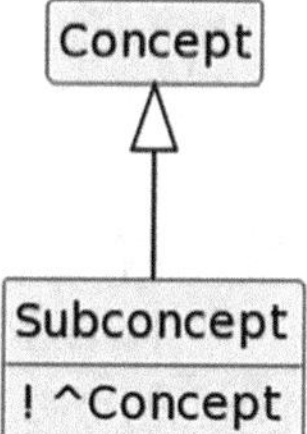

In words, the sub-concept refers to the overall concept, and different instances of the sub-concept refer to different instances of the overall concept. From a modelling perspective, however, it is not always necessary to distinguish such sub-concepts.

5.7 Validation of a Conceptual Data Model via Natural Language

This section presents a way to prepare validation of a conceptual data model by a user organization, namely, by systematically *generating* from the conceptual data model a description in natural language, plain English in this case.

The translation of a property P of a concept C in a conceptual data model depends on whether P is a *Yes/No*-property, a verb phrase, or a noun phrase and whether C represents a human being or not. The rules of the English language lead to the following translations for a property P:

Table 5.3 Translations of a property in a conceptual data model

Form of P	*Situation*	*Concept represents a non-human*	*Concept represents a human being*
α	no Yes/No-property	**its** α	**his/her** α
α?	α is a verb phrase	**whether it is** α	**whether (s)he is** α
α?	α is a noun phrase and starts with a consonant sound	**whether it is a** α	**whether (s)he is a** α
α?	α is a noun phrase and starts with a vowel sound	**whether it is an** α	**whether (s)he is an** α

(1) An alternative for **'his/her** α' is **'their** α'.
(2) For really correct English, **'is'** should sometimes be replaced by **'has'**.

Some examples to illustrate Table 5.3:

Property	*Situation*	*Concept represents a non-human*	*Concept represents a human being*
address	no Yes/No-property	**its** address	**his/her** address
accepted?	verb phrase	**whether it is** accepted	**whether (s)he is** accepted
preferred client?	noun phrase with a consonant sound	**whether it is a** preferred client	**whether (s)he is a** preferred client
active customer?	noun phrase with a vowel sound	**whether it is an** active customer	**whether (s)he is an** active customer

We also need translation rules for '^', '[' and ']', '!', and '%', which can occur around a property in a conceptual data model. For them, we add the following rules:

- We recall from Sect. 5.2 that a *referencing* property is indicated by '^' in front. In that case, we replace '^' by **'a reference to'**.
- We also recall that if a value for a property is *optional*, it is indicated by '[' and ']' around it. In that case, we omit the brackets and write **'optionally'** in front.
- For the moment, we neglect the '!' or '%' in front of a *primary* property.

As an example, a property expression of the form '[!^P]' translates to **'optionally a reference to '** followed by the translation of property P itself (according to Table 5.3).

We will now indicate the translation for a property expression E (i.e., possibly including '^', '[' and ']', '!', and/or '%') by T(E). If a conceptual data model consists of concept C_1 with property expressions $E_{1,1}$, . . ., $E_{1,n1}$, concept C_2 with property expressions $E_{2,1}$, . . ., $E_{2,n2}$ (etc.), until concept C_m with property expressions $E_{m,1}$, . . ., $E_{m,nm}$, then our mapping to English is:

The system needs to contain:

- **For each relevant** C_1**:** T($E_{1,1}$)**, . . ., and** T($E_{1,n1}$)**.**
- **For each relevant** C_2**:** T($E_{2,1}$)**, . . ., and** T($E_{2,n2}$)**.**

⋮

- **For each relevant** C_m**:** T($E_{m,1}$)**, . . ., and** T($E_{m,nm}$)**.**

We added the word **'relevant'** because not each C-instance might be relevant for the user organization.

Furthermore, for each property (combination) P_1, . . ., P_k of a concept C_i which is uniquely identifying within that concept, we add the sentence

– **The same value** [**combination**] **for** P_1**, . . ., and** P_k **should not occur twice.**

after the sentence **'For each relevant** C_i**: . . . . '**. The word **'combination'** can be left out if k = 1 (so, if one property in itself is uniquely identifying).

Example 5.3: Explanation of a Conceptual Data Model in Natural Language

This example has one *human being* concept (*Student*), two *non-human being* concepts (*Course* and *Course Enrolment*), some *Yes/No*-properties, some *optional* properties, some *primary* properties, some *referencing* properties, and some *combinations* thereof.

There are two uniqueness conditions consisting of one property and two uniqueness conditions consisting of two properties:

Student: !Student number, Name, [Phone number], [Freshman?], Birth date
Course: !Course code, %Name, %Faculty, [Master course?], Description
Course Enrolment: !^Student, !^Course, Accepted?

If you apply our mapping rules to this conceptual data model, the result is:

The system needs to contain:

- **For each relevant** Student:
  his/her Student number,
  his/her Name,
  optionally his/her Phone number,
  optionally whether (s)he is a Freshman, **and**
  his/her Birth date.
  - **The same value for** Student number **should not occur twice.**
- **For each relevant** Course:
  its Course code,
  its Name,
  its Faculty,
  optionally whether it is a Master course, **and**
  its Description.
  - **The same value for** Course code **should not occur twice.**
  - **The same value combination for** Name **and** Faculty **should not occur twice.**
- **For each relevant** Course Enrolment:
  a reference to its Student,
  a reference to its Course, **and**
  whether it is Accepted.
  - **The same value combination for** Student **and** Course **should not occur twice.**

We could extend the explanation by also mentioning the value possibilities per property (i.e., its data type), say by replacing $E_{j,k}$ by expressions such as:

$E_{j,k}$ **(being** Yes **or** No),
$E_{j,k}$ **(being a date)**,
$E_{j,k}$ **(being a time)**,
$E_{j,k}$ **(being a date and time)**,
$E_{j,k}$ **(being an integer)**,
$E_{j,k}$ **(being a decimal number)**,

$E_{j,k}$ **(being a string)**,
$E_{j,k}$ **(being a string of exactly *n* characters)**, etc.

We could even go further and extend the generation with all data type details, e.g., ***being a string of at most 20 characters (a digit, '+', '-', '.', or ' ')***, but that might be too much detail in an early stage. That could be generated in a later stage.

Example 5.4: Explanation Including the Value Possibilities per Property
For *Student* it could result in something like:

For each relevant Student:
his/her Student number **(being an integer),**
his/her Name **(being a string),**
optionally his/her Phone number **(being a string of at most** 20 **characters),**
optionally whether he/she is a Freshman **(being** Yes **or** No**), and**
his/her Birth date **(being a date).**

The translation generates easily understandable sentences in plain English. The explanation should be well understandable by end users. In principle, the users should be able to confirm or correct the resulting statements.

A simple legend explaining notions like *optionality*, *reference*, and *uniqueness conditions* could be added, but is in fact not necessary.

We note that the translation to natural language is one-to-one, in the sense that the original conceptual data model can be uniquely reconstructed from the translation result. Furthermore, it turns out that the translation result in natural language (NL) is also (very) suitable for the user organization to express their adaptions. Consequently, the NL-result is a suitable 'communication vehicle' for further discussions and adaptions of the conceptual data model.

Note that all those enumerations do not have limitations on the number of concepts, properties, or relationships. Hence, also 'large' conceptual data models can be handled, i.e., conceptual data models with a large number of concepts, properties, and/or relationships. In that case, we get long enumerations of (simple) statements.

For large conceptual data models, it might be useful to spread the concepts over sections ('sub-areas'), such as *Shipping*, *Warehousing*, and *Production*, and maybe also a section *General*.

5.8 Summary

This chapter treated the notion of *Conceptual Data Model* and its ingredients. It explained how to come from a domain model to a conceptual data model in a stepwise manner, first by means of an example (in Sect. 5.2) and then in general

(Sect. 5.3). This chapter also introduced and explained the different kinds of arrows we use in conceptual data models (Sect. 5.4). Section 5.5 discussed functional dependencies and a few normal forms.

Similar to Sect. 4.3, Sect. 5.6 elaborated on various special modelling cases such as graphs, trees, concepts related to themselves, generalization and specialization, and individual items versus 'catalogue' items.

Finally, Sect. 5.7 presented rules to systematically translate a conceptual data model to natural language. It is a way to prepare and facilitate validation of a conceptual data model by a user organization, but it can subsequently be used for explanation, discussion, and documentation as well.

Chapter 6
Directions for Implementation

Abstract We want to emphasize that a specification should be implementation-independent. A given specification should still be implementable in different technologies. To illustrate this, over the last four centuries, our running university example has been implemented with several—and very different—technologies. Section 6.1 sketches an implementation using parchment scrolls, quill pens, slates, slate pencils, and a sponge. Section 6.2 mentions an implementation using (paper) notebooks. Section 6.3 explains the important general MVC design pattern (Model-View-Controller), a basic principle for interacting with a software system. The emphasis is on Sect. 6.4, which works out in more detail how to specify an implementation using an SQL database, i.e., a database that 'understands' the language SQL. Alternatively, Sect. 6.5 explains how to generate an initial class diagram from a conceptual data model (using Plantuml).

6.1 Parchment Scrolls

In the beginning of our university—more than 400 years ago—the administration of courses, students, and their enrolments was implemented using parchment scrolls and a quill pen (being a 'write-head' for the scrolls), as well as slates, slate pencil, and sponge; see Fig. 6.1. Scrolls and slates are essentially different 'technologies': A slate can be considered as 'rewritable memory', while a parchment scroll is a 'write-once' data storage device, in principle.

There were three parchment scrolls, one for the courses, one for the students, and one for the course registrations (i.e., enrolments). A servant—in other words, a 'human server' or 'processor'—used a quill pen to write down the courses, the students, and the enrolments on the proper scrolls. The servant used a slate, being 'rewritable memory', a slate pencil, and a sponge to keep track of the next unused student number. For the parchment scrolls, the servant used an extra thick quill pen to cross out any outdated info ('deletion') because a parchment scroll was actually a1 'write-once device'. For 'updates', the servant said to use 'indexes' (?), invented by some clever monk. Nobody else understood it, and therefore the system was commonly known as *Miracle*. All in all, Miracle was a 'Scroll Oriented Management

B. de Brock, *Developing Information Systems Accurately*,
https://doi.org/10.1007/978-3-031-16862-8_6

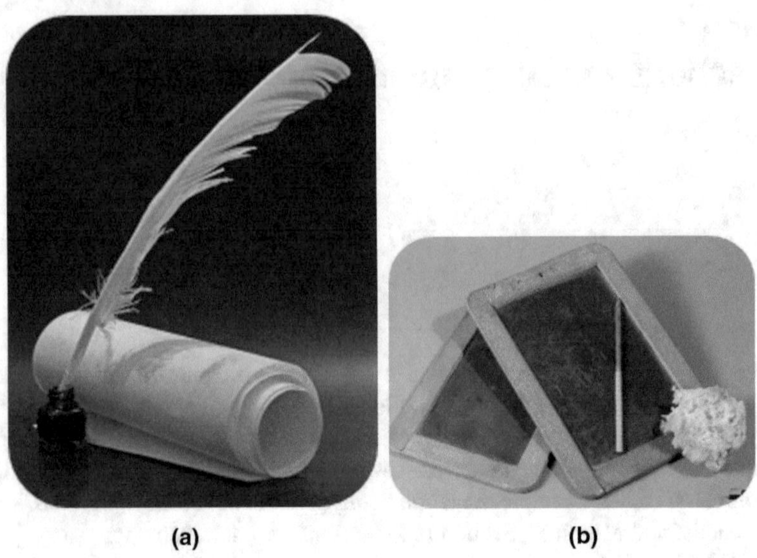

Fig. 6.1 (**a**) Parchment scroll and quill pen. *Photograph by Mushki Brichta.* (**b**) Slate, slate pencil, and sponge. *Photograph by Museum. Flehite, Amersfoort (NL)*

System'. Miracle started with three empty scrolls and the number '1' on the slate ('initialization').

The 'business process' of *course registration* consisted of two phases ('use cases') and ran as follows: Upon a course registration requested by a student, it was the duty of the operating servant to check whether the course and the student were 'known', i.e., written on the course-scroll and student-scroll, respectively ('constraints checking'). Later on, a course registration had to be officially accepted by a professor. Therefore, upon a course registration request, the servant first wrote down a '–' by default. Once the professor accepted the registration request, the servant could easily change the '–' into a '+' on the scroll (an 'in situ' update, not needing those 'indexes'). If the professor refused the registration request, then the servant crossed out the request with that thick quill pen (so, a 'deletion').

They even had what we would now call a 'declaration language', which was named *Structured Scroll Language* (SSL). As the name already suggested, in SSL, you could describe the structure of a scroll: the name of the scroll and for each column to be drawn on the scroll the name above that column, whether the values should be numbers or text (possibly with a maximum number of characters), and whether values are required (never absent) or optional (might be absent). In SSL you could also indicate the uniqueness conditions within a scroll and the references to other scrolls and columns the servant had to guard. Moreover, you could indicate which slates you needed and which 'type' of values should be writable on that slate. Actually, SSL looked very much like SQL, as Example 6.1 shows.

Example 6.1: Specification of *Miracle* in SSL

The specification of our university's Miracle in SSL must have been as follows:

```
CREATE ADMINISTRATION StudentRegistration  /* The state space

CREATE SCROLL  STUD                         /* The student scroll
(SNR        INTEGER        REQUIRED,
 NAME       VARCHAR        REQUIRED,
 ADDR       VARCHAR        OPTIONAL,
 UNIQUE ( SNR ) )

CREATE SCROLL  CRS                          /* The course scroll
(CID        VARCHAR(7)     REQUIRED,
 CNAME      VARCHAR        REQUIRED,
 UNIQUE ( CID ),
 ALSO UNIQUE ( CNAME ) )

CREATE SCROLL  REG                 /* The course registration scroll
(CID        VARCHAR(7)     REQUIRED,
 SNR        INTEGER        REQUIRED,
 JUDGED?    ('-', '+')     REQUIRED,
 UNIQUE ( CID, SNR ),
 (CID) REFERENCES CRS(CID),
 (SNR) REFERENCES STUD(SNR) )

CREATE SLATE  NUSN         INTEGER     /* The slate for the next
                                       /* student number to be used
```

6.2 Paper Notebooks

Much later, the administration of courses, students, their enrolments, etc. was implemented using (paper) notebooks. In principle, there was a separate notebook for each and every concept. If a certain notebook was full, then an additional notebook was bought ('memory expansion'). The notebooks were uniquely numbered, independent of the concept. Each instance was written on a separate line. The implementation of a reference consisted of the combination of the book number, the page number, and the line number (Fig. 6.2).

Fig. 6.2 Storage structure a century ago

6.3 Interaction with a (Software) System

When going from analysis to (software) system design, then as a first step, the *system*—as a 'black box'—can be split into an *interface* and a *kernel*. So, the 'black box' is becoming a 'gray box'. The generic 'analysis-SSD' in Fig. 6.3 then transforms into the 'design-SSD' in Fig. 6.4, where the system is indeed depicted as a gray box. The first step in the analysis-SSD will then be split into two steps in the design-SSD: from user to interface and from interface to kernel. Also the third step in

Analysis-SSD

1 User ➡ System: A
2 System ➡ System: B
3 System ➡ User: C

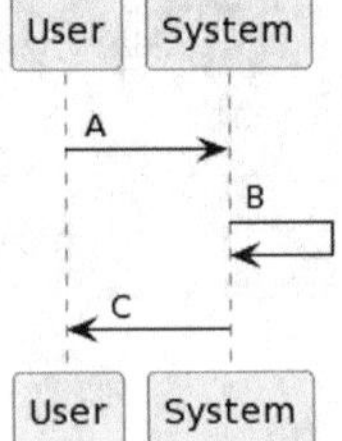

Fig. 6.3 An 'analysis-SSD'

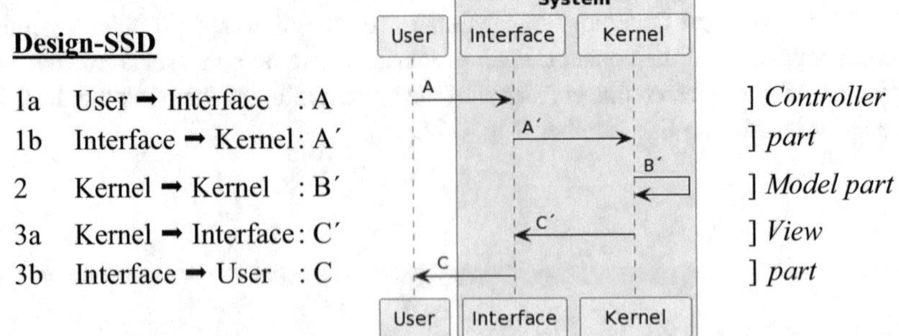

Fig. 6.4 A corresponding 'design-SSD'

1 User ➡ Interface: A
2 Interface ➡ Interface: B
3 Interface ➡ User: C

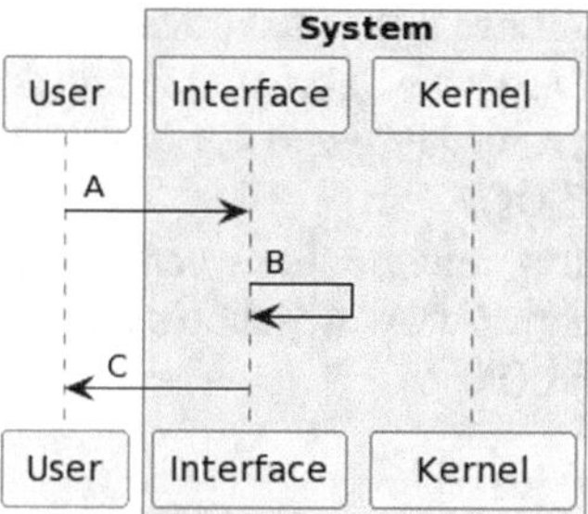

Fig. 6.5 When the interface can handle the incoming request itself

the analysis-SSD will be split into two steps in the design-SSD: from the kernel back to the interface and from the interface back to the user (Fig. 6.4).

This is related to the general **Model-View-Controller** (MVC) design pattern, an important basic software design pattern that divides the related program logic in order to separate internal representations of information from the ways information is presented to and accepted from the user [SWE]. Step 1a and 1b in Fig. 6.4 is the step for the *Controller*, step 2 for the *Model*, and step 3a and 3b for the *View*.

Usually there is communication between the interface and the kernel. But sometimes the interface can handle the incoming request itself. This results in Fig. 6.5.

Each 'call' to the kernel must subsequently be worked out in detail (becoming a 'white box') in the programming language concerned, e.g., SQL or Java. The next sections in this chapter concentrate on the kernel, not on the interface(s).

6.4 SQL-Databases

This section works out how to implement our specifications in the language SQL. It does this for *conceptual data models* in Sect. 6.4.1, for *modification* in Sect. 6.4.2, for *retrieval* in Sect. 6.4.3, and for *textual SSDs* in Sect. 6.4.4. Although SQL is a standard language for databases, each DBMS (Database Management System) might have its own dialect. So, always check the documentation of your own DBMS!

The standards site https://www.itl.nist.gov/div897/ctg/dm/sql_info.html of the US government agency NIST (https://www.nist.gov, National Institute of Standards and Technology) says the following about SQL:

> *The basic structure is a table, consisting of rows and columns. Data definition includes declaring the name of each table to be included in a database, the names and data types of all columns of each table, constraints on the values in and among columns [. . .] Tables can be accessed by inserting new rows, deleting or updating existing rows, or selecting rows that satisfy a given search condition for output. [. . .] Referential integrity allows specification of primary and foreign keys with the requirement that no foreign key row may be inserted or updated unless a matching primary key row exists. Check clauses allow specification of inter-column constraints to be maintained by the database system.*

We will use these (and other) notions in this section: *tables* in Sect. 6.4.1 (Data Model); *inserting*, *updating*, and *deleting* rows in Sect. 6.4.2 (Modification); *selecting* rows in Sect. 6.4.3 (Retrieval); and *stored procedures* in Sect. 6.4.4 (for textual SSDs).

We also refer to https://crate.io/docs/sql-99/en/latest/index.html, to the SQL tutorial https://www.w3schools.com/sql, and to Chap. 9 of *Foundations of Semantic Databases* [Bro].

6.4.1 *From* Conceptual Data Models *to* Data Models in SQL

Once you have a detailed conceptual data model, it is pretty straightforward to transform it to an SQL-database, i.e., a database that 'understands' the language SQL.

First of all, you must replace each reference to a concept with a uniqueness condition consisting of more than one property by those referenced properties. In the example in Fig. 6.6a, a stripped fragment of the larger example in Chap. 8, this applies to the references to Study Enrolment, Course Enrolment, and Exam, where each uniqueness condition consists of two properties. Working from the top downward, this results in Fig. 6.6b.

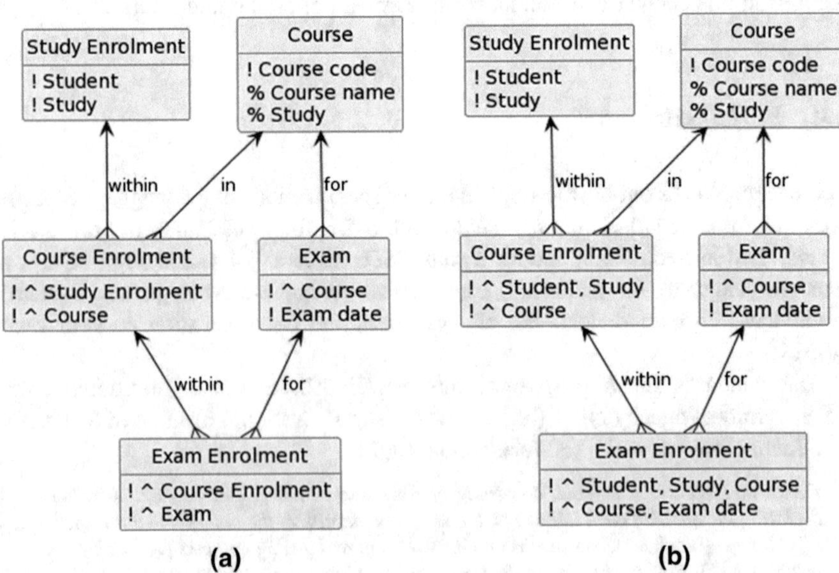

Fig. 6.6 (**a**) Before. (**b**) After

The resulting property sequences—such as *Student, Study, Course* in Exam Enrolment—should be converted into separate properties. After this, the adapted data model leads to a default SQL-specification in the following way:

- First, a declaration CREATE DATABASE <database name> is introduced.
- Each concept translates to a *table*.
- Each property of a concept translates to an *attribute*—a.k.a. *column* or *field*—in that table, followed by the corresponding *data type*, which represents the set of allowed values. The precise syntax of these data types might be implementation-dependent. Besides the available basic data types, 'sub-data types' can be defined by 'creating' so-called *domains*.
- The data type of a property is followed by 'NOT NULL' if a value is always *required* (never absent) for that property, else followed by 'NULL', if a value is *optional* (i.e., might be absent).
- Each remaining constraint within a row in a table, be it on a column (but not yet covered by its data type or domain) or among its columns, translates to a *check* constraint, a.k.a. a *check clause*.
- Each uniqueness condition translates to a *primary key* constraint or a *unique* constraint, each specified by one or more properties. Each table should have one primary key.
- Each reference condition translates to a *foreign key* constraint, implying '*the requirement that no foreign key row may be inserted or updated unless a matching primary key row exists*', to cite the NIST-text.
- Each extra constraint *between* rows within a table or *between* tables translates to an *assertion*.
- In SQL, table names and attribute names cannot contain hyphens ('-') or spaces. They are often replaced by underscores ('_') or left out while turning the next letter into a capital, hence making each name one readable word.

In summary, after a CREATE DATABASE declaration, ingredients of the adapted data model translate to SQL-ingredients as indicated in Table 6.1.

Table 6.1 Correspondence between CDM-ingredients and SQL-ingredients

Conceptual Data Model (CDM)	**Data Model in SQL**
concept	table
property	attribute
set of allowed values for a property	basic data type or domain for the attribute
optional / required	`NULL / NOT NULL`
remaining constraint within a row	CHECK-constraint
uniqueness constraint	PRIMARY KEY constraint or UNIQUE-constraint
reference constraint	FOREIGN KEY constraint
remaining constraint between tables or between rows within a table	ASSERTION

Now we will work out these translations. A *concept* C with *properties* $P_1, \ldots, P_n$ can be implemented in SQL by a CREATE TABLE statement as follows, with C' being the corresponding *table name* and $P'_1, \ldots, P'_n$ the corresponding *attribute* names:

```
CREATE TABLE C'
(P'1   <data type>    [NOT] NULL,
  ⋮
 P'n   <data type>    [NOT] NULL,
 <check-constraints>,
 <uniqueness constraints>,
 <reference constraints> )
```

The order of those three types of constraints can mutually be changed.

Assertions must be created separately, not within a CREATE TABLE, because an assertion can span more than one table, as explained later.

SQL has many 'standard' basic data types. However, their implementation details are DBMS-dependent. Nevertheless, we enumerate some important examples:

o	CHAR(n)	Strings of exactly n characters
o	VARCHAR(n)	Strings of at most n characters
o	VARCHAR	Strings of 'any' length
o	INTEGER	Integers
o	FLOAT	Decimal numbers
o	DATE	Calendar dates
o	TIME	Times (usually hours, minutes, and seconds)
o	DATETIME	Combinations of a date and a time
o	BOOLEAN	The values TRUE and FALSE

Usually, a DBMS has many other data types as well, for instance, SMALLINT, TINYINT, TEXT, IMAGE, and BLOB (*Binary Large Object*, such as image, audio, video, sound, etc.). See, e.g., https://www.w3schools.com/sql/sql_datatypes.asp for more details.

It might be useful in your application to define a 'sub-data type' of a 'basic data type', e.g., when that 'sub-data type' is used more than once. The SQL-format is

```
CREATE DOMAIN <domain name> AS <basic data type>
CHECK( <constraint on @VALUE> )
```

For example, a grade or a rating might be a natural number from 0 up to 10, those values included, or the integers limited to the positive integers only. So you could define the following domains:

```
CREATE DOMAIN ScoreSet AS INTEGER
CHECK( 0 <= @VALUE AND @VALUE <= 10 )

CREATE DOMAIN PosNumSet AS INTEGER
CHECK( @VALUE > 0 )
```

In some DBMSs, a constraint might/must get a name as well. We will use and illustrate such a version with names. Below we give the syntax for a CHECK-constraint, a PRIMARY KEY constraint, a UNIQUE-constraint, and FOREIGN KEY constraint, respectively. A table has only one PRIMARY KEY constraint but zero or more UNIQUE-constraints.

- CONSTRAINT <constraint name> CHECK (<constraint>)
- CONSTRAINT <constraint name> PRIMARY KEY (<attributes>)
- CONSTRAINT <constraint name> UNIQUE (<attributes>)
- CONSTRAINT <constraint name> FOREIGN KEY (<attributes>)
  REFERENCES <table name> (<primary key attributes of the referred table>)

The following example, of a CREATE TABLE, concerns a concept *Study*, having a unique study code (consisting of five characters), a unique name, a description, maybe a promotion video, a level (‘Ba’ or ‘Ma’), a study size (a positive number of credits), maybe an overall rating, and referring to its Faculty (another table).

```
CREATE TABLE Study
(StudyCode       CHAR(5)        NOT NULL,
Name             VARCHAR(50)    NOT NULL,
Description      VARCHAR        NOT NULL,
PromoVideo       BLOB           NULL,
Level            CHAR(2)        NOT NULL,
StudySize        PosNumSet      NOT NULL,
OverallRating    ScoreSet       NULL,
Faculty          VARCHAR(5)     NOT NULL,
CONSTRAINT K1 PRIMARY KEY (StudyCode),
CONSTRAINT U1 UNIQUE (Name),
CONSTRAINT C1 CHECK ( Level IN (‘Ba’, ’Ma’) ),
CONSTRAINT R1 FOREIGN KEY (Faculty)
 REFERENCES Faculty(Abbreviation) )
```

The foregoing constraints are local to one table, except FOREIGN KEY constraints. So-called **assertions** can be created in order to express other ‘inter-table’ constraints, i.e., constraints between more than one table. Assertions can also be used to express constraints *between* rows within one table. Their syntax is:

- CREATE ASSERTION <constraint name> CHECK (<database constraint>)

Those 'inter-table' constraints often have the form

'*For each <concept> x: <constraint on x>*'

This cannot be directly translated to SQL since the language SQL is 'set oriented'. But this is logically equivalent to

'*There does not exist a <concept> x for which <constraint on x> does not hold*'

This is based on the following logical equivalence:

$\forall x \in C: \varphi(x) \Leftrightarrow \neg \exists x \in C: \neg \varphi(x)$

Therefore, we will use the following general pattern for such assertions:

```
CREATE ASSERTION ... CHECK
(NOT EXISTS (SELECT * FROM ... WHERE ...))
```

more specifically

```
CREATE ASSERTION <assertion name> CHECK
(NOT EXISTS (SELECT * FROM <tables> WHERE <condition>))
```

where `<condition>` consists of the correspondence(s) that connect the tables, plus the negation of the original constraint.

We refer to https://crate.io/docs/sql-99/en/latest/chapters/20.html#create-assertion-statement (for instance) for more details about assertions.

Unfortunately, many database management systems do not (yet) provide assertions. In that case, so-called *triggers* can be used to enforce such constraints. A **trigger** is a stored program in a database which automatically fires/executes when some events occur. See https://crate.io/docs/sql-99/en/latest/chapters/24.html for further details.

Chapter 8 contains an extensive example of a database, including assertions.

6.4.2 Modification

Three important basic possibilities to change the state of an information system are distinguished, essentially the CUD in the acronym CRUD:

(a) *adding* information, (b) *changing* information, and (c) *removing* information.

We will now treat each of these three types, starting from a proper textual SSD regarding a concept C.

(a) *Adding/Creating* information:
Essentially, an atomic step in a textual SSD of the form

System ➡ System: Register a new C with the value v_1 for property p_1, …,
and value v_n for property p_n

can be translated to the SQL-statement

```
INSERT INTO C'(p'1, …, p'n) VALUES(v'1, …, v'n)
```

where C' is the corresponding table name, $p'_1, \ldots, p'_n$ are the corresponding attributes, and $v'_1, \ldots, v'_n$ are their respective values expressed in SQL.

For example, for a concept *Course* with properties *Code*, *Name*, *Level*, *Work Load*, and *Number of Expected Students (NES for short)*:

System ➡ System: Register a master course named
Advanced OO-programming II, with code CSMa007,
150 expected students, and a workload of 100 hours

can be translated to the SQL-statement

```
INSERT INTO Course(Code, Name, NES, WL, Level)
VALUES('CSMa007', 'Advanced OO-programming II', 150, 100, 'Ma')
```

(b) *Changing/Updating* information:
Essentially, an atomic step in a textual SSD of the form

System ➡ System: Change for each C that satisfies condition φ the value of
property p_1 into v_1, …, and the value of property p_k into v_k

can be translated to the SQL-statement

```
UPDATE C' SET p'1 = v'1, …, p'k = v'k WHERE φ'
```

where C' is the corresponding table name, $p'_1, \ldots, p'_k$ are the corresponding attributes to be updated, $v'_1, \ldots, v'_k$ are the corresponding SQL-expressions *in terms of the old values* (!) indicating their new values, and φ' is the SQL-representation of φ. For example, for the concept *Course* under (a):

System ➡ System: Increase for each master course
the number of expected students by 10% and
the work load by 5%

can be translated to the SQL-statement

```
UPDATE  Course
SET     NES = 1.10 * NES,    /* Number of Expected Students
        WL  = 1.05 * WL      /* Work Load
WHERE   Level = 'Ma'
```

(c) *Removing/Deleting* information:
Essentially, an atomic step in a textual SSD of the form

System ➡ System: Remove all Cs satisfying condition φ

can be translated to the SQL-statement

`DELETE FROM` C' `WHERE` φ'

where C' is the corresponding table name and φ' is the SQL-representation of φ. For example,

System ➡ System: Remove all course enrolments of the student with ID 12232

can be translated to the SQL-statement

`DELETE FROM` CourseEnrolment `WHERE` StudentID = 12232

6.4.3 Retrieval

An atomic tSSD-step indicating *retrieval* has essentially the following form:

System ➡ System: Retrieve <information>

Instead of *Retrieve*, you might encounter words such as *Read*, *View*, *Select*, *See*, *Search*, *Get*, etc. A retrieval is also known as a *query*.

The information requested can have many different forms. This section treats the main (basic) forms, indicated by (F1), (F2), and (F3). For a more extensive and formal treatment, we refer to Chap. 9 of our book [Bro].

(F1) Straightforward Sets

Often, an information request asks for some set { A | B [and C] } where A expresses *what is asked for*, B expresses the *base set(s)* where the information is coming from, and—optionally—C expresses some additional *condition(s)* for selection (when needed). A specification of the form { A | B [and C] } basically translates to the following SQL-statement:

```
SELECT DISTINCT <what is asked for>
FROM            <base set(s) >
[WHERE          <condition(s)>]
```

This general form represents a wide variety of information requests.

Example 6.2: A Basic Retrieval Example
Suppose you have a data structure containing (at least)

- A table called *Courses* with attributes *courseID*, *name*, *ECTS*, *exam-date*, and *study* the course belongs to, where *courseID* is uniquely identifying
- A table called *Grades* with attributes *studentID*, *courseID*, and *grade*, where the combination *studentID* and *courseID* is uniquely identifying

Expressed orderly and compactly:

Courses: ! courseID, name, ECTS, exam-date, study
Grades: ! studentID, ! courseID, grade

ECTS indicates the number of credit points for the course; see [ECTS]. And suppose that we happen to have the following (over-specific) textual SSD:

System ➡ System: Retrieve the course results of student 123453

Suppose that this request actually asks for *course name*, *exam-date*, *ECTS*, *study*, and *grade* (the 'A-part'), from the base sets *Courses* and *Grades* (the 'B-part'), where it concerns the course results of *student 123453* (the 'C-part'). This textual SSD basically translates to the following SQL-statement:

```
SELECT DISTINCT c.name, c.exam_date, c.ECTS, c.study, g.grade
FROM   Courses c, Grades g
WHERE  g.courseID = c.courseID AND g.studentID = 123453
```

where the 'instance variables' c and g vary over the courses and grades, respectively. An occurrence of an instance variable can be dropped where it is unambiguously clear to which table it applies.

In general, we recommend to use the keyword DISTINCT because otherwise the SELECT-statement also delivers all duplicate results. The keyword DISTINCT avoids redundant results. But if you are sure that duplicate results cannot occur or if duplicate results do not matter, you might drop the keyword DISTINCT. (It might improve the performance of the execution of the SQL-statement as well.) In Example 6.2, for instance, we could drop the keyword DISTINCT because for a fixed student, duplicate results cannot occur since the combination *student*, *course* is uniquely identifying there.

(F2) One Cumulative Value as Result

We now treat some forms of specification that are related to { A | B [and C] }:

1. | { A | B [and C] } | means: the number of elements of that set
2. min({ A | B [and C] }) means: the minimum A-value in that set
3. max({ A | B [and C] }) means: the maximum A-value in that set
4. ∑ B [and C] : A means: the sum of the As of all Bs [satisfying C]
5. Avg B [and C] : A means: the average of the As of all Bs [satisfying C]

In general, where { A | B [and C] } translates to `SELECT DISTINCT` A' `FROM` B' [`WHERE` C'] then:

1. | { A | B [and C] } | translates to `SELECT COUNT(DISTINCT` A') `FROM` B' [`WHERE` C']
2. min({ A | B [and C] }) translates to `SELECT MIN(`A') `FROM` B' [`WHERE` C']
3. max({ A | B [and C] }) translates to `SELECT MAX(`A') `FROM` B' [`WHERE` C']
4. ∑ B [and C] : A translates to `SELECT SUM(`A') `FROM` B' [`WHERE` C']
5. Avg B [and C] : A translates to `SELECT AVG(`A') `FROM` B' [`WHERE` C']

If the set { A | B [and C] } is empty, i.e., if there are no Bs (satisfying C), then the minimum, maximum, and average are not defined. In some SQL-implementations, the sum is not defined either. Otherwise, each of the foregoing expressions delivers only one value as result.

The operators COUNT, MIN, MAX, SUM, and AVG are called *set functions* in SQL. They can be used within WHERE-clauses in SELECT-statements as well.

In the cases of MIN and MAX, the keyword DISTINCT can be dropped because duplicates do not influence the answer. In the cases of SUM and AVG, the keyword DISTINCT *must* be dropped, because otherwise you would take the sum or average over only all *distinct* As. In the COUNT-case, the keyword DISTINCT is essential (unless you are sure that duplicate results cannot occur).

Example 6.3: Examples of the Use of *Set Functions* in SQL

As an illustration, let us suppose that we got the following five retrieval requests:

1. The number of courses student 123453 passed
2. The lowest grade student 123453 ever got
3. The highest grade student 123453 ever got
4. The total number of credit points (ECTS) student 123453 earned
5. The average grade of student 123453, excluding the failed ones

They are related to the five *set functions* we just described. We note that a student passed a course and earned the credit points when the grade is larger

(continued)

Example 6.3 (continued)
than 5. Request 4 is the only one that needs data outside the table *Grades*. All in all, the five retrieval requests translate to the following SQL-statements:

```
1. SELECT COUNT (DISTINCT courseID) FROM Grades
   WHERE studentID = 123453 AND grade > 5
2. SELECT MIN(grade) FROM Grades WHERE studentID = 123453
3. SELECT MAX(grade) FROM Grades WHERE studentID = 123453
4. SELECT SUM(ECTS) FROM Courses c, Grades g
   WHERE g.courseID = c.courseID AND studentID = 123453 AND grade > 5
5. SELECT AVG(grade) FROM Grades WHERE studentID = 123453 AND grade > 5
```

We dropped every occurrence of an instance variable when it was clear to which table it applied. We could have left out the keyword DISTINCT in the first SQL-statement because duplicate results could not occur there.

(F3) A Set of Cumulative Values as Result

In the fourth retrieval request in Example 6.3, we asked for the total number of earned credit points for one particular student. But you might want to have a list of the total number of earned credit points *per* student instead, not for just one student:

Give the total number of earned credit points (ECTS) *per* student

We recall the original data structure from Example 6.2:

Courses: ! courseID, name, ECTS, exam-date, study
Grades: ! studentID, ! courseID, grade

So, we want to group the set of all earned credit points *per* student and to sum the earned credit points *per* student (so *per* such group). But we might be interested in only the students who earned less than 60 credit points. This leads to:

```
SELECT    studentID, SUM(ECTS)                       -- the information asked for
FROM      Courses c, Grades g                        -- the base table(s) with info
WHERE     g.courseID = c.courseID AND grade > 5      -- excluding certain rows
GROUP BY  studentID                                  -- attribute(s) for grouping
HAVING SUM(ECTS) < 60                                -- excluding certain groups
```

As a second example, suppose that you want to know the total number of earned credit points *per* student but now split *per* study (and dropping the requirement of less than 60 credit points in order to get a complete overview), including the average grade (i.e., *per* student *per* study). Now you need the combination of two attributes (*studentID* and *study*) for composing the groups:

```
SELECT studentID, study, SUM(ECTS), AVG(grade)   -- the information asked for
FROM   Courses c, Grades g                        -- the base table(s) with info
WHERE  g.courseID = c.courseID AND grade > 5      -- excluding certain rows
GROUP BY studentID, study                         -- attributes for grouping
```

Now we explain the general case, where there are two optional parts:

```
SELECT A        -- the information asked for (1)
FROM   B        -- the base table(s) where the information is coming from
[WHERE C]       -- condition(s) to exclude certain rows (if needed)
GROUP BY D      -- a set of one or more attributes as grouping criterion
[HAVING E]      -- condition(s) to exclude certain groups (if needed)
```

(1) The SELECT part typically consists of the attribute(s) from the GROUP BY and of one or more *set functions*.

Views

A query can get a name, serving as an 'abbreviation' of that query. Such a 'named query' can be translated to a so-called **view** in the language SQL. If n is the name to be assigned to a conceptual query Q, then the abbreviation can be expressed in the language SQL as follows:

```
CREATE VIEW n AS Q'
```

where Q' is the SQL-translation of the conceptual query Q. For instance, it might be handy to give a name to the overview of all credit points earned by our individual students, say consisting of studentID, courseID, course name, ECTS, and grade:

```
CREATE VIEW CreditPointsEarned AS
   SELECT g.studentID, c.courseID, c.name, c.ECTS, g.grade
   FROM   Courses c, Grades g
   WHERE  g.courseID = c.courseID AND g.grade > 5
```

We left out the keyword DISTINCT because it was not necessary here.

Another example, though debatable, would be to give a request in Example 6.3 a name, for instance, the fourth one:

```
CREATE VIEW CreditPoints AS
   SELECT SUM(ECTS)
   FROM Courses c, Grades g
   WHERE g.courseID = c.courseID AND studentID = 123453 AND grade > 5
```

This example is debatable because we would like to parameterize over studentID in order to give the total number of credit points for an *arbitrary* student, of course. For that, you need SQL's stored procedures, discussed in the next section.

6.4.4 *From* Textual SSDs *to* Stored Procedures

The interaction with the system in a textual SSD can be implemented by one or more *stored procedures* in the language SQL. A **stored procedure** consists of a sequence of SQL-statements mixed with language constructs for control-of-flow. A basic minimal syntax, expressed informally:

```
CREATE PROCEDURE <procedure name> [<parameters>]
AS <SQL-statements mixed with control-of-flow constructs>
```

Parameters are optional but, if present, every parameter has the form:

```
@<parameter name> <data type>
```

So, a stored procedure can contain one or more SQL-statements, most notably SELECT-, INSERT-, UPDATE-, and/or DELETE-statements. A stored procedure can also contain language constructs for *control-of-flow*, constructs such as an IF, an IF...ELSE, a BEGIN-END, and a WHILE. Most CREATE-statements are not allowed in a stored procedure.

A stored procedure can also have global and local parameters and can call other stored procedures too. After a stored procedure has been run for the first time, the system saves a so-called **execution plan**, a compiled plan how to optimally execute the stored procedure. Such pre-compilation makes subsequent execution of a stored procedure very fast, much faster than stand-alone statements. Therefore, it might make sense to rewrite a view into a stored procedure. The conversion is very simple:

Convert CREATE VIEW n AS Q' into CREATE PROCEDURE n AS Q'

Stored procedures have more possibilities and advantages as well. For instance, they can return status values and parameter values to a calling procedure or batch, and they can be executed on remote SQL servers.

Example 6.4: A Simple Parameterized Stored Procedure in SQL
You can parameterize over studentID in the CreditPoints-example at the end of Sect. 6.4.3 using a stored procedure in SQL:

```
CREATE PROCEDURE CreditPointsOf @x INTEGER AS
  SELECT SUM(ECTS)
  FROM Courses c, Grades g
  WHERE g.courseID = c.courseID AND studentID = @x AND grade > 5
```

Example 6.5 shows how a textual SSD can be implemented by a stored procedure. In general, however, a textual SSD can have several interactions with the system and might therefore need more than one stored procedure.

Example 6.5: A Stored Procedure Implementing a Textual SSD
This example refers back to the example in Fig. 2.6, which contains a complete development path for a functional requirement. The underlying parameterized user wish (pUW) is:

pUW: Register a student *with a given name, address, country, birth date, ...*

The example contains two alternative scenarios, AS1 (the student is a foreigner) and AS2 (he/she was a student before), resulting in the following structure for the textual SSD:

User → System: <pUW> ;
if student is a foreigner
  then ..... *(even if the foreigner was a student before, as the customer told us)*
  else **if** (s)he was not a student before
      then System → System: generate new student number ;
        System → System: fulfil <pUW + new student number>
      else .....
    end
end ;
System → User: result *(e.g., registered data including the generated student number)*

The stored procedure implementing this textual SSD simply follows the structure of the textual SSD:

```
CREATE PROCEDURE RegisterStudent  @n VARCHAR(50), @a VARCHAR,
                 @c VARCHAR(20), ...., @out VARCHAR OUTPUT  AS
BEGIN
 IF @c <> 'NL'            -- if the student is a foreigner
 THEN .....               -- AS1
 ELSE IF .....            -- if (s)he was not a student before
     THEN BEGIN INSERT INTO Student(name, address, country, ...)
                     VALUES(@n, @a, @c, ...)
                SELECT @out = 'Done. New student nr. is '+ <...>
          END
     ELSE .....           -- AS2
END
```

The keyword OUTPUT in the SQL-code indicates that @out is declared as a return parameter. Let's suppose that in the underlying 'CREATE Student' statement, *student number* was declared as a so-called AUTO-INCREMENT primary key field; see below.

An **AUTO-INCREMENT field** in a table automatically generates a unique number when a new row is inserted in that table. By default, the starting value is 1, and it will increment by 1 for each new row. In several DBMSs, however, the starting value and the increment can be chosen. For the various AUTO-INCREMENT dialects, see, for instance, https://www.w3schools.com/sql/sql_autoincrement.asp.

See https://crate.io/docs/sql-99/en/latest/index.html for further SQL-details.

6.5 Generating an Initial Class Diagram

As an alternative to SQL, a conceptual data model can easily be transformed into a 'Version 0.0' of a corresponding *class diagram*. You can start with the Plantuml-code for the conceptual data model and remove the hide-commands: 'hide circle', 'hide (empty) members', and 'hide methods'. For our example in Fig. A.1 in Sect. A.3 of this Plantuml tutorial, containing all our notational conventions, this results in the class diagram in Fig. 6.7.

The green ©-circle in each 'concept box' indicates that it is a *class*. The third part in each concept box is meant for the *methods*. From this 'Version 0.0' on, you can add methods, derived attributes, managers, etc. The methods can be used to implement the interactions with the system described in a textual SSD. They typically include GET- and SET-statements. Derived attributes can sometimes be used to improve performance. The managers are meant to manage the different objects in a class, i.e., creating, updating, deleting, and finding and retrieving them.

As an illustration, we zoom in on Concept E and its sub-concept Concept F in Fig. 6.7 and add some properties and methods: Method MethA has no parameters, MethB has one parameter, MethC has two parameters, and MethD has three parameters; see Fig. 6.8.

The methods MethA, MethB, and MethC apply to all instances of Concept E and Concept F (generalization/specialization), while method MethD applies only to all

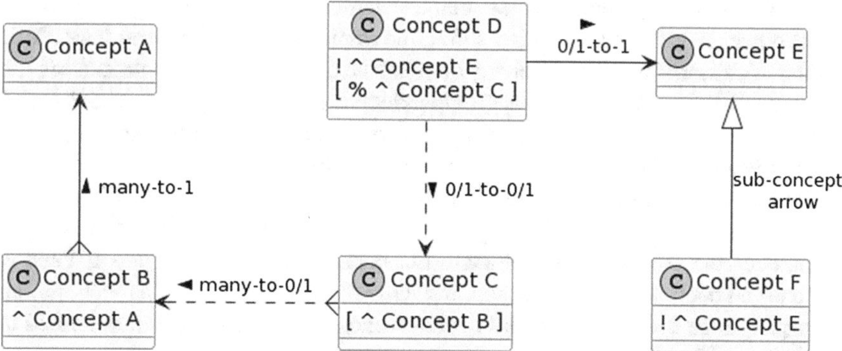

Fig. 6.7 A class diagram containing all our notational conventions

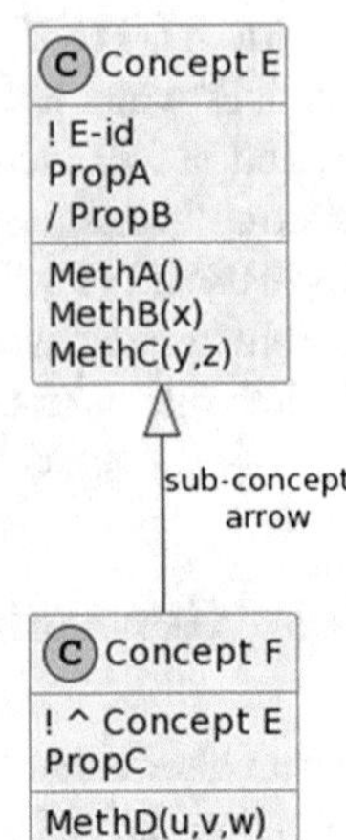

Fig. 6.8 Which properties and methods apply to which concepts?

instances of Concept F. Similarly, the properties E-id, PropA, and PropB apply to all instances of Concept E and Concept F (generalization/specialization), while property PropC applies only to all instances of Concept F.

The '/' in front of PropB indicates that PropB is a derivable property, i.e., its value can be computed from the other data. You might do the same for a derivable concept or method, i.e., putting a '/' in front.

For a (minimal) further elaboration of the class diagram, you might add a manager for every concept that does not have an outgoing arrow. For the conceptual data model in Sect. 8.5, for instance, you might add at least a 'Student-manager' and a 'Study-manager'. This easily leads to a 'Version 0.1' of the class diagram. For efficiency reasons, other managers might be needed as well.

See https://plantuml.com/class-diagram for further possibilities.

6.6 Summary

We want to emphasize and illustrate that a specification should be implementation-independent. A given specification should be implementable in several ways. This chapter illustrated this by sketching completely different implementations of the same specification, e.g., by means of parchment scrolls, (paper) notebooks, and SQL-databases, respectively. This chapter also presented the general and important *Model-View-Controller* (MVC) software design pattern.

Section 6.4 worked out in detail how to implement our specifications in an SQL-database. As an alternative, e.g., for preparing an Object-Oriented implementation, Sect. 6.5 sketched how to transform a conceptual data model into a 'Version 0.0' and 'Version 0.1' of a corresponding *class diagram*. The methods sections can subsequently be used to implement the interactions with the system as described in the textual SSDs.

Chapter 7
Organizing and Managing the Development Process

Abstract The previous chapters treated the 'contents' of IS development, i.e., how to *do* IS development, to put it this way. This chapter discusses how to *organize* and *manage* an IS-development process, from the point of view of a *technical manager*, not that of a general manager. Section 7.1 recalls the organizational and managerial problems mentioned in Sect. 1.7. Section 7.2 sketches some history, emphasizing some useful ideas from the past, in order to understand the current situation: '*Where are we now, and why?*' Finally, Sect. 7.3 discusses some wider management issues, e.g., 'agile contracting' and the Unified Process.

7.1 Sketch of the Problem Area

Section 1.7 sketched the problem area of developing information systems. Here we shortly recall those problems:

(A) Users' language (informal unbounded natural language) and way of thinking (in terms of business processes, often neglecting the underlying data structures) might be quite different from the language and formal way of thinking of developers (schema's, models, data, input/output, parameters, procedures, etc.).
(B) For several reasons, the set of user wishes is initially unclear and most likely incomplete, growing and changing over time, and might be(come) inconsistent.
(C) There might be very, very many requirements.
(D) Usually, a new system has to interact with other, existing (or not yet existing) systems. However, often, there is no—or poor or only outdated—documentation of existing systems.
(E) The development of the system might change the organization itself: the requirements analysis and/or (pilot) system might trigger new opportunities, new wishes, and new requirements.
(F) Developing information systems went from supporting known processes to enabling entirely new business models, often even yet to start. This leads to *concurrent development* of a business and its enabling information systems.
(G) The 'times to market' should become shorter and shorter.

B. de Brock, *Developing Information Systems Accurately*,
https://doi.org/10.1007/978-3-031-16862-8_7

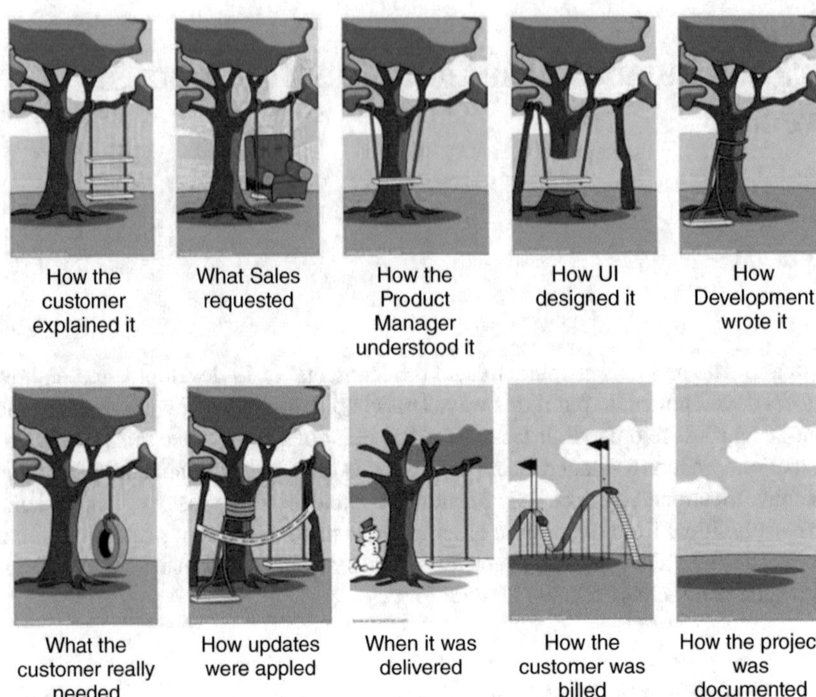
How the customer explained it
What Sales requested
How the Product Manager understood it
How UI designed it
How Development wrote it
What the customer really needed
How updates were appled
When it was delivered
How the customer was billed
How the project was documented

Fig. 7.1 The problem area

(H) In the meantime, circumstances in the organization and its environment might change, maybe partly due to the introduction of the information system itself.

So, there is—and stays—much uncertainty, *increased speed and flexibility in development is needed*, and the requirements are clear only *by the end* of the project.

These problems have severe consequences for an IS development project, which might therefore be failing on all three basic requirements for a project:

(1) The project delivers inadequate functionality (too little)
(2) The project is not within time (too late)
(3) The project is not within budget (too costly)

Or even worse: The project has to be ended prematurely, after a lot of time and money has been spent, and without delivering any working functionality.

Figure 7.1 repeats Fig. 1.2 which illustrated some of the problems very nicely, as explained in Sect. 1.7.

So, all in all, there are *communication* problems as well as *management* problems everywhere. The communication problems were addressed in Chaps. 2–5. This chapter addresses the management problems.

7.2 Some History and Trends

To understand the current situation ('*Where are we now, and why?*'), we sketch some history, emphasizing some ideas from the past. Some ideas are still useful today, while others do not apply anymore. We also mention some recent trends.

7.2.1 Waterfall Methods

In the beginning of mainstream computerization, well-established, well-understood, and stable manual processes were automated. The development of the *complete* (!) system used to be done in a few *successive* phases, similar to engineering projects in other areas at that time:

(1) **Analysis**:	Describing the (business) domain and *all* user requirements
(2) **Design**:	Creating a logical model of the system to-be (a 'blueprint')
(3) **Implementation**:	Writing the programs and building the system
(4) **Verification**:	Testing whether each separate unit as well as the integration result works according to the original specification
(5) **Maintenance**:	Fixing issues and releasing new versions with issues solved

This is also known as a **waterfall method**. Waterfall methods strictly follow a linear development path:

(1) Analysis, (2) Design, (3) Implementation, (4) Verification, (5) Maintenance

The phases might be named differently, e.g., *Requirements Engineering* instead of *Analysis* or *Testing* instead of *Verification*.

It is called a '*waterfall method*' because progress flows from the top to the bottom, just like a cascading waterfall, as in Fig. 7.2. Every phase produces a report on which every party agrees. Then the phase is closed, and, in principle, a closed phase is never reopened, just as the water in a waterfall never goes back. The next phase is based on the reports/results of the previous phase(s).

This is a typical, classical engineering approach which turned out to be (very) successful in many situations outside software development, e.g., for building bridges. The users are involved only in the Analysis phase, when finding out what the system must be able to do. Managers like to use a waterfall-based project management methodology, because management concerns such as planning, scheduling, milestones, deadlines, progress measurement, resource allocation, cost estimation, etc. become relatively simple and clear. Moreover, software development contractors were often forced to use a waterfall method by their (big) clients, e.g., by the US Department of Defense, as in their standard DOD-STD-2167 of 1985.

A linear method such as a waterfall method assumes, among others:

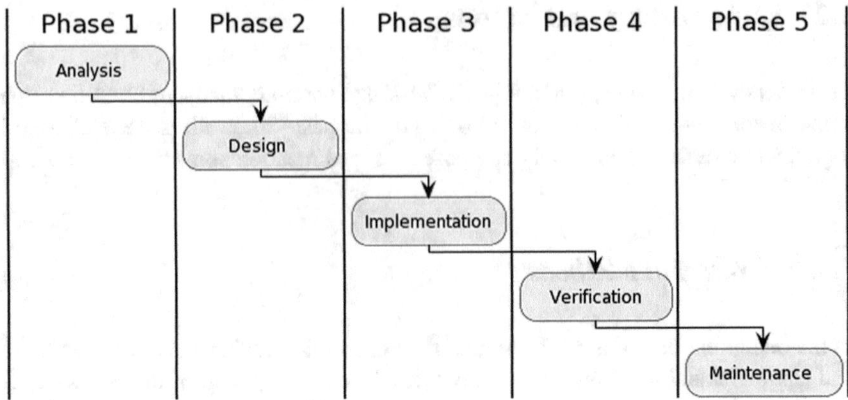

Fig. 7.2 The waterfall phases

- Well-established, well-understood, and stable processes to be automated
- A clearly defined/definable problem
- A clearly solvable problem
- No changes in the problem during the development period (!)

However, following a waterfall method can also lead to several severe problems:

P1. Neither the user nor the designer is capable of describing the new system *completely*, *in detail*, and *upfront*.
P2. Requirements must be identified and 'frozen' long before programming and delivery.
P3. Design must be completely specified before programming begins.
P4. There often is a (very) long time between system proposal and delivery of the new system. Meanwhile, the world changes and the requirements might therefore change as well.
P5. When developing a system, also—the insight into—the problem domain develops, as well as the environment, and maybe the organization itself as well.
P6. At the end of the development period, a large, new system is dropped in its entirety on the desk of the user ('big bang').
P7. Usually more than 50% of the early requirements is not used after all.

Over time there arose various refinements of—and alternatives to—waterfall methods, which could also be used in combination. We will now explain some of them.

7.2.2 Parallel Development

One way to speed up the process and shorten the development time is **parallel development**: After a carefully made—and convincing—global design, the system might turn out to be dividable into (reasonably) independent subsystems. In that

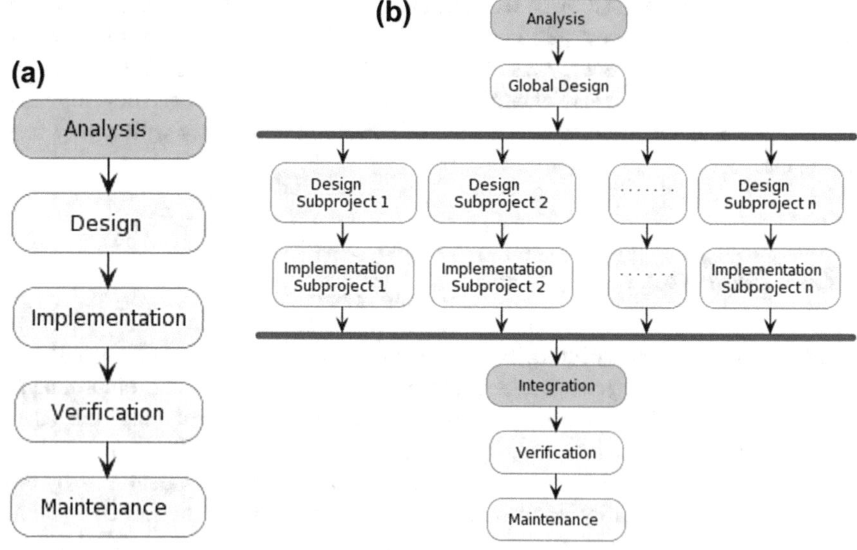

Fig. 7.3 (**a**) Standard waterfall. (**b**) Parallel development

case, different teams can further develop those subsystems in parallel, i.e., working out design and implementation in parallel subprojects. But then an integration phase has to be added, colored blue in Fig. 7.3. The phase(s) with user involvement are colored green.

Although parallel development speeds up the development process, addressing problem P3, it does not solve the other problems, although it softens P2.

7.2.3 CASE Tools, CASE Workbenches, and CASE Environments

Another way to speed up the process and shorten the development time is the use of CASE tools, where **CASE** stands for *Computer-Aided Software Engineering*.

CASE tools are software tools used to speed up design and implementation of software applications. For instance, there are CASE tools for generating code from high-level—'fourth generation'—programming languages, for debugging, for supporting specific tasks with graphical modelling, and for analyzing code for complexity, performance, or correctness w.r.t. a specification. But there are also CASE tools to support project managers, e.g., in their planning, scheduling, or task assignments.

CASE workbenches integrate two or more CASE tools to completely cover a specific part of the software life cycle. Finally, **CASE environments** cover the complete software life cycle.

Although CASE tools, CASE workbenches, and CASE environments can speed up the development process—see problem P3—they do not solve most of the other problems mentioned in Sect. 7.2.1. Moreover, instead of speeding up the development process, they might also enlarge flaws and implicit problems in a development project, just as a situation might spin out of control more quickly with a very fast racing car.

7.2.4 *Prototyping*

A **prototype**, or more specifically a *software* prototype, is a (relatively quickly made) simple, limited version of—a part of—the intended system, emphasizing only the *functionality* (and *usability*) of the system. With prototyping, the other quality requirements (such as security, performance, maintainability, recoverability, etc.) will be ignored initially. The purpose of prototyping is the evaluation—by the users—of the functionality and usability of (that part of) the envisioned system. Prototyping is especially useful for systems that have much interaction with (human) users. The two most important kinds of software prototyping are *evolutionary prototyping* and *throw-away prototyping*. They are explained below and illustrated in Fig. 7.4a, b.

An **evolutionary prototype** is a simple, limited version of the intended software system developed on—a copy of—the operational platform. A **throw-away prototype** is a simple, limited version of the intended software system as well, but not developed on—a copy of—the operational platform but on a different development platform, say an easier, handier, cheaper, or better known one. In that case, an extra Redesign phase is needed (see Fig. 7.4b), after which the prototype is 'thrown away'. Throw-away prototyping could even be done 'with pencil and paper', but then you cannot experience the functionality 'at work'.

The development phases within these kinds of prototyping are now as follows:

- **Analysis**: Describing (a subset of) the business domain and user requirements
- **Design**: Creating a logical model of (that part of) the system to-be ('blueprint')
- **Prototype implementation**: Making/adapting the prototype
- **Prototype evaluation**: Evaluating the functionality (and usability) of the prototype by (future) users

The above steps should be *iterated* until the result is satisfying enough for the users. Then the next steps follow:

- **Redesign**, but only in case of a *throw-away prototype*: Redesigning the program for the intended operational platform, colored blue in Fig. 7.4b
- **Implementation on operational platform**: Writing the program and building the system, taking care of the other quality requirements as well
- **Maintenance**: Fixing issues and releasing new versions with issues solved, as before

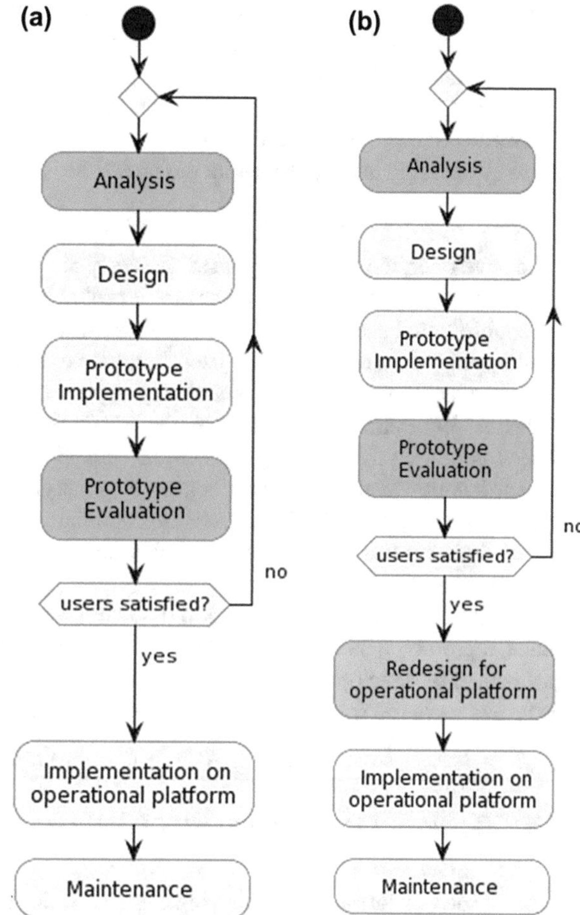

Fig. 7.4 (**a**) Evolutionary prototyping. (**b**) Throw-away prototyping

In Fig. 7.4a, b the phases with user involvement are colored green. Note that user involvement is not limited to the first phase anymore but also happens in between. The *prototype evaluations* by the users will likely lead to refinements.

Prototyping is an *iterative* process: An **iterative process** is a process that makes progress through successive refinements [Cohn2]. Because of the intermediate feedback from the users, there is no need for a separate verification phase anymore.

We use the criterion 'satisfying?' and not 'perfect?' or so, because 'satisfying' is usually good enough. Don't spend ~~much~~ time on making the *prototype* system itself perfect: For example, if in each 'round' (iteration), you do only 80% right or at least 'satisfying', then after two rounds, more than 95% is 'satisfying', and after three rounds, more than 99% is 'satisfying'. This is because 20% is left after the first round, 4% left after round 2, and 0.8% left after round 3. If in each round you do only 70% right or at least 'satisfying', then after three rounds, more than 97% is 'satisfying', and after four rounds, more than 99% is 'satisfying'. This is because

30% is left after round 1, 9% left after round 2, 2.7% left after round 3, and 0.81% left after round 4 .... So, make clear appointments when to stop changing.

Some of the many advantages of prototyping are to get valuable feedback from the users and to discover misunderstandings (or were it mis-explanations?) in an early stage of the project. But also to become aware of useful extra functionalities because after seeing and experiencing the prototype, the user might react as follows:

'Nice. Very nice! But, eh, . . ., after seeing all this, would it also be possible to . . .?'

For the developer, the '*Nice. Very nice!*' is (very) nice to hear, but the '*would it also be possible to . . .?*' is very useful, because it probably contains new or improved or more sophisticated user wishes. It clearly illustrates the advantages of prototyping.

Prototyping requires intensive user involvement, in particular of the (most) knowledgeable people. So, not some newly appointed juniors or trainees as a kind of 'proxies' but (various) domain experts. But those experts are usually the most occupied people in the user organization as well. So, it can be (very) hard to have them sufficiently available. Nevertheless, it is necessary in order to get a good quality of the system to be developed. Our company, Remmen & De Brock, even required their sufficient availability by contract (!), in order to guarantee a good quality of the system.

Theoretically, a single prototype could cover the complete system at once, but in practice, a prototype initially covers only a part of the intended system, typically the 'next' part to be developed. This makes prototyping an *incremental* process as well. This brings us to the explanation of *iterative* and *incremental* development.

7.2.5 Iterative Development and Incremental Development

The basic idea of **incremental development** is to develop and deliver the system 'piece by piece'; see Figs. 7.5 and 7.7. Hence, with incremental development, the system 'grows' over time.

The basic idea of **iterative development** is to improve 'the same piece' through successive refinements (Figs. 7.6 and 7.7), as we saw in the case of prototyping. So, the basic idea is that results do not necessarily need to be 'the first time right'.

Although the notions of *incremental* development and *iterative* development are different, they are usually applied hand in hand. Waterfall development (Fig. 7.3a) is neither iterative nor incremental.

Since the notions *incremental* development and *iterative* development are often confused, Figs. 7.5–7.7 might clarify the notions. In the figures, each next 'piece' is an extension of the system, an extension that follows after the previous pieces.

A combination of iterative and incremental development might look as in Fig. 7.7.

When iterative and incremental development are combined, there might not be a pre-set 'last' piece, as Fig. 7.7 already suggests.

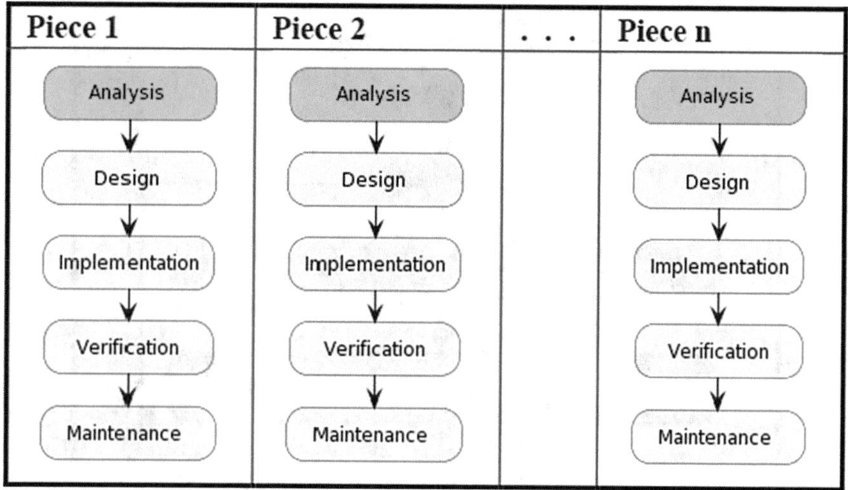

Fig. 7.5 **Incremental** but not iterative

You don't have to finish a 'piece' completely before starting to work on the next piece, as Fig. 7.7 might suggest. It might be sensible to start working on a next piece of functionality even though the current piece is not ideal yet. For instance, it might be sufficient to start and deliver a 'first version', say consisting of the Main Success Scenario and a few important alternative scenarios. Moreover, future and/or changing requirements might shed new light on the current piece of functionality.

Some advantages of incremental development and iterative development are listed below.

Some advantages of *iterative* development:

- Early signalling and solving of problems.
- Better user participation, with early feedback, fast adjusting, and fast repairing.
- Users and developers learn about the system with each iteration.
- Improved customer relations.

Some advantages of *incremental* development:

- Quicker delivery of useful subparts of the system.
- Earlier return on investment.
- Measurable sub-products.
- Improved progress monitoring.
- Reduction of complexity.
- Easier error location.
- No overwhelming 'big bang'.
- Users and developers learn about the system with each increment.
- Improved customer relations.

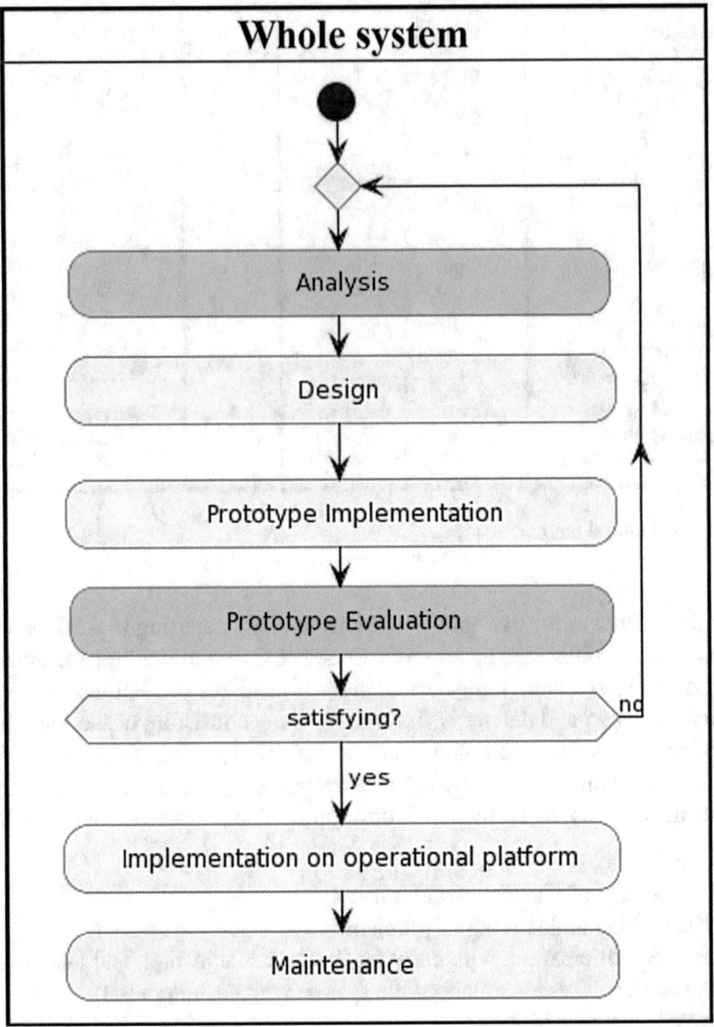

Fig. 7.6 **Iterative** but not incremental

When you combine iterative and incremental development, you have all these advantages together, so '*the best of both worlds*'. And in combination, you also have the advantages of frequent user feedback and short feedback loops.

How Large or Small Is a 'Piece'?

As stated before, a system could be developed and delivered 'piece by piece'. But how large or small should a 'piece' be? A so-called *module* is a good candidate: By a **module**, we mean a '*functional unit of independent utility*'. It could cover the tasks—or one task—of a (sub)department, for instance. A module might contain a

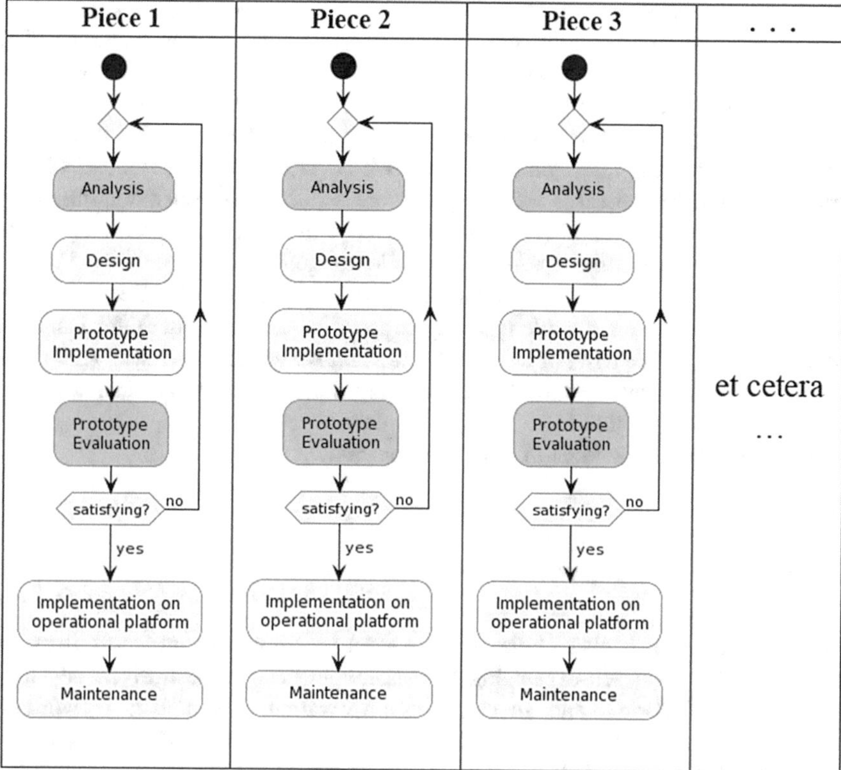

Fig. 7.7 **Iterative** and **incremental**

handful to a dozen of user wishes. Looking back at the advantages of incremental development mentioned earlier, delivery of a module means delivery of a useful, measurable sub-product and an early return on (time) investment (and also a good moment to send a bill ☺). Delivery of a module contributes to the relation with the customer as well.

A 'student registration module' for the 'student registration department' of a university or school might be an example: Before entrance of that university or school, the new student has to be registered. Registration typically includes personal data (name, address, birth date, etc.), additionally data about his/her previous education (preliminary training), and maybe some payment data. But it must also be possible to *browse* for a particular student, to *update* the data, and to *delete* (or *archive*) a student who leaves the university, so, in fact basic CRUDA-functionality. It is probably also one of the first modules needed.

And another example: Our company had to develop a system for a business partnership of five heart-lung surgeons within a hospital. The most important part of the system to-be was the part about the very operations, with an emphasis on the blood-fluid balance. However, it turned out that the best module to develop first was the module for the generation of the waiting lists. Waiting lists are very important in case of heart-lung surgery and should be produced frequently and very carefully, based on much (medical) info per patient and following strict rules. It was a very time-consuming task for them. After the delivery of that module, the waiting lists could be generated by the system. It saved the partnership almost one full secretary, a clear example of early return on investment. We developed the other modules in the order of the steps a patient is following: anamnesis, diagnosis, operation, intensive care, and follow-up (i.e., after the patient left the hospital). Each module in this sequence needs the information from the earlier modules.

However, a 'piece' of development and delivery could also be (much) smaller than a module (where a module typically supports several use cases), for instance, covering only *one use case*, or even only *one scenario* within a use case. And if the development is iterative as well, the user might see and evaluate that use case (scenario) even a few times.

This brings us to the topic of *agile development*.

7.2.6 Agile Development

Agile development is characterized by frequent user involvement; short, iterative development cycles; self-organizing teams; simple designs; test-driven development; code refactoring; and an emphasis on creating a demonstrable working product with each development cycle, as it is formulated in the *Software Engineering Body of Knowledge* [SWE] or as written in the *Manifesto for Agile Software Development* (http://agilemanifesto.org/):

> We are uncovering better ways of developing software by doing it and helping others do it. Through this work we have come to value:
>
> **Individuals and interactions** over *processes and tools*
> **Working software** over *comprehensive documentation*
> **Customer collaboration** over *contract negotiation*
> **Responding to change** over *following a plan*
>
> That is, while there is value in the items on the right, we value the items on the left more.

In agile development, requirements and design are not considered completed before implementation. Well-known examples of agile software approaches are Scrum (https://www.scrum.org) and XP (eXtreme Programming, see http://www.extremeprogramming.org or [Beck]).

For instance, XP advocates **pair programming**, i.e., working in groups of two programmers (one computer, one table, two chairs): One programmer writes code, while the other one reviews each line of code as it is typed in and thinks about the next step and the direction of the work as well. XP requires **on-site customer (s)**—'*The Customer is Always Available*', cf. http://www.extremeprogramming.org/rules/customer.html—but that is not realistic. As explained in Sect. 7.2.4, you need the most knowledgeable people, i.e., the domain experts. But they are usually the most occupied people in the user organization as well. So, you cannot require to have them available all the time. Using a so-called proxy of the customer/user, that is, someone else who acts *on behalf of* the customer, does not work when it comes to the details.

Instead of *on-site customer(s)* or proxies, you should have **on-site developers**, i.e., developers who are always available on the customer site. One way or the other, on-site customers as well as on-site developers provide the possibility of (almost) *continuous validation*.

For example, in one of our projects, we had to build an Aggregate Data Drug Information System (ADDIS) for a very busy rapporteur of the *European Medicines Agency* (https://www.ema.europa.eu/en). ADDIS was meant as an evidence-based decision support system for healthcare policy decision-making concerning alternative treatment options. The rapporteur was also a medical professor and researcher and at that time head of the clinical trial coordination center of the university hospital as well. The system to-be should support his advanced ideas about how to considerably improve the quality of the work of a rapporteur. It is obvious that we needed himself—and not some junior or trainee as a 'proxy'—but that we could not require to have him available all the time. First of all, we negotiated ('fought for') 1 h/week in his agenda, and soon we could also move our developers to a (negotiated) room next to him: So, *on-site developers*. And, as a—foreseen—consequence, the developers could also occasionally drop by, at the end of the day. And besides that, there are also the joint coffee machine and lunches ☺. By now, ADDIS (https://addis.drugis.org/#) is applied and cited very frequently.

Agile Planning

Planning in agile development is not fixed beforehand—neither predictive nor prescriptive—but *adaptive*. It could consist of three levels of planning, for instance:

- <u>Macro</u> Global plan for the entire project (say, a few years):
  - Rough goals, milestones, and time path at a high macro/project level
- <u>Meso</u> High-level plan for the next 'module' (say, for 3 months). For instance:
  - Goals, milestones, and time path for the next quarter ('quarter n + 1')
  - Global goals for the quarter thereafter ('quarter n + 2')
- <u>Micro</u> Concrete plan for the next iteration (say, for 2 weeks):
  - Concrete goals, milestones, and time path for the next iteration

So, planning always stays one stage ahead of the work in progress. It is a kind of '*rolling planning*'. That makes it easy to adapt the planning to new circumstances.

To give an example from our project for the rapporteur of the *European Medicines Agency* (EMA*) who had* advanced ideas on how to improve the quality of their EMA-reports: All of a sudden, the EMA (comparable to the US Food and Drug

Administration, https://www.fda.gov/) announced a new '*Summary of Efficacy Table*' template for the so-called *Day 80 (assessment) report*. Until then we never even heard of a 'Day 80 Report'. Anyway, after some explanation, it was very clear that this was a golden opportunity to draw attention to—and to promote—the system under development. This EMA-announcement came in the middle of the execution of a quarterly (meso-level) plan. We decided to finish that meso-level plan as foreseen, because that had its merits too, but to change our plans for the next quarter(s) completely, such that our system would asap be able to generate the contents of a '*Summary of Efficacy Table*' according to the new EMA Day 80 report template. If you are interested, click on *Show table* in the reference [SET] to see a partly filled in *Day 80 Summary of Efficacy Table*.

How to Rank Requirements?

Well, there is no unequivocal answer to that question, except '*It depends on the circumstances*'. There may well be several relevant criteria, also concurrently. . .

For instance, *business value* (versus *development effort*) or *urgency/need* for that functionality or *criticality*: How critical is this part for the system as a whole? Or *risk*: The chance that the project fails. *Quick wins* first? *Impact* is another criterion. But high impact ones first, or last? Or *dependency* on other (external) systems that still must be developed or delivered and may be delayed.

And *dependencies* among the parts of the system under development is another important criterion. For example, there might be a 'natural'—sequential or partial—order in the 'modules' to be developed, as you saw in the example of the heart-lung surgery at the end of Sect. 7.2.5. In that example, each module in the sequence needed the info from the earlier modules. Formulated more generally: The order of development might follow the order of the business process, but not necessarily. This might be dealt with at the macro-level of the 'rolling planning'. Anyway, the good news is that you don't have to rank all the requirements upfront.

Another relevant criterion might be *(departmental) readiness*: In a large governmental organization for which our company worked a long time ago, the departments had largely independent tasks. Therefore, there was no 'natural' order of the 'modules' to be developed. However, some departments were (mentally) ready for support of their tasks by software, while others were quite resistant. But once we delivered (sub)systems to some of the 'ready' departments, other departments became interested too.

But there might also be (mutual) dependencies on the *micro-level* of user wishes: User wishes for retrieving 'reports', 'overviews', and 'summaries' (etc.) presuppose the presence of CRUDA functionality—at least Creates—for the elementary data on which those reports and overviews (etc.) are based. On the other hand, the CRUDA functionality for the elementary data—especially the Creates—might depend on the (summarized) data that should be produced in those reports/overviews/summaries. For example, the user wish '*Retrieve all Xs over period p*' presupposes a date for the Xs, which might not have been needed until this user wish came up.

And finally there are the sudden, unforeseen, and sometimes disruptive changes. For instance, the user organization is 'merged with' or taken over by another organization, which happened even twice within one of our projects! Or some (completely) new functionality rushes in from outside, with the highest priority (a change triggered by the 'environment'), as you saw with that 'Day 80 report', or the upswing of a world-wide pandemic, what happened in 2020 with COVID, which might profoundly change the priorities of the functionalities still to be developed and might change the functionalities themselves too.

The relatively good news is that you don't have to plan and rank everything in detail beforehand with agile planning: At the micro-level, for instance, you need a concrete plan for only the next iteration (say, 2 weeks). And at the meso-level, you need a high-level plan for only the next quarter and global goals for the quarter thereafter. But even then, things might change before 'the next quarter' or 'the quarter thereafter' is there, as our example with the EMA Day 80 report illustrated. And we could easily adapt our planning to new circumstances in that case.

Business Value Versus Development Effort

A concrete approach to the earlier mentioned issue of '*business value* versus *development effort*' is as follows: The customer indicates the business value of each 'unit of functionality' foreseen for the 'next round'. As 'unit of functionality' you can take a user wish, user story, use case, use case scenario, or so. The customer can express it in terms of money—probably after some complicated computations—but it can also be expressed on a simple 5-point scale (Likert scale). Furthermore, the developer indicates the expected development effort for each such unit. That can be in hours/days, simple Likert scale, function points, story points, or so. After that, you can determine the business value *per* unit of development effort—so, in a sense, the 'value for money'—for each functionality. Subsequently, you can order them accordingly, to determine which one(s) to develop next, but of course taken their dependencies into account. This is what we did in our EMA-project (Van Valkenhoef et al, *Quantitative release planning in extreme programming*, [Val]).

7.2.7 DevOps

Until now we mainly addressed the gaps between *customers* and *developers*. Although beyond the scope of this book, we want to mention a more recent, additional trend called *DevOps*. DevOps addresses the gaps between software development (*Dev*) and the daily IT operations (*Ops*). **DevOps**, combining SW-development and IT-operations, intends to streamline SW development and IT operations in order to speed up the delivery of (software) applications. The goal of DevOps is to shorten the development life cycle and to provide *continuous delivery*. Putting them behind each other, you get a 'software production line' including *continuous integration* and *continuous delivery*, which might even be several times a day or via 'nightly builds'. DevOps contributes to shortening the 'time to market' (Problem E in Sect. 7.1).

DevOps requires a very close collaboration between the different groups in the 'software production line', such as future users, requirements analysts, developers, programmers, testers, implementers, and the actual users. In terms of Sect. 7.2.5, the 'pieces' (i.e., increments) of functionality can be very, very small with DevOps. But it is important to take privacy and security issues into account as well during such a streamlined, continuous delivery!

7.2.8 *History and Trends in Conclusion*

To conclude Sect. 7.2: Be ready and open for *change*, because software development implies *frequent adaptions*. Software development is NOT about translating frozen requirements into the design of <u>the</u> system NOR about continuously changing everything all the time. It is important to stimulate—even to require—user participation, to overcome resistance, to listen to feedback, and to adjust when and where necessary. Often, information systems in practice are continuously under development ('under construction'), just like a city.

Therefore, we prefer to use an *iterative*, *incremental*, and *agile* development process, being an evolutionary process with *frequent user feedback* and *short feedback loops*, building increments from iterative stages. Be open and ready for change, or as some say, '*embrace change*' [Beck].

7.3 Wider Management Issues

Besides the management issues we mentioned until now, there are other management issues as well. We want to highlight the following issue in particular.

Agile Contracting

How should an *agile contract*, i.e., a contract for an agile development project, be formulated? Note that in an agile development project, the requirements are not completely spelled out beforehand, can be supplemented later on, and can also be changed during development. Also note that the customer must have the freedom to change his/her mind. Consequently, you cannot specify the deliverables beforehand. We explain how we formulated it in our latest agile project.

Well, the customer's requirements should not jump around all the time, but they have to 'converge'. This led us to the (accepted) contract clause that '*It is the intention that the set of requirements converges to an end point and that the system under development converges to the final set of requirements*'. Furthermore, the contract stipulated to work by means of a series of intermediate versions of the system to be developed (one version per quarter) as well as a series of intermediate versions of the set of requirements. The project was for 4 years, so 16 deliveries. We also added the clause '*This way of working assumes that the right persons are sufficiently available for deliberation*', similar to the clause we used earlier with the company Remmen & De Brock.

In line with the agile planning described in Sect. 7.2.6, we also wrote that in order to achieve the intended convergence, the deliverables of each Milestone N will consist of:

1. The agreed result
2. A detailed set of requirements for Milestone N + 1
3. A global set of requirements for Milestone N + 2

The contract also specified the agreed result for the first milestone and the set of requirements for the second milestone.

Furthermore, the contract stipulated that the detailed set of requirements and the global set of requirements for the next two milestones will always be drawn up in mutual deliberation with the customer.

The **Unified Process** (UP) is a system development 'framework' (with variants) intended to cover 'all' management issues. It distinguishes several *disciplines*, usually eight (see Jacobson, Booch, and Rumbaugh, *The Unified Software Development Process*, [JBR]):

1. Business modelling
2. Requirements analysis
3. Design
4. Implementation (programming, installation, etc.)
5. Testing
6. Deployment (daily operations)
7. Configuration and change management
8. Project management

There exist refinements and variations too, e.g., also including a discipline called *(Development) Environment*. The disciplines might also be named differently, e.g., *Verification* instead of *Testing*. The UP framework combines many existing 'best practices' and can be applied in many different ways: waterfall, iterative, agile, etc.

To put this textbook in perspective, this book concentrates on the disciplines **Requirements analysis** and **Design**, although Chap. 6 covers part of *Implementation* and the current chapter touches upon the discipline *Project management*, in particular from the point of view of a *technical manager*. With respect to requirements analysis, we concentrate on the *functional* requirements, not on the other requirements, a.k.a. *quality* requirements or 'non-functional' requirements.

For an example of some high-level quality requirements for our earlier mentioned system ADDIS, we refer to https://github.com/drugis/drugis.org/blob/master/software/addis/requirements.md, and for some of its design decisions to https://github.com/drugis/drugis.org/blob/master/software/addis-desktop/retrospective.md.

7.4 Summary

This chapter considered the development of an information system from a technical manager's point of view. First, Sect. 7.1 recalled the problems you may encounter when developing information systems:

(A) Users' language (unbounded natural language) and way of thinking are often quite different from the developers' language and way of thinking.
(B) The *individual* user wishes might be unclear, explained wrongly, understood wrongly, and/or prone to change. Also, *the set of* user wishes might be unclear, incomplete, growing over time, and be(come) inconsistent.
(C) There might be very many requirements.
(D) Often there is no, or poor, or only outdated documentation of existing systems with which the new system has to interact.
(E) The development/introduction of the system might change the organization too: People awake, and it might trigger new opportunities, wishes, and requirements.
(F) New processes in existing organizations must be automated, though they might not be well established or well understood. Or you might even need to develop systems for businesses which still have to be developed too. That is *concurrent development* of a business (model) and its enabling information systems.
(G) The times to market must become shorter and shorter, putting more pressure on the development: new products must appear constantly, and meanwhile product variation and personalization are increasing.
(H) Circumstances within the customer organization and in its environment might change (very) quickly nowadays and consequently the (set of) requests as well.

Subsequently, Sect. 7.2 sketched some history, emphasizing some ideas from the past and some recent trends, e.g., DevOps. We explained which ideas are still useful and why others do not apply anymore, for example, why a linear, 'big bang' method such as a pure *waterfall method* does not work under the circumstances we sketched. Those circumstances require *flexibility in development.*

Anyway helpful are *parallel development*—developing (reasonably) independent subsystems in parallel—*CASE tools*, *CASE workbenches*, and *CASE environments* (productivity tools for the SW engineer) and *prototyping*, i.e., quickly making a simple, limited version of (a part of) the intended system for the user to try out.

However, we emphasized *incremental development* (developing and delivering the system 'piece by piece') and *iterative development* (improving 'the same piece' through successive refinements), using an *agile rolling planning*: global plan for the entire project, high-level plan for the next 'module', and concrete plan for the next iteration. We also zoomed in on the possible size of a 'piece', e.g., a 'module' (a 'functional unit of independent utility'), a user wish, or maybe only one use case scenario.

Ranking the—already known—requirements upfront might be difficult: There might be several relevant criteria, concurrently. Moreover, ranking *all* requirements upfront is unnecessary in case of *incremental* development, i.e., developing and delivering the system 'piece by piece'.

Finally, Sect. 7.3 pointed out that there exist other management issues as well, besides the ones treated in this book. We discussed *agile contracts* and mentioned the system development framework called *Unified Process* (UP).

Part II
Case Studies

Part II contains three (use) case studies. The first case study concerns a university, for which the author is a domain expert himself. In that case study, the emphasis is on the *statics*. The second one concerns the case study in Larman's book *Applying UML and Patterns*. In that case study, the emphasis is on the *dynamics*. The third 'use case study' comes from several discussions the author had with a domain expert on energy control systems. It illustrates the *interplay* between the dynamics and the statics of the system under development.

Chapter 8 work out step by step the development of a simple domain model towards a full-fledged conceptual data model and a specification for implementation in the database language SQL as well, hence illustrating Chaps. 4, 5, and 6.

Chapter 9, a study concerning the conversion of use cases, converts the well-known nontrivial use case *Process Sale* from Larman's book into a textual SSD (Sect. 9.1). For validation purposes, we subsequently translate that textual SSD (back) into natural language (Sect. 9.2) and into a graphical SSD (Sect. 9.3). Chapter 9 illustrates several parts of Chap. 2.

Chapter 10 illustrates the typical development situation where the requirements are constantly changing, also because of new opportunities and a growing customer base. It also shows the application of our approach to a *control system*.

In summary, Chapter 8 illustrates domain models and conceptual data models and their possible SQL-implementation. Chapter 9 shows the conversion of use cases to textual SSDs and the subsequent conversion of textual SSDs to natural language and to graphical SSDs. Chapter 10 illustrates the interplay between the dynamics and the statics, the application of our approach to a control system, and how to deal with the typical situation that requirements are changing all the time.

An overview of what the case studies cover:

Case studies	
Analysis and Specification	*Implementation*
Ch. 8 and 10: Statics Ch. 9 and 10: Dynamics	Ch. 8: Statics

Chapter 8
A Non-trivial University Example Worked Out

Abstract The example in this chapter will demonstrate the full path from an informal sketch of a problematic situation via a simple domain model toward a precisely specified conceptual data model, including the path to validation and implementation. We illustrate how you could analyze such an informal situation sketch and how subsequent questions may then arise. This chapter mainly illustrates Chaps. 4–6.

The development from the initial situation sketch to a simple domain model will be treated first (Sects. 8.1–8.3), followed by the development of a conceptual data model (Sects. 8.4–8.9). After a section about validation of the conceptual data model through explanation in natural language (Sect. 8.10), the implementation of the conceptual data model in the database language SQL will be worked out (Sect. 8.11).

This substantial example is partly inspired by the various university-related fragments presented until now. This example also illustrates that a larger example quickly becomes more subtle in practice. Although the example is not particularly large, it contains all kinds of subtleties as you may encounter them in practice.

8.1 Initial Sketch of the Situation

A student can enrol for a study, a.k.a. a study program. After that, the student can enrol for several courses within that study and can subsequently participate in those courses (although an enrolment will not always be followed by actual participation). Later on, a student can enrol for an exam of that course and might afterward get graded for that exam. Later on, the student gets the opportunity to rate the course. One more thing: Upon enrolment for a course, a student is supposed to have passed all prerequisite courses of that course.

8.2 Analysis of the Initial Situation Sketch

Now we will analyze the initial situation sketch in Sect. 8.1 phrase by phrase. Per phrase, we make one or more comments.

B. de Brock, *Developing Information Systems Accurately*,
https://doi.org/10.1007/978-3-031-16862-8_8

1. ‘*A student can enrol for a study, a.k.a. a study program*’:
    (a) This seems association between *student* and *study*. It is unclear whether it is a many-to-many or a many-to-one association. So, ask it. Suppose that the answer is that a student can enrol for several studies. Then it is a many-to-many association.
2. ‘*After that, the student can enrol for several courses within that study*’:
    (a) This implies not only an association between *student* and *course* but also an association between *course* and *study*. The first one is probably many-to-many, but check it. We emphasize the fact that, in the end, errors made in the beginning of a development project are the most costly ones!
    (b) The second association could be many-to-many or many-to-one. So, ask it. Suppose that the answer is that a course belongs to only one study.
    (c) The phrase ‘After that, ...’ indicates that a student can enrol for a course only after she/he has enrolled for that study.
3. ‘... *and can subsequently participate in those courses*’:
    (a) Suggests a second association between *student* and *course*.
    (b) The word ‘subsequently’ indicates that a student can participate in a course only if she/he enrolled for that course.
4. ‘... *although an enrolment will not always be followed by actual participation*’:
    (a) So, there can be course enrolments without subsequent participation.
5. ‘*Later on, a student can enrol for an exam of that course*’:
    (a) An association between *student* and *exam*, probably many-to-many, but (probably) also a many-to-one association between *exam* and *course*.
    (b) The phrase ‘Later on, ...’ indicates that a student can enrol for an exam only if (s)he enrolled for that course.
6. ‘... *and might afterward get graded for that exam*’:
    (a) An association between *student* and *exam* again.
    (b) The word ‘afterward’ indicates that a student can get a grade only if she/he enrolled for that exam.
7. ‘*Later on, the student gets the opportunity to rate the course*’:
    (a) An association between *student* and *course* again.
    (b) The phrase ‘Later on, ...’ suggests that a student can rate a course only afterwards. But when? Which condition applies? After she/he enrolled for that course, or after participation in the course, or after getting graded? Again, ask it. Suppose that the answer is: After participation.
8. ‘*Upon enrolment for a course, a student is supposed to have passed all prerequisite courses of that course*’:

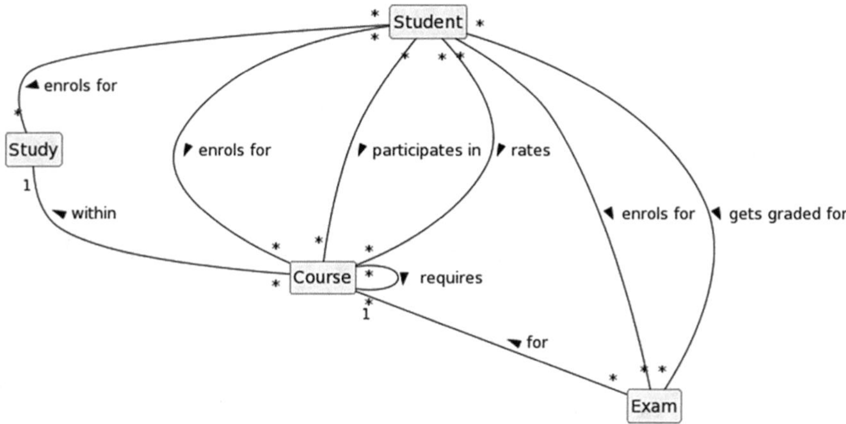

Fig. 8.1 A simple domain model

(a) What is the status of this remark? Is it a warning, or a hard condition? Suppose that the answer is that it is a warning but not a hard condition. Then this warning should appear, indeed, 'Upon enrolment for a course'.
(b) The phrase 'prerequisite courses of that course' indicates an association between courses, probably many-to-many.

8.3 A Simple Domain Model for the Situation

The simple domain model in Fig. 8.1 constitutes an informal and suggestive description, containing four concepts and nine associations, and covers many of the points made, but not all of them.

Actually, the domain model covers the points 1a, 2a, 2b, 3a, 5a, 6a, 7a, and 8b. Point 4a is a remark we can take notice of, but it does not have consequences for us. Point 8a should be handled in the appropriate use case(s).

The domain model does not cover the points 2c, 3b, 5b, 6b, and 7b. We will come back to these points in Sects. 8.5 and 8.9.

8.4 From Domain Model to an Initial Conceptual Data Model

From here on, we will more or less follow the steps mentioned in Sect. 5.3. Following step 1 of Sect. 5.3, you can simply replace each of the seven many-to-many associations by a new, formerly hidden concept with two many-to-one associations. Together with the original 4 concepts and the other 2 many-to-one associations, it gives the 11 concepts and 16 references depicted in Fig. 8.2.

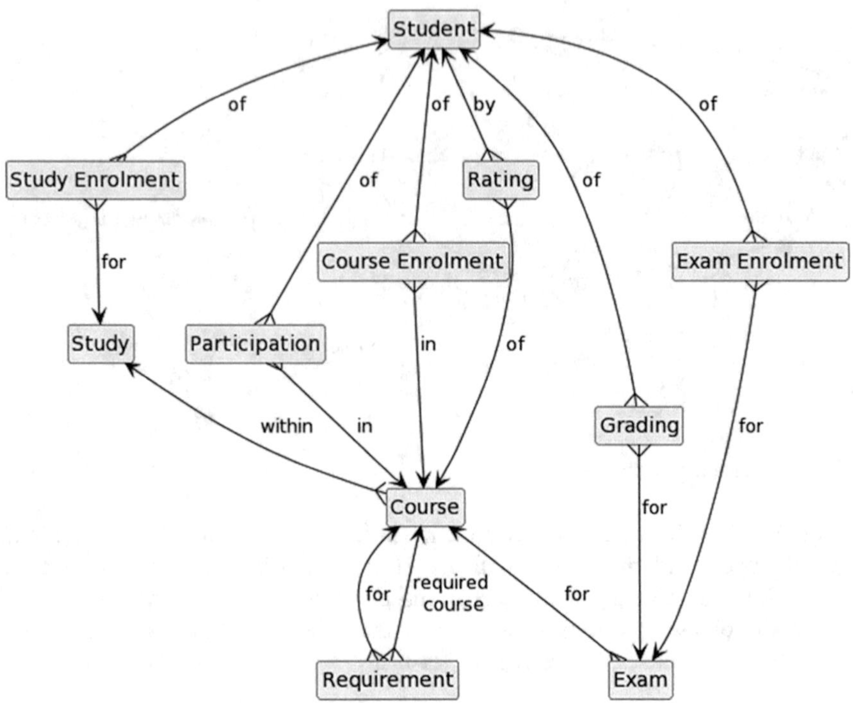

Fig. 8.2 An initial conceptual data model

8.5 A Refined Conceptual Data Model Including References

Now we come back to the points 2c, 3b, 5b, 6b, and 7b, which were not covered yet.

Point 2c implies that a course enrolment should refer to an underlying study enrolment. Hence a course enrolment implicitly refers to the student as well, making the explicit reference to the student superfluous.

Similarly, point 5b implies that an exam enrolment should refer to an underlying course enrolment. Hence an exam enrolment implicitly refers to the student as well, making the explicit reference to the student superfluous.

Point 6b implies that a grading should refer to an underlying exam enrolment. Hence a grading implicitly refers to the student and exam as well, making the two explicit references superfluous.

Similarly, point 3b implies that a participation should refer to an underlying course enrolment. Hence a participation implicitly refers to the student and course as well, making the two explicit references superfluous.

Similarly, point 7b implies that a rating should refer to an underlying participation. Hence a rating implicitly refers to the student and course as well, making the two explicit references superfluous.

Hence, because of these points, six of the original seven many-to-many associations are mutually associated; see Fig. 8.3.

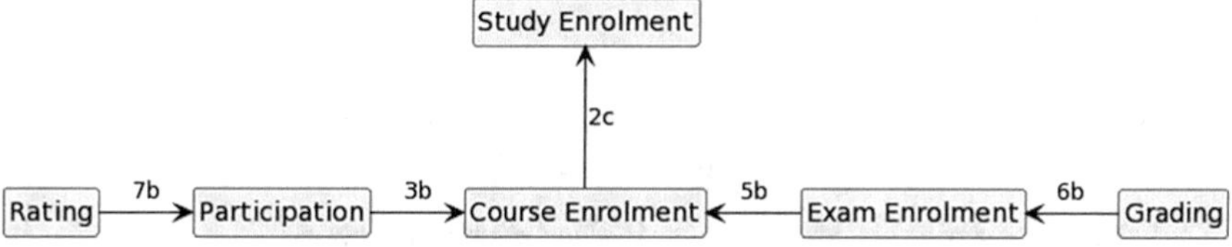

Fig. 8.3 Six of the original many-to-many associations are mutually associated

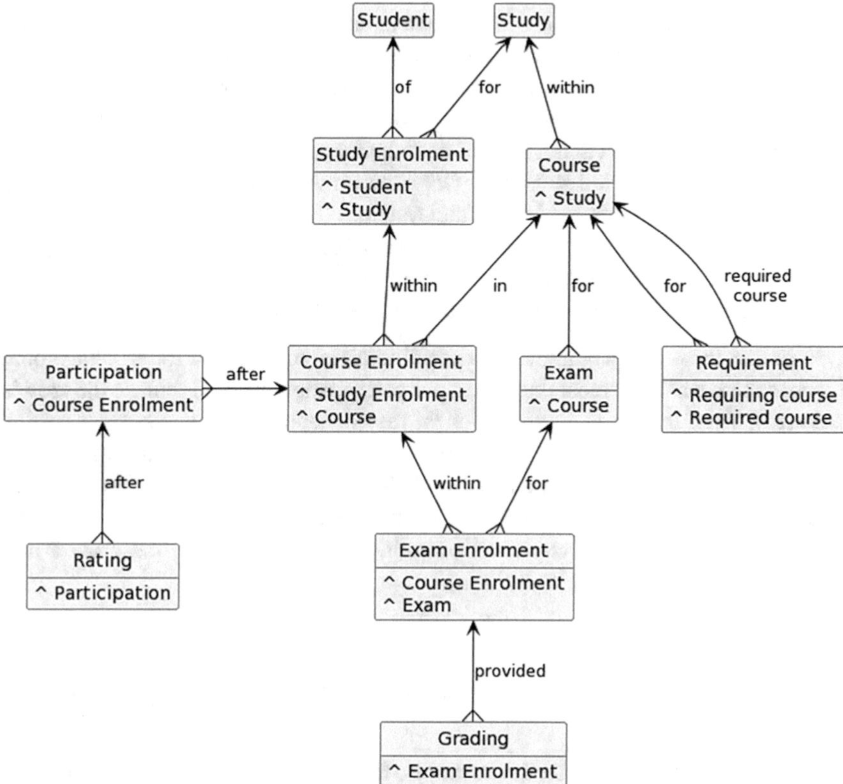

Fig. 8.4 A refined conceptual data model including references

All in all, this leads to the improved conceptual data model in Fig. 8.4, with the references explicitly mentioned in the concepts, as advised in Sect. 5.3, Step 2.

We note that the date ordering constraints were not treated yet (e.g., that a course enrolment date should not be before the date of the study enrolment concerned). We will come back to that in Sect. 8.9.

8.6 Uniqueness Constraints

Now we consider the uniqueness conditions, i.e., step 3 of Sect. 5.3. Suppose that we obtained the following answers from the university:

1. A student is uniquely identified by his/her student number.
2. A study is uniquely identified by its study code (a.k.a. its CROHO-code).
3. Both the full name and the abbreviation of a faculty are unique.
4. A student can enrol for any study only once.
5. A course has a unique course code and a name which is unique within the study.
6. After a study enrolment, there is no use to enrol twice for an individual course.
7. There cannot be two exams of the same course on the same day.
8. There is no use to mention a required course twice for a requiring course.
9. The university stated that a student participates after course enrolment if there is at least one registered presence. Only the number of registered presences is considered relevant to register in the system.
10. Per participation there can be at most one rating.
11. Within a course enrolment there is no use to enrol twice for an exam.
12. For a given exam enrolment there can be at most one grading.

Note that there are two uniqueness conditions for courses and for faculties too.

Since there can be at most one rating per participation, we will replace the crow's foot arrow from Rating to Participation in the conceptual data model by a normal arrow; see Table 5.1. Similarly, since there can be at most one grading for a given exam enrolment, we also replace that crow's foot arrow by a normal arrow. Since all participations related to a given course enrolment are taken together, there is at most one 'participation' for a given course enrolment, so we replace that crow's foot arrow by a normal arrow as well.

8.7 Conceptual Data Model with 'All' Relevant Properties

Until now we concentrated on the concepts, their associations/references, and their uniqueness conditions. Now we look at some additional properties to be taken into account. In line with step 4 of Sect. 5.3, we also (implicitly) indicate whether a value is optional. Further elicitation revealed the following:

According to the university, the relevant data to register about a student are his/her name, address, gender (if the student allows it), birth date, phone number (if applicable), university e-mail address (called his/her 'U-mail'), and date of first registration at the university, independent from any study she/he will follow. A student will then get a student number. If a student leaves the university, his/her data are kept 'on file'. But it will be registered that the student has left the university. On our suggestion to register the *date* the student left the university, the university reacted that is not always clear *when* the student left the university.

A study (program) has a level, in particular Bachelor or Master. It also has a 'size', expressed in the number of credit points (a.k.a. 'ECTS', cf. [ECTS]) that a student must earn. A Bachelor's program usually consists of 180 ECTS, while a Master's program typically consists of 60 or 120 ECTS. A study is offered by a *faculty*, another important concept within a university.

A faculty has a full name, a main physical address, a central e-mail address, a central phone number, and its founding year is of interest as well. Besides its full name, each faculty also has an abbreviation which is commonly used. For instance, the Faculty of Economics and Business is also known as FEB, and the Faculty of Science and Engineering is known as FSE.

A course belongs to a 'study year' (first year, second year, etc.) and a 'study block': A study year is divided into four blocks. Courses also have a description and an ECTS-size (often five ECTS). A course in a study is given under the responsibility of a faculty, not necessarily the faculty that offers that study. For example, a mathematics course in a business study might be given by a science faculty.

All enrolments should have an enrolment date. And an exam should have an exam date. An enrolment date should not be before the date of the enrolment it refers to. So, a course enrolment should not be before the study enrolment concerned, and an exam enrolment should not be before the course enrolment concerned. Moreover, a study enrolment date should not be before the student's registration date. On the other hand, an exam enrolment should be at least 7 days before the exam date.

Finally, a grading should of course contain the grade itself, and a rating should contain the rate value given. A course requirement might have a further explanation, but not necessarily.

The resulting conceptual data model might now be as presented in Fig. 8.5. It consists of 12 concepts, 15 references, and 47 properties.

8.8 Possible Values for the Properties

In line with step 5 of Sect. 5.3, you have to determine the *possible values* per property, according to the user organization. Well, according to various sources in the university, the possible values for the properties are as follows, where we go through the concepts in the order in which they appear in the picture:

1. A *faculty name* and *course name* are a string of at most 50 characters.
2. A *faculty abbreviation* consists of at most five characters.
3. A *faculty address*, *student name*, and *student address* can be any string.
4. A *U-mail* and *e-mail address* can be any string of the form X@Y.Z.
5. A *phone number* is a string of at most 20 characters (a digit, '+', '-', '.', or ' ').
6. A *founding year* is a year after 1600.
7. A *student number* is a natural number consisting of 6 digits and divisible by 11 (meant for simple checks).

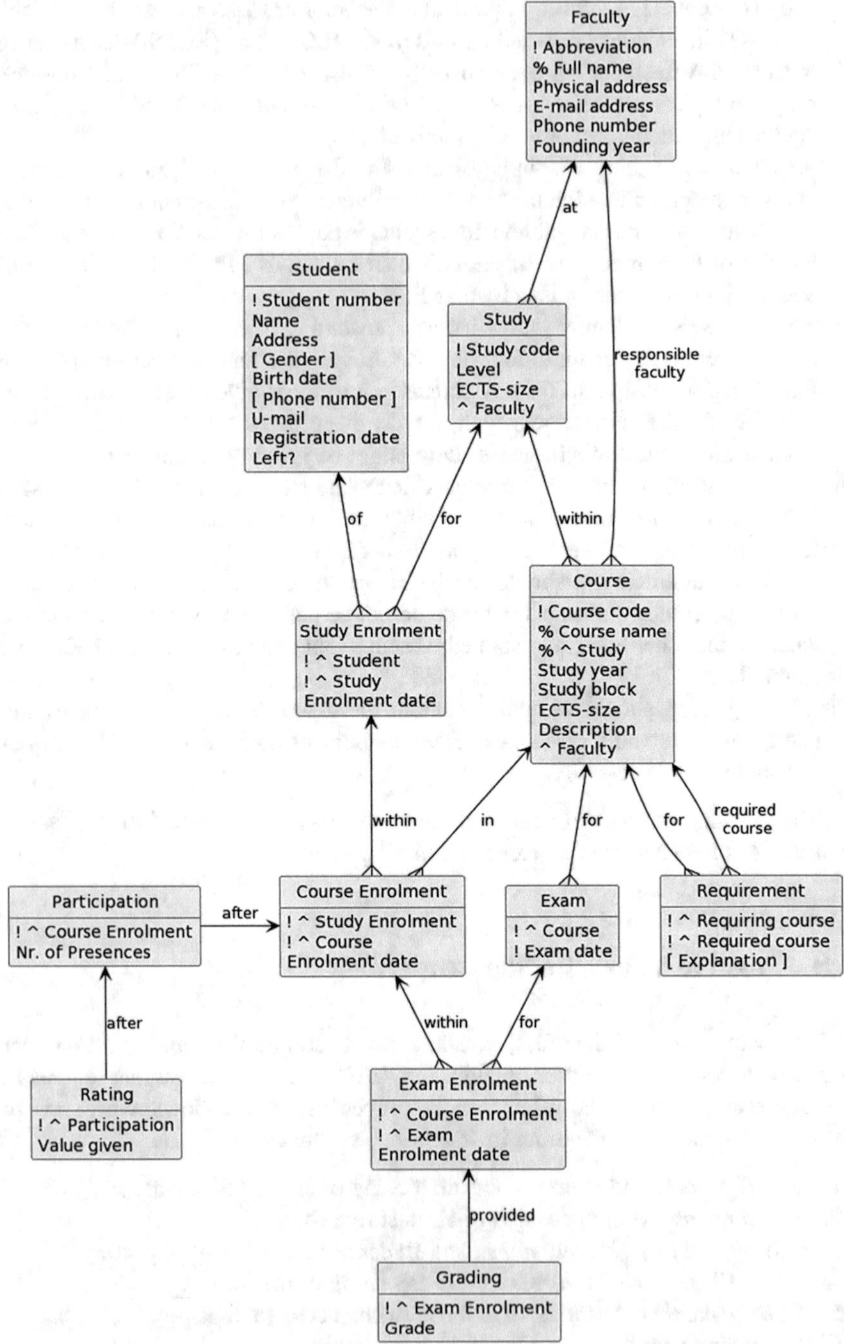

Fig. 8.5 Conceptual data model with the relevant properties

8. Two *genders* are distinguished (until now): ♂ (Male) and ♀ (Female).
9. A *birth date* can be any past date, in principle (but likely at least 17 years ago). The remark between brackets is meant as only a warning, because sometimes the university gets very young but very smart students.
10. A *registration date* can be any date, but not a date in the future.
11. The property *Left?* has two possible values: *Yes* and *No*.
12. A *study code* is a natural number consisting of five digits.
13. The *level* of a study is either *Ba(chelor)* or *Ma(ster)*, at least until now.
14. An *ECTS-size* is a natural number larger than 0.
15. A *study-* or *course-enrolment date* can be any date not in the future.
16. A *course code* consists of a combination of exactly nine letters and digits.
17. The *study year* of a course can be *1*, *2*, or *3*; *3* for only a Bachelor study.
18. There are four *study blocks*: 1–4.
19. A *course description* can be any string (usually about half a page).
20. The *number of presences* of a participation is a natural number larger than 0.
21. An *exam date* can be any date, also a future date.
22. The *explanation* of a requirement can be any string (say a few lines, if present).
23. The *value given* at a rating is a natural number, but at most 10.
24. An *exam enrolment date* can be any date since September 2010, when the university started to keep track of exam enrolments, but it cannot be a future date.
25. A *grade* is a natural number from 0 up to 10, those values included (although some lecturers principally refuse to give a '0').

8.9 Remaining Integrity Rules

According to step 6 in Sect. 5.3, you must add remaining *integrity rules*, provided that they are there. In Sect. 8.9.1 we informally discuss them, and in Sect. 8.9.2, we write them out formally.

8.9.1 Informally

There are indeed some remaining integrity rules.

1. Further elicitation confirmed our conjecture that the prerequisite courses of a course must all be 'earlier', that is, scheduled in earlier years or in earlier blocks of the same year.
2. As stated in Sect. 8.8, point 17, a year 3 can apply to only a Bachelor study.
3. As mentioned in Sects. 8.2 and 8.7, an enrolment date should not be before the date of the other enrolment it refers to; see also Fig. 8.5. Below we recall the remaining 'date ordering' integrity rules from Sects. 8.2 and 8.7. For referential

purposes, we abbreviated the relevant dates. The ordering is 'more or less chronologically':

(a) In 8.7: a study enrolment (SE) should not be before the student's registration (SR)
(b) 2c in 8.2: a course enrolment (CE) should not be before the study enrolment (SE) concerned
(c) 3b in 8.2: a student can participate (PA) in a course only after enrolment for that course (CE)
(d) 7b in 8.2: a student can rate (RA) a course only after participation (PA)
(e) 5b in 8.2: an exam enrolment (EE) should not be before the course enrolment (CE) concerned
(f) 6b in 8.2: a student can get a grade (GR) for an exam only after enrolment for that exam (EE)

Schematically: SR $\leq$ SE $\leq$ CE $\leq$ PA $\leq$ RA and CE $\leq$ EE and EX $\leq$ GR

However, Participation (PA), Rating (RA), and Grading (GR) do not contain a date... We will come back to this in Sect. 8.9.2.

4. We might have missed the following subtlety in point 2 of Sect. 8.2: 'After study enrolment, the student can enrol for several courses *within that study*', so, not any course, but only courses *within that study*.

   In other words, the study of the course enrolled for must be the same as the study of the study enrolment underlying that course enrolment; cf. Fig. 8.5.

Formulated differently, Point 4 says that all directed paths from *Course Enrolment* to *Study* in Fig. 8.6a lead to the same result. This is indicated by the circle in the middle of the diagram.

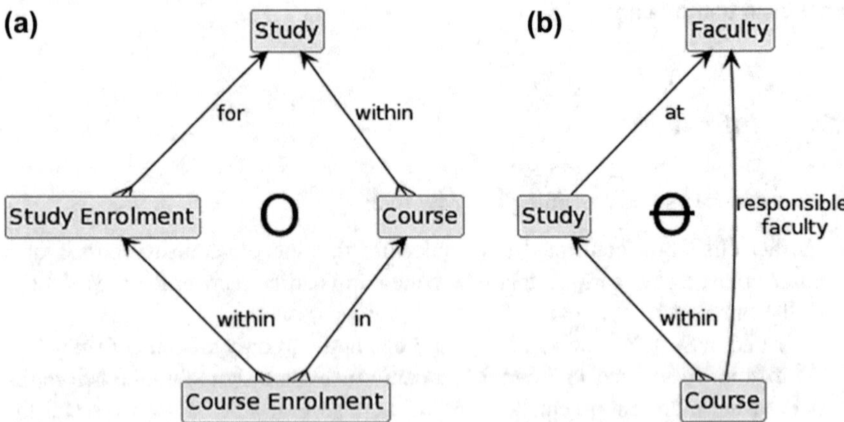

Fig. 8.6 (**a**) A commutative diagram. (**b**) A non-commutative diagram

In mathematics, this is called a **commutative diagram**, i.e., a diagram in which all directed paths with the same start- and endpoints lead to the same result.

The diagram in Fig. 8.6b is not commutative because the faculty responsible for a course does not need to be the faculty that offers that study; see Sect. 8.7. This is indicated by the crossed-out circle in the middle of the diagram.

Exercise 8.1
Similarly, we also missed the following subtlety in point 5 of Sect. 8.2: 'Later on, a student can enrol for an exam *of that course*', so, only exams *of that course*. This suggests another commutative diagram.

Determine and generate that commutative diagram. For the generation part, we refer to Sect. A.3.2 of the Appendix, our Plantuml tutorial.

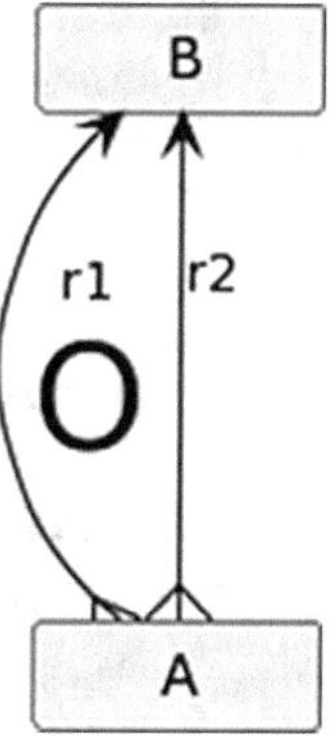

Fig. 8.7 What does this commutative diagram say?

Exercise 8.2
What does the commutative diagram in Fig. 8.7 say?

What is your conclusion?

8.9.2 More Formally

Now we try to formalize the remaining constraints. For readability reasons, some words below are written in **bold**. Furthermore, *year* stands for *Study year*, *block* for *Study block*, *Rdate* for *Registration date*, and *Edate* for *Enrolment date*:

1. For each course Requirement r:
   (c1.year < c2.year) **or** (c1.year = c2.year **and** c1.block < c2.block),
   where c1 indicates the Requir*ed* course and c2 indicates the Requir*ing* course

2. For each Course c: **not** (c.year = 3 **and** s.Level ≠ 'Ba'), where s indicates the study the course belongs to (i.e., s = c.Study)

3(a) For each Study Enrolment e: s.Rdate ≤ e.Edate, where s indicates the enrolling student

3(b) For each Course Enrolment ce: se.Edate ≤ ce.Edate, where se indicates the underlying study enrolment

3(c) Although there seem to be internal lists where teaching assistants register the presence of students enrolled for the course concerned, only the *final* number of presences of a student in a course is relevant. Therefore, no 'participation days' are registered, and hence there is no 'date ordering' integrity rule needed in this case.
On the other hand, there is referential integrity rule R9 (see Sect. 8.11), requiring that a 'participation' should refer to a course enrolment

3(d) The actual date of a course rating is not considered relevant by our university, only that the rating was done by a student who actually participated.
But that is already covered by referential integrity rule R10 (see Sect. 8.11), requiring that a rating should refer to a participation.

3(e) For each Exam Enrolment ee: ce.Edate ≤ ee.Edate, where ce indicates the underlying course enrolment

3(f) The actual registration of a grade does not have (and, as we heard, will not get) a registration date associated to it, so there is no applicable 'date ordering' integrity rule in this case, only referential integrity rule R13 (see Sect. 8.11), requiring that a grading should refer to an exam enrolment.

4. For each Course Enrolment ce: c.Study = se.Study where c indicates the course enrolled for and se indicates the underlying study enrolment

Hence, all in all, only the constraints 1, 2, 3(abe), and 4 remain.

8.10 The Conceptual Data Model Explained in Natural Language

You can systematically map/translate the conceptual data model to natural language (plain English in this case), e.g., for validation and explanation reasons. We follow the mapping rules of Sect. 5.7 though we left out the comma's and '**and**'. The texts in bold are the general texts, while the regular texts are application specific.

The system needs to contain:

For each relevant Faculty:
its Full name
its Abbreviation
its Physical address
its E-mail address
its Phone number
its Founding year.
The same value for Full name **should not occur twice.**
The same value for Abbreviation **should not occur twice.**

For each relevant Student:
his/her Student number
his/her Name
his/her Address
optionally his/her Gender
his/her Birth date
optionally his/her Phone number
his/her U-mail
his/her Registration date
whether (s)he is Left.
The same value for Student number **should not occur twice.**

For each relevant Study:
its Study code
its Level
its ECTS-size
a reference to its Faculty.
The same value for Study code **should not occur twice.**

For each relevant Study Enrolment:
a reference to its Student
a reference to its Study
its Enrolment date.
The same value combination for Student **and** Study **should not occur twice.**

For each relevant Course:
its Course code
its Course name
a reference to its Study
its Study year
its Study block
its ECTS-size
its Description
a reference to its Faculty.
The same value for Course code **should not occur twice.**
The same value combination for Course name **and** Study **should not occur twice.**

For each relevant Course Enrolment:
a reference to its Study Enrolment
a reference to its Course
its Enrolment date.
The same value combination for Study Enrolment **and** Course **should not occur twice.**

For each relevant Exam:
a reference to its Course
its Exam date.
The same value combination for Course **and** Exam date **should not occur twice.**

For each relevant Participation:
a reference to its Course Enrolment
its Nr. of Presences.
The same value for Course Enrolment **should not occur twice.**

For each relevant Rating:
a reference to its Participation
its Value given.
The same value for Participation **should not occur twice.**

For each relevant Exam Enrolment:
a reference to its Course Enrolment
a reference to its Exam
its Enrolment date.
The same value combination for Course Enrolment **and** Exam **should not occur twice.**

For each relevant Grading:
a reference to its Exam Enrolment
its Grade.
The same value for Exam Enrolment **should not occur twice.**

For each relevant Requirement:
a reference to its Requiring course
a reference to its Required course
optionally its Explanation.
The same value combination for Requiring course **and** Required course **should not occur twice.**

8.11 Specification in SQL

This section presents a specification in the database language SQL corresponding to our conceptual data model. We use the guidelines given in Sect. 6.4.1. But first, each reference to a uniqueness that consists of more than one property must be replaced by those referenced properties. This results in Fig. 8.8.

Note that 'Course' occurs twice in Exam Enrolment and hence also in Grading. However, according to point 5 of Sect. 8.2 'After course enrolment, the student can enrol for an exam *of that course*', so, not any exam, only exams *of that course*. In other words, the course of the exam enrolled for must be the course in the course enrolment underlying that exam enrolment. So, you need only one field 'Course'.

Note that Exam date and Enrolment date now both occur in Exam Enrolment. So, the requirement that an exam enrolment should be at least 7 days before the exam date (see Sect. 8.7) can be expressed within Exam Enrolment. We express this in Constraint C6, using the SQL-expression `DATEADD(DAY,-7,ExamDate)`, which indicates the seventh `DAY` *before* `ExamDate`.

We recall from Sect. 6.4 that although SQL is a standard language for databases, each DBMS (Database Management System) might have its own dialect. So, check the documentation of your own DBMS!

Since table names and attribute names cannot contain hyphens ('-') or spaces in SQL, we replace '-' by '_', and we leave spaces out while turning the next letter into a capital, making each name one recognizable word.

First we create the database *Student Tracking System*, which represents our state space. Then we introduce several special *domains*, i.e., 'sub data types' of basic data types; see Sect. 6.4.1. For example, domain `StudNumSet` concerns all six-digit integers divisible by 11. Domain `CrsCodeSet` expresses that it concerns all nine-character strings that do not contain a character which is not a letter or a digit. Finally, domain `PhoneNumSet` expresses that it concerns all strings of at most 20 characters that do not contain a character which is not a digit, '+', '-', '.', or a space.

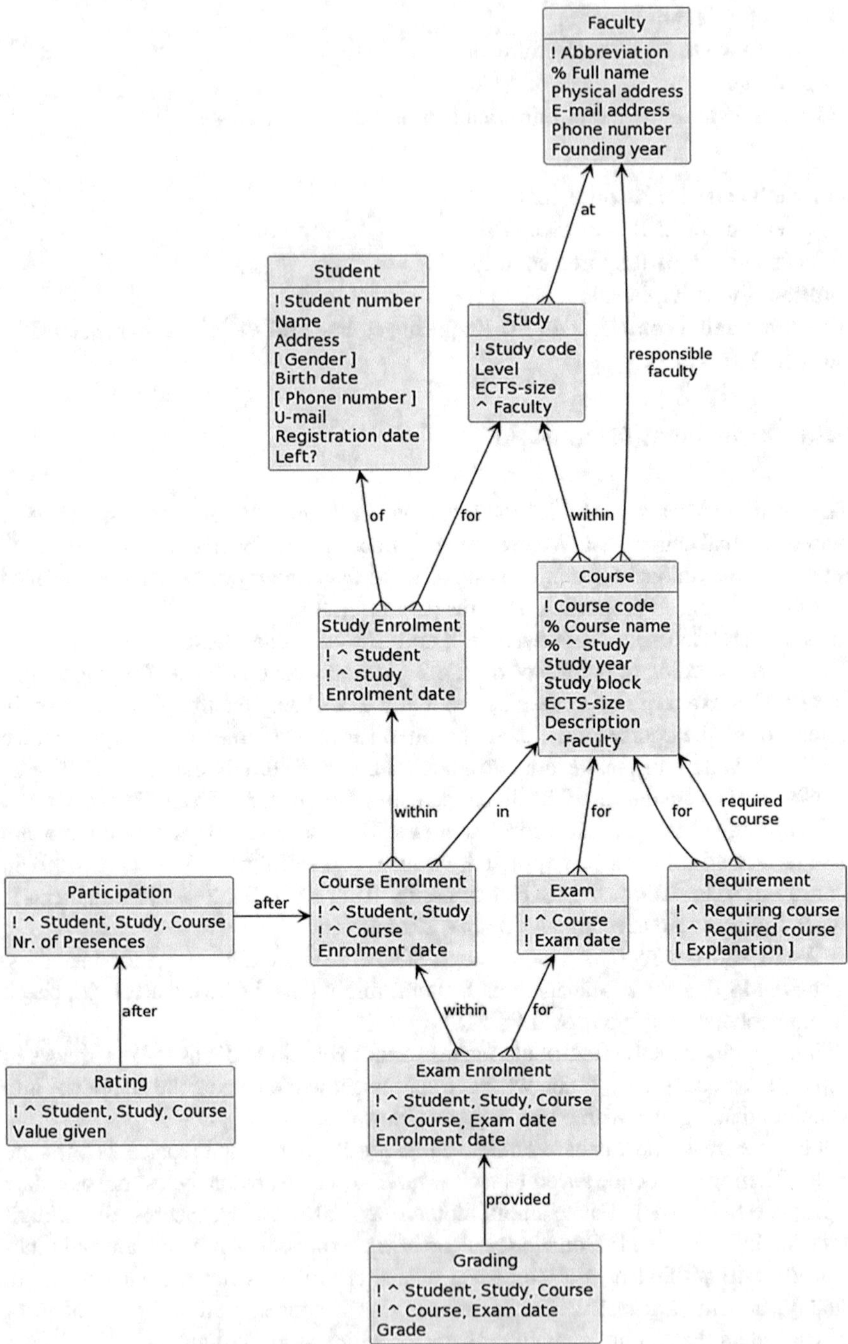

Fig. 8.8 The adapted conceptual data model

Subsequently, for each of the concepts, which are written in yellow, we define a CREATE TABLE. Together they contain all the constraints per table mentioned up to now. When called upon, CURDATE() in constraint C2 and domain DateUpToNow refers to the date at that moment. For clarity, primary keys consisting of more than one attribute are marked blue.

```
CREATE DATABASE Student Tracking System;

CREATE DOMAIN GenderSet AS CHAR(1)
CHECK( @VALUE IN ('♂', '♀') );

CREATE DOMAIN LevelSet AS CHAR(2)
CHECK( @VALUE IN ('Ba', 'Ma') );

CREATE DOMAIN YesNoSet AS VARCHAR(3)
CHECK( @VALUE IN ('No', 'Yes') );

CREATE DOMAIN PosNumSet AS INTEGER
CHECK( @VALUE > 0 );

CREATE DOMAIN ScoreSet AS INTEGER
CHECK( 0 <= @VALUE AND @VALUE <= 10 );

CREATE DOMAIN CROHO_code AS INTEGER
CHECK( 10000 <= @VALUE AND @VALUE < 100000 );

CREATE DOMAIN StudNumSet AS INTEGER
CHECK( 100000 <= @VALUE AND @VALUE < 1000000
    AND @VALUE % 11 = 0 );

CREATE DOMAIN DateUpToNow AS DATE
CHECK( @VALUE <= CURDATE() );

CREATE DOMAIN EMailSet AS VARCHAR
CHECK( @VALUE LIKE '%@%.%' );

CREATE DOMAIN CrsCodeSet AS CHAR(9)
CHECK( @VALUE NOT LIKE '%[!a-z0-9]%' );

CREATE DOMAIN PhoneNumSet AS VARCHAR(20)
CHECK( @VALUE NOT LIKE '%[!0-9+-. ]%' );
```

```
CREATE TABLE Faculty
(Abbreviation          VARCHAR(5)    NOT NULL,
FullName               VARCHAR(50)   NOT NULL,
PhysicalAddress        VARCHAR       NOT NULL,
E_mailAddress          EMailSet      NOT NULL,
PhoneNumber            PhoneNumSet   NOT NULL,
FoundingYear           INTEGER       NOT NULL,
CONSTRAINT K1 PRIMARY KEY (Abbreviation),
CONSTRAINT U1 UNIQUE(FullName),
CONSTRAINT C1 CHECK (FoundingYear > 1600) );

CREATE TABLE Student
(StudentNumber         StudNumSet    NOT NULL,
Name                   VARCHAR       NOT NULL,
Address                VARCHAR       NOT NULL,
Gender                 GenderSet     NULL,
BirthDate              DATE          NOT NULL,
PhoneNumber            PhoneNumSet   NULL,
U_mail                 EMailSet      NOT NULL,
RegistrationDate       DateUpToNow   NOT NULL,
Left?                  YesNoSet      NOT NULL,
CONSTRAINT K2 PRIMARY KEY (StudentNumber),
CONSTRAINT C2 CHECK ( BirthDate < CURDATE() ) );

CREATE TABLE Study
(StudyCode             CROHO_code    NOT NULL,
Level                  LevelSet      NOT NULL,
ECTS_size              PosNumSet     NOT NULL,
Faculty                VARCHAR(5)    NOT NULL,
CONSTRAINT K3 PRIMARY KEY (StudyCode),
CONSTRAINT R1 FOREIGN KEY (Faculty)
    REFERENCES Faculty(Abbreviation) );

CREATE TABLE StudyEnrolment
(Student               StudNumSet    NOT NULL,
Study                  CROHO_code    NOT NULL,
EnrolmentDate          DateUpToNow   NOT NULL,
CONSTRAINT K4 PRIMARY KEY (Student, Study),
CONSTRAINT R2 FOREIGN KEY (Student)
    REFERENCES Student(StudentNumber),
CONSTRAINT R3 FOREIGN KEY (Study)
    REFERENCES Study(StudyCode) );
```

```
CREATE TABLE Course
(CourseCode            CrsCodeSet    NOT NULL,
CourseName             VARCHAR(50)   NOT NULL,
Study                  CROHO_code    NOT NULL,
StudyYear              INTEGER       NOT NULL,
StudyBlock             INTEGER       NOT NULL,
ECTS_size              PosNumSet     NOT NULL,
Description            VARCHAR       NOT NULL,
Faculty                VARCHAR(5)    NOT NULL,
CONSTRAINT K5 PRIMARY KEY (CourseCode),
CONSTRAINT U2 UNIQUE(CourseName, Study),
CONSTRAINT C3 CHECK (1 <= StudyYear AND StudyYear <= 3),
CONSTRAINT C4 CHECK (1 <= StudyBlock AND StudyBlock <= 4),
CONSTRAINT R4 FOREIGN KEY (Study)
    REFERENCES Study(StudyCode),
CONSTRAINT R5 FOREIGN KEY (Faculty)
    REFERENCES Faculty(Abbreviation) );

CREATE TABLE CourseEnrolment
(Student               StudNumSet    NOT NULL,
Study                  CROHO_code    NOT NULL,
Course                 CrsCodeSet    NOT NULL,
EnrolmentDate          DateUpToNow   NOT NULL,
CONSTRAINT K6 PRIMARY KEY (Student, Study, Course),
CONSTRAINT R6 FOREIGN KEY (Student, Study)
    REFERENCES StudyEnrolment(Student, Study),
CONSTRAINT R7 FOREIGN KEY (Course)
    REFERENCES Course(CourseCode) );

CREATE TABLE Exam
(Course                CrsCodeSet    NOT NULL,
ExamDate               DATE          NOT NULL,
CONSTRAINT K7 PRIMARY KEY (Course, ExamDate),
CONSTRAINT R8 FOREIGN KEY (Course)
    REFERENCES Course(CourseCode) );

CREATE TABLE Participation
(Student               StudNumSet    NOT NULL,
Study                  CROHO_code    NOT NULL,
Course                 CrsCodeSet    NOT NULL,
NrOfPresences          PosNumSet     NOT NULL,
CONSTRAINT K8 PRIMARY KEY (Student, Study, Course),
CONSTRAINT R9 FOREIGN KEY (Student, Study, Course)
    REFERENCES CourseEnrolment(Student, Study, Course) );
```

```
CREATE TABLE Rating
(Student                StudNumSet    NOT NULL,
Study                   CROHO_code    NOT NULL,
Course                  CrsCodeSet    NOT NULL,
ValueGiven              ScoreSet      NOT NULL,
CONSTRAINT K9 PRIMARY KEY (Student, Study, Course),
CONSTRAINT R10 FOREIGN KEY (Student, Study, Course)
    REFERENCES Participation(Student, Study, Course) );

CREATE TABLE ExamEnrolment
(Student                StudNumSet    NOT NULL,
Study                   CROHO_code    NOT NULL,
Course                  CrsCodeSet    NOT NULL,
ExamDate                DATE          NOT NULL,
EnrolmentDate           DateUpToNow   NOT NULL,
CONSTRAINT K10 PRIMARY KEY (Student, Study, Course, ExamDate),
CONSTRAINT C5 CHECK ('2010-09-01' <= EnrolmentDate),
CONSTRAINT C6 CHECK(EnrolmentDate <= DATEADD(DAY,-7,ExamDate)),
CONSTRAINT R11 FOREIGN KEY (Student, Study, Course)
    REFERENCES CourseEnrolment(Student, Study, Course),
CONSTRAINT R12 FOREIGN KEY (Course, ExamDate)
    REFERENCES Exam(Course, ExamDate) );

CREATE TABLE Grading
(Student                StudNumSet    NOT NULL,
Study                   CROHO_code    NOT NULL,
Course                  CrsCodeSet    NOT NULL,
ExamDate                DATE          NOT NULL,
Grade                   ScoreSet      NOT NULL,
CONSTRAINT K11 PRIMARY KEY (Student, Study, Course, ExamDate),
CONSTRAINT R13 FOREIGN KEY (Student, Study, Course, ExamDate)
  REFERENCES ExamEnrolment(Student, Study, Course, ExamDate));

CREATE TABLE Requirement
(RequiringCourse        CrsCodeSet    NOT NULL,
RequiredCourse          CrsCodeSet    NOT NULL,
Explanation             VARCHAR       NULL,
CONSTRAINT K12 PRIMARY KEY (RequiringCourse, RequiredCourse),
CONSTRAINT R14 FOREIGN KEY (RequiringCourse)
    REFERENCES Course(CourseCode),
CONSTRAINT R15 FOREIGN KEY (RequiredCourse)
    REFERENCES Course(CourseCode) )
```

Now we want to express the remaining constraints in SQL. We will use SQL-*assertions* for those 'inter-table' constraints. Each remaining constraint has the form

'*For each <concept> x: <constraint on x>*'

As explained in Sect. 6.4.1, this cannot be directly translated to SQL since SQL is *set oriented*. But this is logically equivalent to

'*There does not exist a <concept> x for which <constraint on x> does not hold*'

Therefore, we will use the following pattern for our assertions:

```
CREATE ASSERTION <assertion name> CHECK
(NOT EXISTS (SELECT * FROM <tables> WHERE <condition>))
```

where `<condition>` consists of the correspondence(s) that join the tables, followed by the *negation* of the original requirement. Below, for readability reasons, those two parts are separated by a capital AND. For <assertion name>, we used the requirement number preceded by the letter 'A' and wrote the name in **bold**.

```
CREATE ASSERTION A1 CHECK
(NOT EXISTS (SELECT * FROM Requirement r, Course c1, Course c2
WHERE (c1.CourseCode = r.RequiredCourse and c2.CourseCode =
r.RequiringCourse) AND not (c1.year < c2.year or (c1.year = c2.year and
c1.block < c2.block))));

CREATE ASSERTION A2 CHECK
(NOT EXISTS (SELECT * FROM Course c, Study s WHERE
 c.Study = s.StudyCode AND (c.year = 3 and s.Level <> 'Ba')));

CREATE ASSERTION A3a CHECK
(NOT EXISTS (SELECT * FROM StudyEnrolment e, Student s
 WHERE s.StudentNumber = e.Student AND
    s.RegistrationDate > e.EnrolmentDate));

CREATE ASSERTION A3b CHECK
(NOT EXISTS (SELECT * FROM CourseEnrolment e, StudyEnrolment s
 WHERE (s.Student = e.Student and s.Study = e.Study) AND
    s.EnrolmentDate > e.EnrolmentDate));

CREATE ASSERTION A3e CHECK
(NOT EXISTS (SELECT * FROM ExamEnrolment e, CourseEnrolment c
 WHERE (c.Student = e.Student and c.Study = e.Study and
 c.Course = e.Course) AND c.EnrolmentDate > e.EnrolmentDate));

CREATE ASSERTION A4 CHECK
(NOT EXISTS
 (SELECT * FROM CourseEnrolment e, Course c, StudyEnrolment s
 WHERE (s.Student = e.Student and s.Study = e.Study and
     c.CourseCode = e.Course) AND c.Study <> s.Study))
```

Chapter 9
Converting a Large Use Case

Abstract In this chapter, as an illustration of Chap. 2, we convert the well-known use case Process Sale from Larman's book *Applying UML and Patterns* into a textual SSD (Sect. 9.1). For validation purposes, we subsequently translate that textual SSD into natural language (Sect. 9.2) and into a graphical SSD (Sect. 9.3). Figure 9.1 schematically shows what will be done in which section.

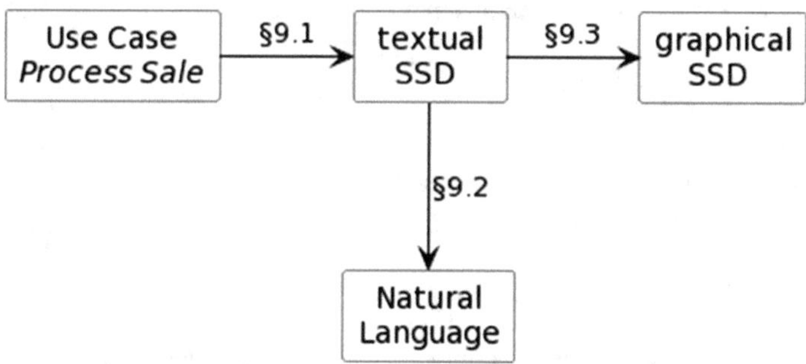

Fig. 9.1 What will be done in which section

9.1 Converting a Large Use Case to a Textual SSD

To illustrate the (sub)structuring and integration of the various scenarios of a use case, which can become quite extensive and complex in practice, we will give a large tSSD-example of such (sub)structuring and integration. The example is based on Larman's use case *Process a Sale* as described in [Lar], Sect. 6.8, and on our understanding of that description. It starts simple with a so-called *brief format* description (where POS stands for *point of sale*):

Process a Sale (Brief Format)

A customer arrives at a checkout with items to purchase. The cashier uses the POS system to record each purchased item. The system presents a running total and line-item

B. de Brock, *Developing Information Systems Accurately*,
https://doi.org/10.1007/978-3-031-16862-8_9

details. The customer enters payment information, which the system validates and records. The system updates inventory. The customer receives a receipt from the system and then leaves with the items.

First we recall the textual SSD for the Main Success Scenario as presented it in Example 2.2, Sect. 2.5 (*System Sequence Descriptions*). The primary actor here is **Cashier**, the word we will use in this concrete example instead of our usual **User**. Secondary actors are **Customer**, **AccSys** (Accounting system), and **InvSys** (Inventory system).

We refer to the step numbers as used in [Lar]. Some of his steps consist of more than one step in the textual SSD, e.g., his Step 4. Then such additional steps are shortly indicated by 'Step 4 too', etc. The two parts of Step 4 can be done in any order. Also the three parts of Step 8 can be done in any order. But the two parts of steps 6 and 7 cannot be done in any order.

Customer ➡ **Customer:** arrive at checkout with items to purchase; /* Step 1
Cashier ➡ **System:** StartNewSale; /* Step 2
repeat **Cashier** ➡ **System:** EnterItem(item-ID); /* Step 3
    System ➡ **System:** RecordSaleLineItem , /* Step 4
    System ➡ **Cashier:** description, price, and running total /* Step 4 too
until cashier indicates done; /*
Cashier ➡ **System:** EndSale; /*
System ➡ **Cashier:** total with taxes; /* Step 5
Cashier ➡ **Customer:** total; /* Step 6
Cashier ➡ **Customer:** request for payment; /* Step 6 too
Customer ➡ **System:** process payment; /* Step 7
System ➡ **System:** handle payment; /* Step 7 too
System ➡ **System:** log completed sale , /* Step 8
System ➡ **AccSys:** sale and payment info , /* Accounting system. Step 8 too
System ➡ **InvSys:** sale and payment info; /* Inventory system. Step 8 too
System ➡ **Cashier:** receipt; /* Step 9
Customer ➡ **Customer:** leave with receipt and goods /* Step 10

Note that the MSS uses only basic steps, sequential composition (';'), arbitrary order (','), and one **repeat**-loop. There are 16 basic steps.

Exercise 9.1
How many external steps, input steps, internal steps, and output steps are there?

Beside the Main Success Scenario, Sect. 6.8 of Larman [Lar] contains also more than 20 alternative scenarios, called *extensions* there. We will now work out almost all of those extensions and number them as done by Larman.

We start with the definition of what we will call the *Main Scenario*, followed by the other definitions referred to. In the *Main Scenario*, we italicized the lines which were changed or new, and we crossed out the lines that were deleted (compared to the *Main Success Scenario* above). The underlined names in blue could constitute clickable links to their definition.

DEFINE ProcessSale **as** /*
Customer → Customer: arrive at checkout with items to purchase; /* Step 1
Cashier → System: StartNewSale; /* Step 2
System → System: *CreateSale;* */* This step wasn't mentioned in [Lar]*
~~**repeat Cashier → System:** EnterItem(item ID); /* Step 3~~
Repeat: Perform *EnterItem;* */* Step 3*
System → System: RecordSaleLineItem , /* Step 4
System → Cashier: description, price, and running total /* Step 4 too
until cashier indicates done; /*
Cashier → System: EndSale; /*
System → Cashier: total with taxes; /* Step 5
Cashier → Customer: total; /* Step 6
Cashier → Customer: request for payment; /* Step 6 too
maybe perform *HandleDiscount* ***end;*** */* Extension 5b*
maybe perform *HandleCredit* ***end,*** */* Extension 5c ⎤ can be done*
maybe perform *HandleCoupons* ***end;*** */* Extension 7f ⎦ in any order*
~~**Customer → System:** process payment; /* Step 7~~
~~**System → System:** handle payment; /* Step 7 too~~
perform *HandlePayment;* */* Extensions 7a,b,c,d*
System → System: log completed sale, /* Step 8
System → AccSys: sale and payment info, /* Accounting system. Step 8 too
System → InvSys: sale and payment info; /* Inventory system. Step 8 too
maybe perform *HandleGiftReceipt* ***end;*** */* Extension 9b*
if *system detects printer is out of paper* */* Extension 9c*
then perform *HandlePaperShortage* ***end;*** */* Extension 9c*
System → Cashier: receipt; /* Step 9
Customer → Customer: leave with receipt and goods /* Step 10
END;

We continue with the definitions referred to.

The '▼' behind the two categories in *EnterItem* indicates that there is a list to choose a value from. The parameter q (for 'quantity') is optional. It comes from Larman's Extension 3b. Its default value is 1.

DEFINE EnterItem **as**
either perform HandleCodedItem(item-ID [; q]) /* Usual case
or Cashier → System: enterPricedItem(P-category▼; price) /* Extension 3c
or Cashier → System: enterWeightItem(W-category▼; weight) /* own extension
end
END;

In *HandleCodedItem*, we shortened Cashier to Cas and System to Sys for reasons of space. To avoid misunderstandings, for each condition in *HandleCodedItem*, we indicate which actor has to check it. This is in line with the extension introduced in Sect. 2.5.1; see in particular Table 2.5.

```
DEFINE HandleCodedItem(item-ID [; q]) as
  Cas ➡ Sys: enterCodedItem(item-ID [; q]) ;                    /* Try this        (A)
  if Sys: quantity parameter q is absent                        /* check by System
    then Sys ➡ Sys: make q equal to 1                           /* 1 is the default
  end ;
  Sys ➡ Sys: determine item i having that item-ID;              /* not in [Lar]
  IF Sys: item-ID is unknown                                    /* Extension 3a
     then Sys ➡ Cas: 'Unknown item ID' ;
          If Cas: there is a human-readable item-ID             /* check by Cashier
            then Cas ➡ Sys: enterManually(item-ID; q)           /* else try this   (B)
            else If Cas: there is a price on the tag            /* check by Cashier
                 then Cas ➡ Sys: enterPrice(price; q) ;         /* else try this   (C)
                        Cas ➡ Sys: applyStandardTaxation
                 else            /* after finally finding out the correct item-ID or price
                   either  Cas ➡ Sys: enterManually(item-ID; q)          /* either (B)
                     or    Cas ➡ Sys: enterPrice(price; q) ;             /* or (C)
                           Cas ➡ Sys: applyStandardTaxation              /*
                   end
                End
          End
  END
END;

DEFINE HandleDiscount as                                        /* Extension 5b
    Cashier ➡ System: applyDiscount(Customer ID);
    System ➡ System: apply discount to sale;
    System ➡ Cashier: new total with taxes
END;

DEFINE HandleCredit as                                          /* Extension 5c
    Cashier ➡ System: applyCredit(Customer ID);
    System ➡ System: apply credit to sale up to price = 0;
    System ➡ System: reduce remaining credit;
    System ➡ Cashier: new total with taxes
END;

DEFINE HandleCoupons as                                         /* Extension 7f
    repeat Cashier ➡ System: record coupon;
           System ➡ System: reduce price with value of coupon;
           System ➡ System: record usage of coupon;
           System ➡ Cashier: new total with taxes
    until coupons are done
END;
```

```
DEFINE HandlePayment as                                /* Extensions 7a,b,c,d
    either perform HandleCashPayment                   /* Extension 7a
        or perform HandleCreditPayment                 /* Extension 7b
        or perform HandleCheckPayment                  /* Extension 7c
        or perform HandleDebitPayment                  /* Extension 7d
    end
END;

DEFINE HandleCashPayment as                            /* Extension 7a
    Cashier ➡ System: Enter(cash amount tendered);
    System ➡ Cashier: balance due;
    System ➡ System: release cash drawer;
    Cashier ➡ System: deposit cash amount tendered;
    Cashier ➡ Customer: cash balance;
    System ➡ System: record cash payment
END;

DEFINE HandleCreditPayment as                                   /* Extension 7b
    Customer ➡ System: MakeCreditPay(credit account info);
    System ➡ Cashier: payment info (for verification);
    Cashier ➡ System: confirm;
    System ➡ AutSys: payment approved?;       /* Payment Authorisation system
    AutSys ➡ System: payment approval;        /* AutSys answers request by return
    System ➡ Cashier: payment approved,                         /*⎤ can be done
    System ➡ System: record credit payment;                     /*⎦ in any order
    ⋮                                                           /*  and so on…
END;

define HandleCheckPayment as … end;           /* Extension 7c. Unspecified in [Lar]

define HandleDebitPayment as … end;           /* Extension 7d. Unspecified in [Lar]

DEFINE HandleGiftReceipt as                                     /* Extension 9b
    Cashier ➡ System: giveGiftReceipt;
    System ➡ Cashier: gift receipt
END;

DEFINE HandlePaperShortage as                                   /* Extension 9c
    System ➡ Cashier: 'Out of paper';
    Cashier ➡ Cashier: replace paper;
    Cashier ➡ System: printReceipt
END;
```

The example in [Lar] also has some extensions that are possible *at any time*, for example, HandleManagerOverride:

```
DEFINE HandleManagerOverride as                          /* Extension *a
    Manager ➡ System: changeModeTo('Manager');
    System ➡ System: change to mode 'Manager';
    Manager ➡ System: <do some ManagerMode operation>;  /* (1)
    System ➡ System: change to mode 'Cashier'
END;
```

(1) E.g., a cash balance change

The example in [Lar] also has some extensions that can arise within a certain range of steps. For example, Extension 2–4a can arise within the range of steps 2 until 4. We give some examples:

```
DEFINE HandleTaxExempt as                                /* Extension 2–4a
    Cashier ➡ System: enterStatusCode('tax-exempt');
    System ➡ System: record Status Code 'tax-exempt'
END;

DEFINE HandleItemRemoval as                              /* Extension 3–6a
    Customer ➡ Cashier: request to remove item;
    IF value of item ≤ cashier-limit
       then Cashier ➡ System: remove item
       else Manager ➡ System: remove item               /* (1)
    END;
    System ➡ System: delete item;
    System ➡ Cashier: new (running) total
END;
```

(1) Actually a HandleManagerOverride

```
DEFINE HandleSaleCancellation as                         /* Extension 3–6b
    Cashier ➡ System: cancel sale;
    System ➡ System: delete sale;
    System ➡ Cashier: 'Done'
END;

DEFINE HandleSaleSuspension as                           /* Extension 3–6c
    Cashier ➡ System: suspendSale;
    System ➡ System: record suspended sale;             /* (2)
    System ➡ Cashier: suspend receipt                   /* (2)
END;
```

(2) with sale ID and all line items so far

9.2 Converting a Large Textual SSD to Natural Language

We will now turn to the issue of validation. As argued in Sect. 2.8, you can facilitate the validation process by a precise translation of a textual SSD into expressions in natural language. It is useful and well doable by the user organization to validate the natural language result.

To illustrate clearly how the generation of natural language texts from textual SSDs works, we give a large practical example based on the textual SSD from Sect. 9.1, which in turn is based on Larman's use case *Process a Sale* [Lar] and is the result of structuring and integrating the MSS and the many alternative scenarios. Beside the MSS, Larman presents also more than 20 alternative scenarios, called *extensions* there. We worked out almost all of them and named them as in [Lar]. We start with the translation of the Main Scenario ProcessSale, followed by the translations of the other definitions referred to. The underlined names could constitute clickable links to their description. The end result of translating the textual SSD back to natural language might be more structured and clearer than the original description was.

```
ProcessSale means:                                                          /*
    The Customer does arrive at checkout with items to purchase.            /* Step 1
    The Cashier asks the System to StartNewSale.                            /* Step 2
    The System does CreateSale.                   /* This step wasn't mentioned in [Lar]
    Repeat: Perform EnterItem.                                              /* Step 3
    The System does RecordSaleLineItem and                                  /* Step 4
    the System sends description, price, and running total to Cashier       /* Step 4 too
    until cashier indicates done.                                  /*
    The Cashier asks the System to EndSale.                        /*
    The System sends total with taxes to Cashier.                  /* Step 5
    The Cashier sends total to the Customer.                       /* Step 6
    The Cashier sends request for payment to the Customer.         /* Step 6 too
    Maybe perform HandleDiscount end.                              /* Extension 5b
    Maybe perform HandleCredit end and                   /* Extension 5c ⎤ can be done
    maybe perform HandleCoupons end.                     /* Extension 7f ⎦ in any order
    Perform HandlePayment.                                         /* Extensions 7a,b,c,d
    The System does log completed sale and                         /* Step 8
    the System sends sale and payment info to AccSys and           /* Accounting system.
    the System sends sale and payment info to InvSys.              /* Inventory system.
    Maybe perform HandleGiftReceipt end.                           /* Extension 9b
    If system detects printer is out of paper                      /* Extension 9c
        then perform HandlePaperShortage end.                      /* Extension 9c
    The System sends receipt to Cashier.                           /* Step 9
    The Customer does leave with receipt and goods                 /* Step 10
end.                                                               /*
```

We continue with the other definitions referred to:

```
EnterItem means:
    Either perform HandleCodedItem(item-ID [; q])                              /* Usual case
      or the Cashier asks the System to enterPricedItem(P-category▼; price)    /* Ext. 3c
      or the Cashier asks the System to enterWeightItem(W-category▼; weight) /* Own ext.
    end
end.

HandleCodedItem(item-ID [; q]) means:
  The Cashier asks the System to enterCodedItem(item-ID [; q]).
  If Sys: quantity parameter q is absent
          then the System does make q equal to 1 end.
  The System does determine item i having that item-ID.
  If Sys: item-ID is unknown
    then the System sends 'Unknown item ID' to Cashier.
         If Cas: there is a human-readable item-ID
           then the Cashier asks the System to enterManually(item-ID; q)
           else if Cas: there is a price on the tag
                then the Cashier asks the System to enterPrice(price; q).
                     The Cashier asks the System to applyStandardTaxation
                else
                  either the Cashier asks the System to enterManually(item-ID; q)
                  or     the Cashier asks the System to enterPrice(price; q).
                         The Cashier asks the System to applyStandardTaxation
                  end
                end
         end
  end
end.

HandleDiscount means:                                                   /* Extension 5b
    The Cashier asks the System to applyDiscount(Customer ID).
    The System does apply discount to sale.
    The System sends new total with taxes to Cashier
end.

HandleCredit means:                                                     /* Extension 5c
    The Cashier asks the System to applyCredit(Customer ID).
    The System does apply credit to sale up to price = 0.
    The System does reduce remaining credit.
    The System sends new total with taxes to Cashier
end.
```

```
HandleCoupons means:                                          /* Extension 7f
    Repeat: The Cashier asks the System to record coupon.
            The System does reduce price with value of coupon.
            The System does record usage of coupon.
            The System sends new total with taxes to Cashier
    until coupons are done
end.

HandlePayment means:                                          /* Extensions 7a,b,c,d
    Either perform HandleCashPayment                          /* Extension 7a
        or perform HandleCreditPayment                        /* Extension 7b
        or perform HandleCheckPayment                         /* Extension 7c
        or perform HandleDebitPayment                         /* Extension 7d
    end
end.

HandleCashPayment means:                                      /* Extension 7a
    The Cashier asks the System to Enter(cash amount tendered).
    The System sends balance due to Cashier.
    The System does release cash drawer.
    The Cashier asks the System to deposit cash amount tendered.
    The Cashier sends cash balance to the Customer.
    The System does record cash payment
end.

HandleCreditPayment means:                                    /* Extension 7b
    The Customer asks the System to MakeCreditPay(credit account info).
    The System sends payment info (for verification) to Cashier.
    The Cashier asks the System to confirm.
    The System sends payment approved? to AutSys.             /* (1)
    The AutSys asks the System to payment approval.           /* (2)
    The System sends payment approved to Cashier and          /* ⎤ can be done
    the System does record credit payment.                    /* ⎦ in any order
    ⋮                                                         /*  and so on…
end.
```

(1) AutSys is a payment authorisation system
(2) AutSys answers the request by return

```
HandleCheckPayment means: … end.        /* Extension 7c. Unspecified in [Lar]

HandleDebitPayment means: … end.        /* Extension 7d. Unspecified in [Lar]
```

```
HandleGiftReceipt means:                                        /* Extension 9b
    The Cashier asks the System to giveGiftReceipt.
    The System sends gift receipt to Cashier
end.
```

```
HandlePaperShortage means:                                      /* Extension 9c
    The System sends 'Out of paper' to Cashier.
    The Cashier does replace paper.
    The Cashier asks the System to printReceipt
end.
```

The example in [Lar] also has some extensions that are possible *at any time*, for example, HandleManagerOverride:

```
HandleManagerOverride means:                                    /* Extension *a
    The Manager asks the System to changeModeTo('Manager').
    The System does change to mode 'Manager'.
    The Manager asks the System to <do some ManagerMode operation>.      /* (1)
    The System does change to mode 'Cashier'
end.
```

(1) E.g., a cash balance change

The example in [Lar] also has some extensions that can arise within a certain range of steps. For example, Extension 2–4a can arise within the range of steps 2 until 4. We give some examples:

```
HandleTaxExempt means:                                          /* Extension 2–4a
    The Cashier asks the System to enterStatusCode('tax-exempt').
    The System does record Status Code 'tax-exempt'
end.
```

```
HandleItemRemoval means:                                        /* Extension 3–6a
    The Customer sends request to remove item to the Cashier.
    If value of item ≤ cashier-limit
      then  the Cashier asks the System to remove item
      else  the Manager asks the System to remove item          /* (1)
    end.
    The System does delete item.
    The System sends new (running) total to Cashier
end.
```

(1) Actually a HandleManagerOverride

```
HandleSaleCancellation means:                                /* Extension 3-6b
    The Cashier asks the System to cancel sale.
    The System does delete sale.
    The System sends 'Done' to Cashier
end.

HandleSaleSuspension means:                                  /* Extension 3-6c
    The Cashier asks the System to suspendSale.
    The System does record suspended sale.                   /* (2)
    The System sends suspend receipt to Cashier              /* (2)
end.

  (2) with sale ID and all line items so far
```

9.3 Converting a Large Textual SSD to a Graphical SSD

We recall from Sect. 2.8 that you might facilitate the validation process by a precise translation of a *textual* SSD into a *graphical* SSD. It might be feasible to validate a textual SSD with the user organization using a graphical representation, provided that they understand graphical representations. Having rewritten Larman's example as a set of textual SSDs in Sect. 9.1, we will now illustrate how to convert those textual SSDs into graphical SSDs.

We start with the Main Scenario *ProcessSale*, followed by the graphical representations of the other definitions referred to. Readability or fitting the page is often a problem with large graphical SSDs, as becomes clear.

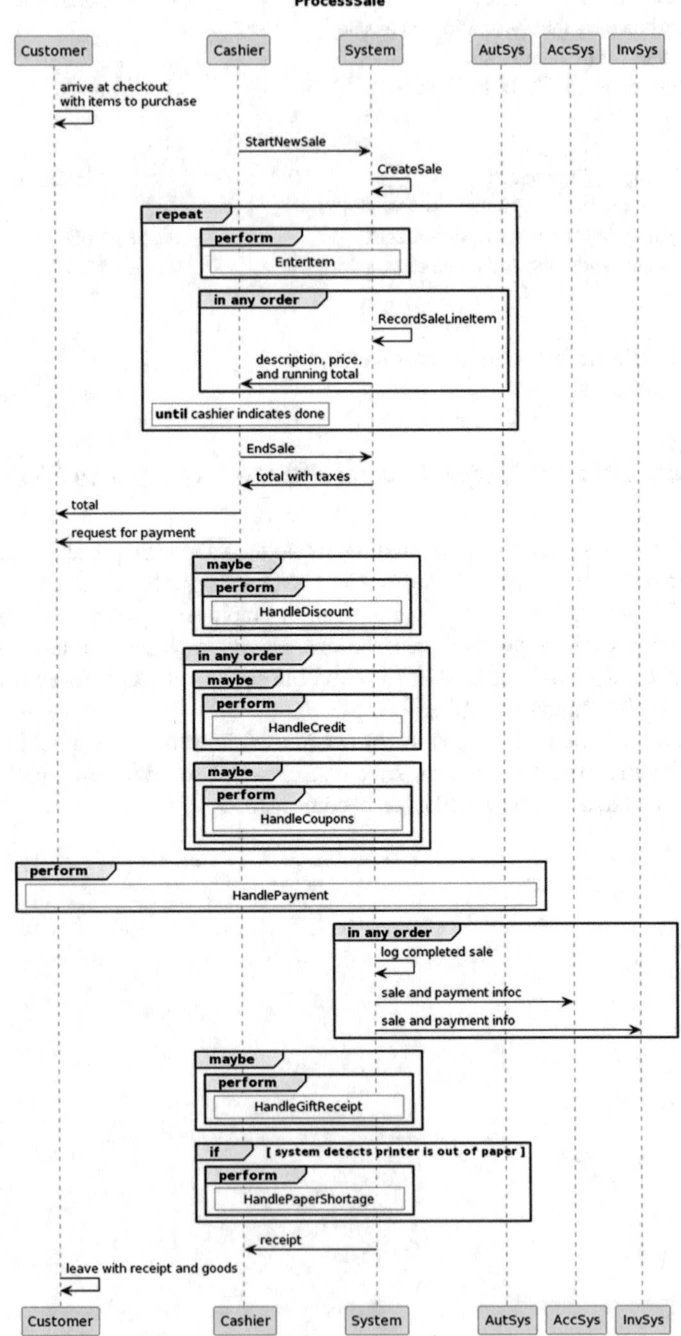
ProcessSale
Customer
Cashier
System
AutSys
AccSys
InvSys
arrive at checkout
with items to purchase
StartNewSale
CreateSale
repeat
perform
EnterItem
in any order
RecordSaleLineItem
description, price,
and running total
until cashier indicates done
EndSale
total with taxes
total
request for payment
maybe
perform
HandleDiscount
in any order
maybe
perform
HandleCredit
maybe
perform
HandleCoupons
perform
HandlePayment
in any order
log completed sale
sale and payment infoc
sale and payment info
maybe
perform
HandleGiftReceipt
if
[system detects printer is out of paper]
perform
HandlePaperShortage
receipt
leave with receipt and goods
Customer
Cashier
System
AutSys
AccSys
InvSys

We continue with the other definitions referred to:

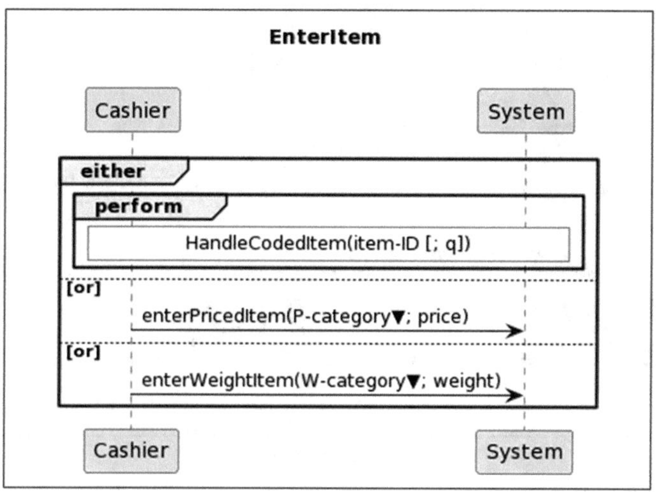

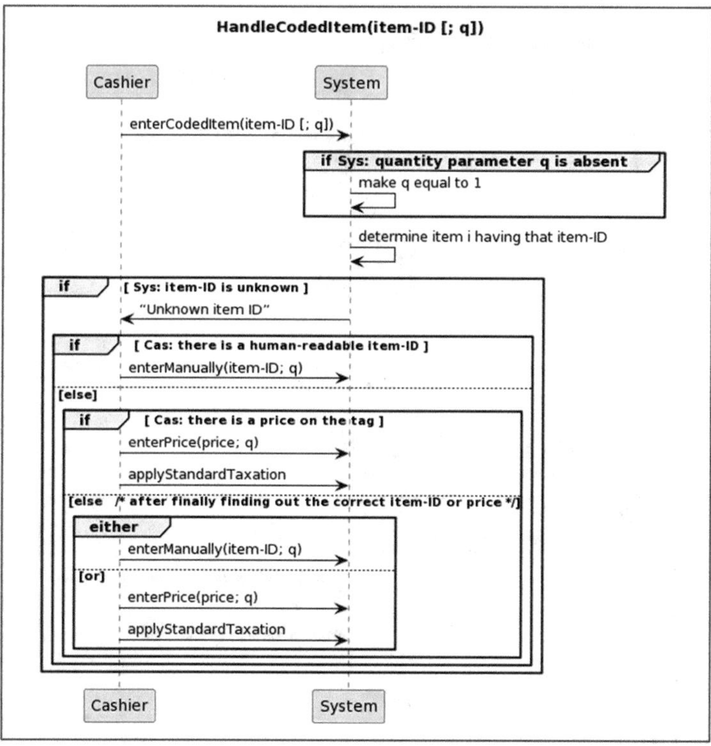

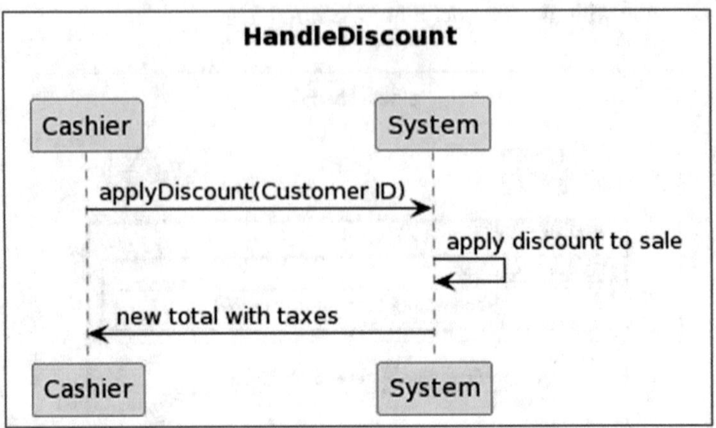
HandleDiscount
Cashier
System
applyDiscount(Customer ID)
apply discount to sale
new total with taxes
Cashier
System

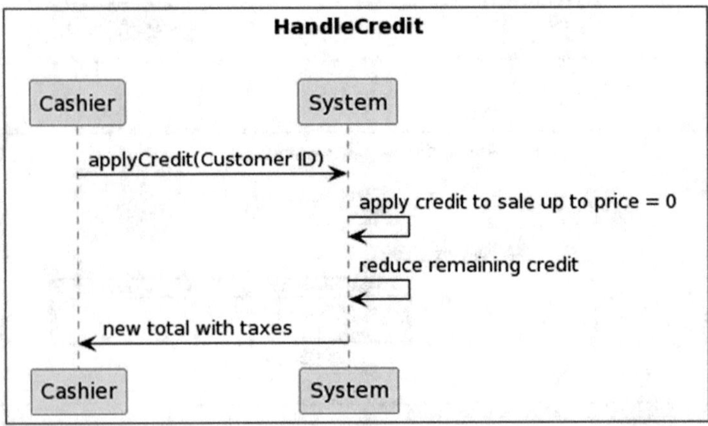
HandleCredit
Cashier
System
applyCredit(Customer ID)
apply credit to sale up to price = 0
reduce remaining credit
new total with taxes
Cashier
System

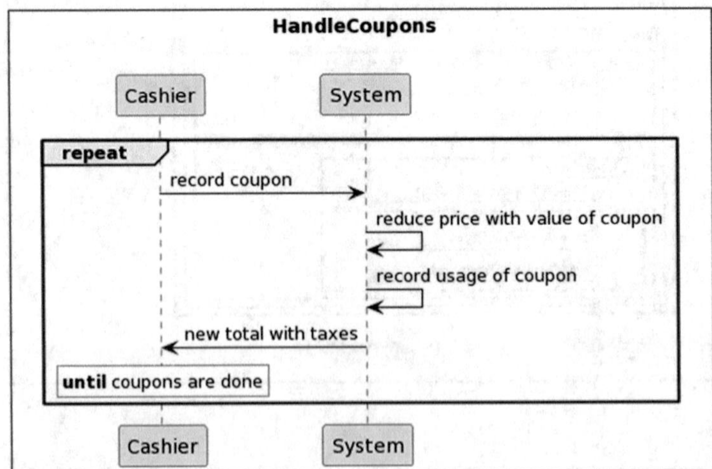
HandleCoupons
Cashier
System
repeat
record coupon
reduce price with value of coupon
record usage of coupon
new total with taxes
until coupons are done
Cashier
System

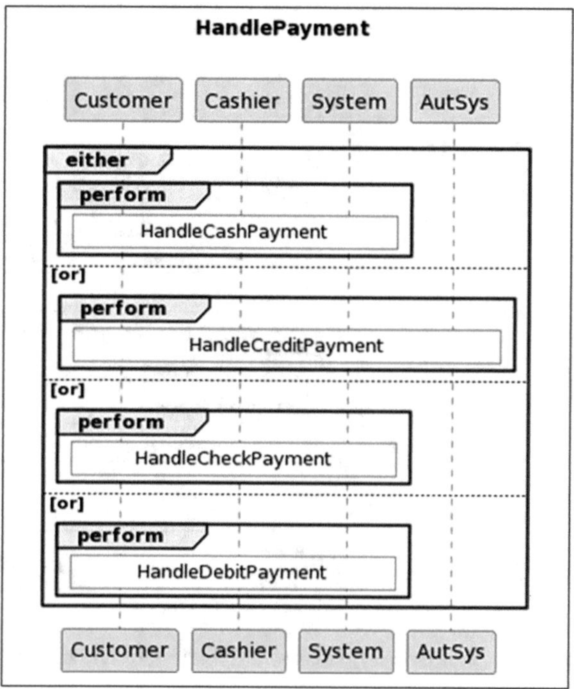
HandlePayment
Customer
Cashier
System
AutSys
either
perform
HandleCashPayment
[or]
perform
HandleCreditPayment
[or]
perform
HandleCheckPayment
[or]
perform
HandleDebitPayment
Customer
Cashier
System
AutSys

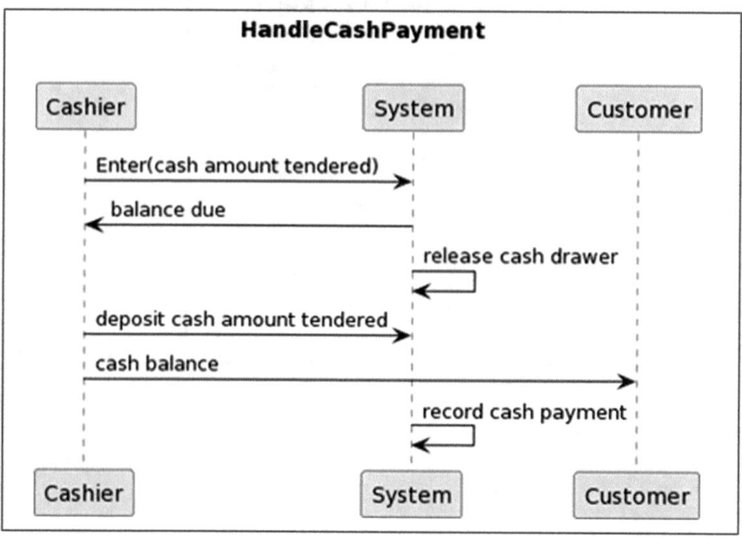
HandleCashPayment
Cashier
System
Customer
Enter(cash amount tendered)
balance due
release cash drawer
deposit cash amount tendered
cash balance
record cash payment
Cashier
System
Customer

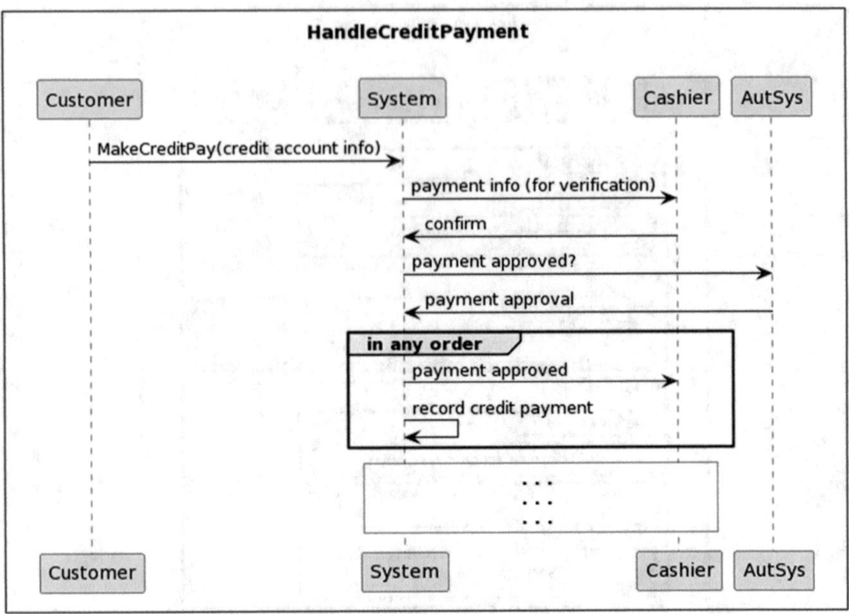

We left out the unspecified *HandleCheckPayment* and *HandleDebitPayment*.

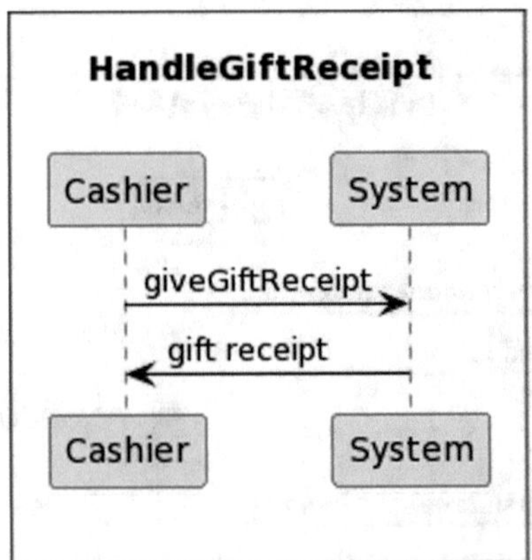

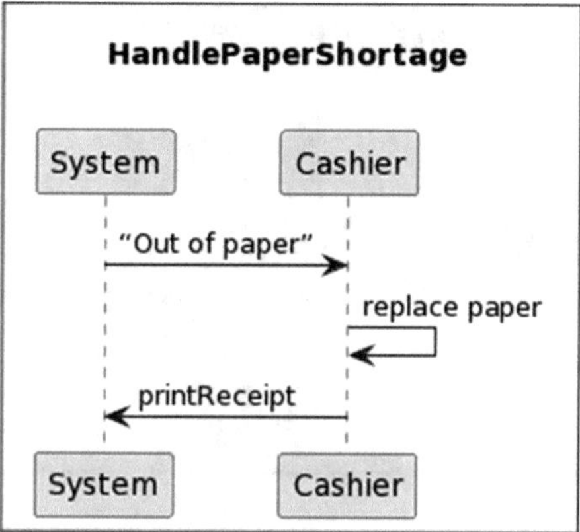

The example in [Lar] also has some extensions that are possible *at any time*, for example, *HandleManagerOverride*:

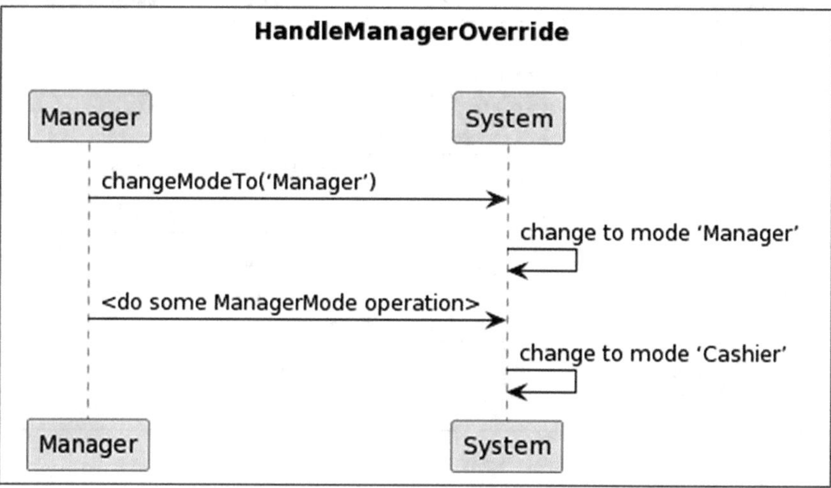

The example in [Lar] also has some extensions that can arise within a certain range of steps. For example, Extension 2–4a can arise within the range of steps 2 until 4. We give some examples:

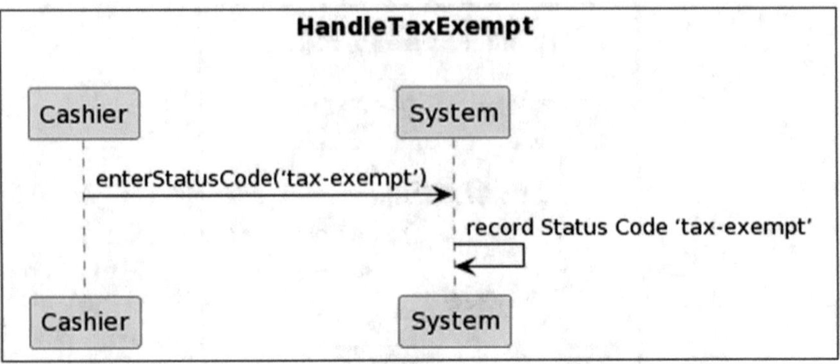
HandleTaxExempt
Cashier
System
enterStatusCode('tax-exempt')
record Status Code 'tax-exempt'
Cashier
System

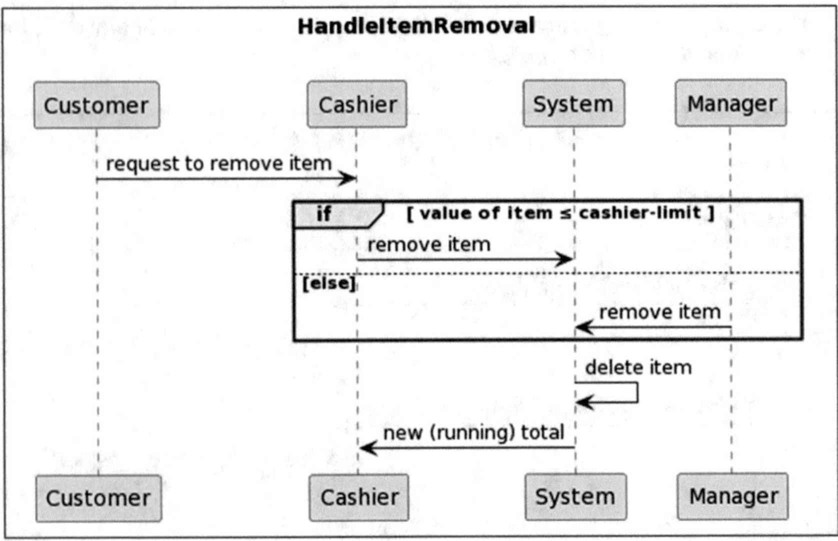
HandleItemRemoval
Customer
Cashier
System
Manager
request to remove item
if
[value of item ≤ cashier-limit]
remove item
[else]
remove item
delete item
new (running) total
Customer
Cashier
System
Manager

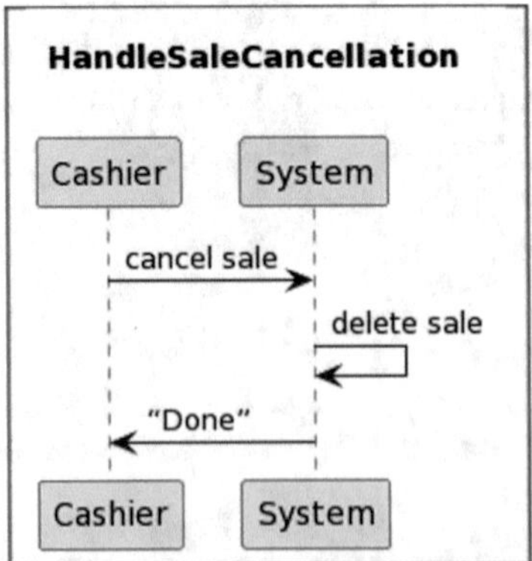
HandleSaleCancellation
Cashier
System
cancel sale
delete sale
"Done"
Cashier
System

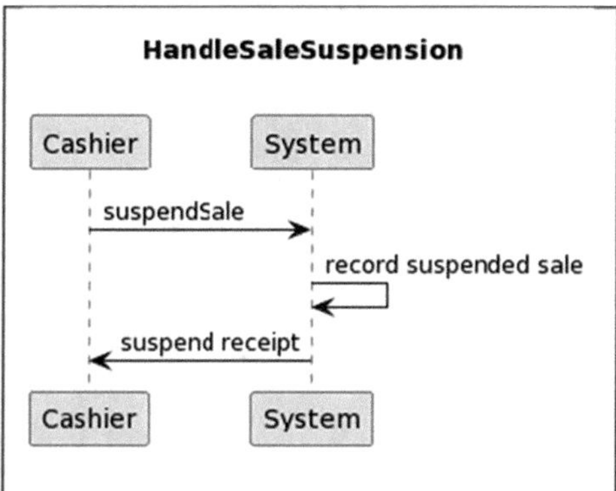
HandleSaleSuspension
Cashier
System
suspendSale
record suspended sale
suspend receipt
Cashier
System

Chapter 10
Development Example Where Requirements Constantly Change

Abstract This case study is meant to illustrate several points. The main ones are:

1. The applicability of our approach to a different kind of system, a *control system*
2. The (mental) process of going from a simple, naïve solution via several more complex ones, probably usually triggered/inspired/guided by brainstorms with the customer and sometimes by your own new—and generalizing—insights
3. How to deal with all those changes

To answer the last point globally: In this case study, we deal with the many changes by usually writing down only the (small) differences with a previous solution, not writing out the new situation completely. Writing out the new situation completely might be done only once in a while, say, when you don't have a good overview of the intermediate result anymore.

Moreover, this case study also illustrates the following points:

4. The *scope issue*: What should be inside and outside the scope of the system?
5. The *maneuverability* ('agility') of our textual SSDs
6. The phenomenon that the data structures are usually more stable than the processes
7. The development of a *generic system*, not a system for one single user organization

10.1 Initial Description

Suppose our system has to regulate the temperature in a building with several rooms (e.g., an office or a school) where the rooms have sensors for measuring the temperature and those rooms might also have heatings and air conditioners. By *actuators* we mean the heatings and the air conditioners in this example. The system to be developed—from here on called 'the system'—must be able to receive temperature measurements from the sensors and, when necessary, start or stop the heatings or air conditioners in that room. So the system is a kind of 'distributed thermostat'.

B. de Brock, *Developing Information Systems Accurately*,
https://doi.org/10.1007/978-3-031-16862-8_10

The initial requirement was that the heating(s) in a room must be started when the temperature in that room drops below 19 °C and must be stopped when the temperature in that room comes above 21 °C and, similarly, the air conditioner (s) in a room must be started when the temperature in that room comes above 25 °C and must be stopped when the temperature in that room drops below 23 °C.

A simple (even naïve) version of the main use case, *Handle measurement*, would then be something like:

1. A sensor sends a measured temperature to the system.
2. If that temp. is below 19 °C, then the system starts the heating(s) in that room.
3. If that temp. is above 21 °C, then the system stops the heating(s) in that room.
4. If that temperature is below 23 °C, then the system stops the air conditioner(s) in that room.
5. If that temperature is above 25 °C, then the system starts the air conditioner(s) in that room.

Consequently, for any measured temperature, one or two of steps 2–5 apply, as shown in the following picture:

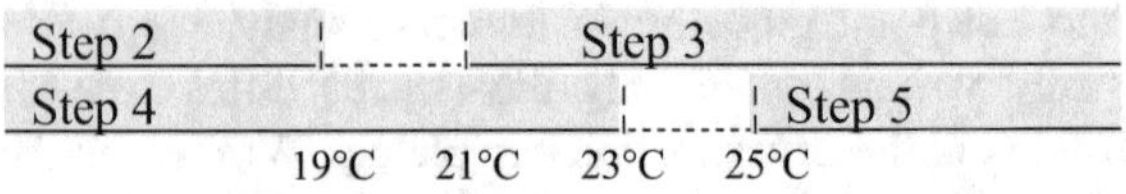

Step 2 Step 3
Step 4 Step 5
19°C 21°C 23°C 25°C

We note that in this example, the sensors are not considered part of the system to be developed. In other words, they are outside the *scope* of the system.

Next, we introduce several extensions/variants/alternatives as they came up.

10.2 No Unnecessary Starts or Stops

We realized that if an actuator is already in the desirable state ('On' or 'Off'), then the system does not need to start or stop that actuator again. So, an improved version of the main use case would be (with the new parts in italics):

1. A sensor sends a measured temperature to the system.
2. If that temperature is below 19 °C *and some heating(s) in that room are 'Off'*, then the system starts those heating(s).
3. If that temperature is above 21 °C *and some heating(s) in that room are 'On'*, then the system stops those heating(s).
4. If that temperature is below 23 °C *and some airco(s) in that room are 'On'*, then the system stops those airco(s).
5. If that temperature is above 25 °C *and some airco(s) in that room are 'Off'*, then the system starts those airco(s).

Which *persistent* data does our system need for this? The system needs to 'know' the sensors, the heatings, the air conditioners, and the rooms they are in. Together we will call this the *configuration structure*. For this improved version of the use case, the system also needs to know the state the heatings and air conditioners are in ('On' or 'Off').

If each sensor has a unique sensor ID (SID), each heating has a unique heating ID (HID), each airco has a unique airco ID (AID), and each room has a unique room ID (RID), then the following concepts and attributes are sufficient for the moment, where the uniquely identifying attributes are indicated by '!':

Sensor: ! SID, RID

Heating: ! HID, RID, State ('On' or 'Off')

Airco: ! AID, RID, State ('On' or 'Off')

Together, *configuration structure* plus *state info*, we call it the *configuration info*.

To relate it to our theory, the following holds for the main use case: An *input* of the system is essentially a (sensor; temperature)-pair, say *Measurement(s, t)*. An *output* of the system is essentially *a set of* (actuator; command)-pairs, where a command can be either 'On!' or 'Off!'. In the corresponding *state change*, the states of the affected actuators change, from 'On' to 'Off' or the other way around.

10.3 Variable Thresholds per Room

On hindsight, the customer was not completely satisfied with this solution: Not all rooms might have the same threshold temperatures, e.g., a corridor might have a minimum threshold of 17 °C instead of 19 °C. Moreover, we realized that, as presented now, those concrete temperatures (19, 21, 23, and 25 °C) might end up 'hard-coded' in the system.

In order to solve these two issues, we now need one more concept ('Room'), having four threshold values, namely, a minimum and a maximum threshold for the heatings and a minimum and a maximum threshold for the aircos. So:

Room: ! RID, Hmin, Hmax, Amin, Amax /* all four thresholds in Celsius

with the condition per room that Hmin ≤ Hmax < Amin ≤ Amax.

10.4 Variable Thresholds per Room Type

Later on, the customer proposed a refined variant, namely, that the thresholds would depend only on the *type of room* (e.g., classroom, gym hall, corridor, etc.) instead of every individual room. Then the extension with 'Room' can be replaced by:

Room Type: ! RTID, Hmin, Hmax, Amin, Amax

Room: ! RID, RTID

The advantage is that the thresholds can be set uniformly for all rooms of the same type. The disadvantage is that the thresholds must be set uniformly for all rooms of the same type…

After all these adaptions, we now have the information structure as depicted in Fig. 10.1. We indicate the identifiers by a '!' and the referencing attributes by a '^'.

Given all these proposed changes, it is time to reconsider—and adapt—the main use case. The new parts are indicated in italics:

1. A sensor sends a measured temperature to the system.
2. If that temperature is below the minimum heating threshold *for the room type concerned* and some heating(s) in that room are 'Off', then the system starts those heating(s) *and adapts their registered state.*
3. If that temperature is above the maximum heating threshold *for the room type concerned* and some heating(s) in that room are 'On', then the system stops those heating(s) *and adapts their registered state.*

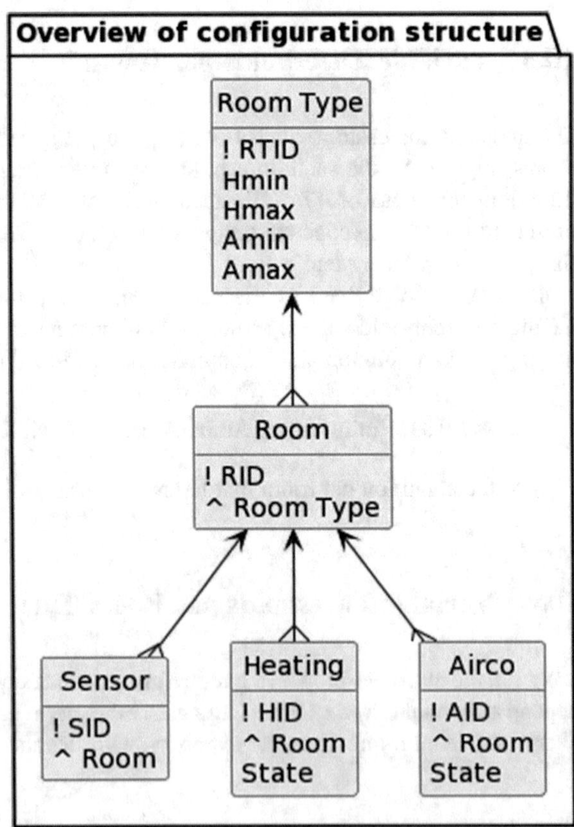

Fig. 10.1 Information structure with variable thresholds per room type

4. If that temperature is below the minimum airco threshold *for the room type concerned* and some airco(s) in that room are 'On', then the system stops those airco(s) *and adapts their registered state.*
5. If that temperature is above the maximum airco threshold *for the room type concerned* and some airco(s) in that room are 'Off', then the system starts those airco(s) *and adapts their registered state.*

Beside the main use case, we also need use cases to *manage* the *configuration info*. In particular, we need use cases to add, remove, and (in some cases) update room types, rooms, sensors, heatings, and aircos. These are more or less standard and relatively simple use cases. Therefore, we will not write them out but only point out some noteworthy considerations and the conditions the system must check:

Add a room type	Check: $Hmin \leq Hmax < Amin \leq Amax$
Add a room	Check: Room type registered. Maybe force the user to choose the proper room type first
Add a sensor	Check: Room registered. Maybe force the user to choose the proper room type and room first
Add a heating	See Add a sensor. Default State-value could be 'Off'
Add an airco	See Add a sensor. Default State-value could be 'Off'

Delete a room type	Check: No rooms of this type are registered
Delete a room	Check: No sensors, heatings, or aircos are registered for this room. Or: delete them as well?
Delete a sensor	Giving a warning might be useful here: If it is the last sensor in that room, that room would not be controlled anymore
Delete a heating	No remarks
Delete an airco	No remarks

Update a room type	Is actually UpdateThresholds from Section 10.10, because there is nothing else to update (for the time being);
Update a room	Boils down to updating its type of room, the only possibility, and hence – implicitly – its thresholds; see Section 10.10
Update a sensor	Boils down, as yet, to updating its room. This use case might include the step: System → sensor: SendTemperature
Update a heating	Updating its state is managed by the system. Because a heating is fixed in a room, updating its room does not make sense
Update an airco	See Update a heating

The five 'Add' use cases might make use of *forms* in order to let the user choose from the proper lists; cf. Sect. 2.6. Furthermore, all IDs might be system generated.

10.5 Storing the Measurements

As a control system, the system handles an incoming measurement by taking the appropriate actions. After that, the control system does not need to 'remember' the incoming measurement anymore, in principle. However, the user organization—as well as the producers and installers of the heatings and aircos—found it useful to be able to look back at the past measurements. Therefore, the incoming measurements must be stored too, together with a timestamp. Then we need one more concept, say 'Measurement', having the following properties (where the combination of *SID* and *Timestamp* is uniquely identifying):

Measurement: ! SID, ! Timestamp, RID, Temperature

The main use case now gets an extra step: Step 1 is replaced by

1. A sensor sends a measured temperature plus timestamp to the system.
1/2. The system stores the measured temp., the sensor, the room, and the timestamp.

These measurements could be stored inside the system under development or in a separate external system. There could be several reasons for that:

- The organization/installer already has a system for that.
- The organization/installer already has a system with data with which the measurement data have to be combined.
- The measurement data have to be combined with other external data (such as weather data).
- The control system might get overloaded when intensive trend analyses on its measurement data will be started, at the expense of ... its controlling function.

Whatever the reason is, Step 1/2 would be replaced by:

1/2′. The system asks the external system to store the measured temperature, sensor, room, and timestamp.

An option that was discussed too—but ignored later on—is to store the actions taken by the system itself as well, not only the incoming measurements. This option might be included in a next version of the control system.

10.6 A Corresponding Textual SSD and Graphical SSD

After all this analysis, it is time to write out the complete textual SSD for our latest use case version, with the parameters made explicit. In the following textual SSD, Measurement(x, t, y) stands for measurement by sensor x of temperature t at timestamp y, and r in Store(x, t, y, r) stands for the room sensor x is in. Strictly speaking, the five steps after Step 1 can be done in any order, which can be indicated by ',' instead of ';' in our grammar:

```
1. Sensor x ➡ System: Measurement(x, t, y);
2. System ➡ External System: Store(x, t, y, r),
3. if t < Hmin of the type of room sensor x is in
   then for each heating h in the room of x in state 'Off'
          do System ➡ h: 'On!' ;
             System ➡ System: Change state of h to 'On'
          end
   end,
4. if t > Hmax of the type of room sensor x is in
   then for each heating h in the room of x in state 'On'
          do System ➡ h: 'Off!' ;
             System ➡ System: Change state of h to 'Off'
          end
   end,
5. if t < Amin of the type of room sensor x is in
   then for each airco a in the room of x in state 'On'
          do System ➡ a: 'Off!' ;
             System ➡ System: Change state of a to 'Off'
          end
   end,
6. if t > Amax of the type of room sensor x is in
   then for each airco a in the room of x in state 'Off'
          do System ➡ a: 'On!' ;
             System ➡ System: Change state of a to 'On'
          end
   end
```

In event-driven terminology, the first step is the *event*, and the other five steps constitute the *event handling*. And presented as a graphical SSD (Fig. 10.2):

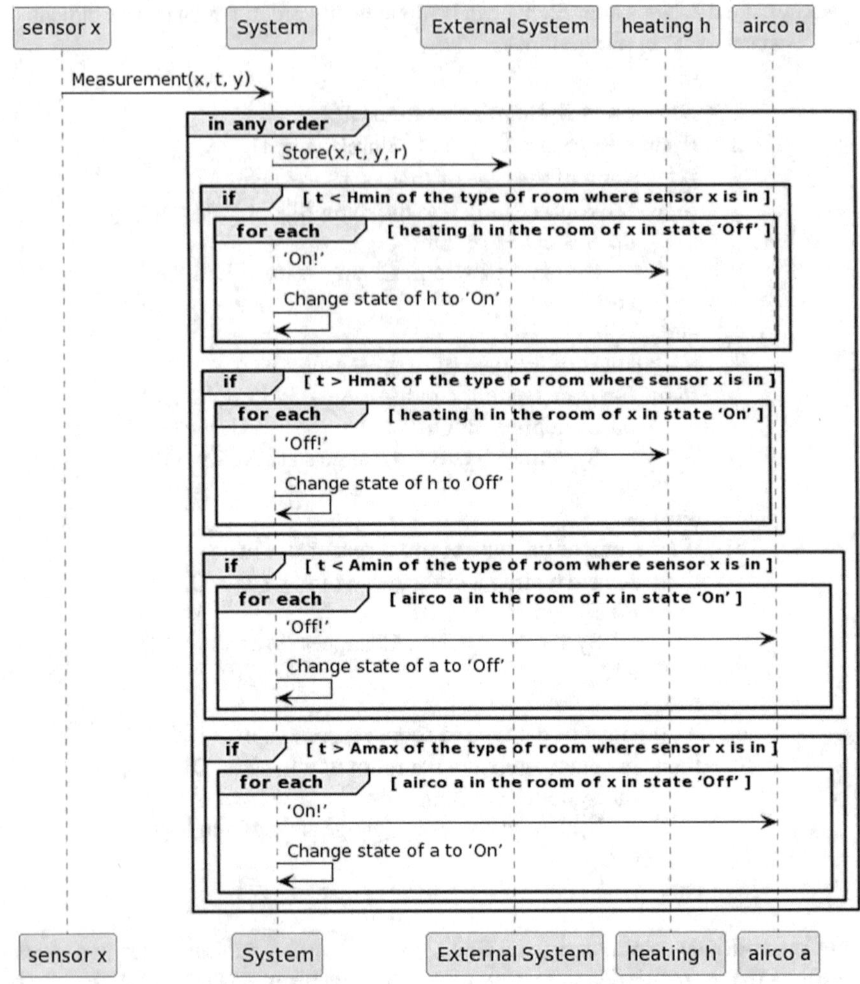

Fig. 10.2 Graphical SSD corresponding to the previous textual SSD

The Plantuml-code for the graphical SSD more or less resembles the textual SSD:

```
@startuml
"sensor x" -> System: Measurement(x, t, y)
group in any order
  System -> "External System": Store(x, t, y, r)
participant h as "heating h"
participant a as "airco a"
  group if [ t < Hmin of the type of room where sensor x is in ]
    group for each [ heating h in the room of x in state 'Off' ]
      System -> h: 'On!'
      System -> System: Change state of h to 'On'
    end
  end
  group if [ t > Hmax of the type of room where sensor x is in ]
    group for each [ heating h in the room of x in state 'On' ]
      System -> h: 'Off!'
      System -> System: Change state of h to 'Off'
    end
  end
  group if [ t < Amin of the type of room where sensor x is in ]
    group for each [ airco a in the room of x in state 'On' ]
      System -> a: 'Off!'
      System -> System: Change state of a to 'Off'
    end
  end
  group if [ t > Amax of the type of room where sensor x is in ]
    group for each [ airco a in the room of x in state 'Off' ]
      System -> a: 'On!'
      System -> System: Change state of a to 'On'
    end
  end
end
@enduml
```

Exercise 10.1
Construct the textual SSDs and the graphical SSDs for the discussed alternatives: No storage of the measurements, internal storage of the measurements, etc.

10.7 Where Does the Timestamp Come from?

In the example until now, it was the sensor that provided the timestamp (of the measurement). However, as our customers pointed out, some sensors are so simple that they cannot provide a timestamp. In that case, the system itself could add a timestamp, i.e., the timestamp of arrival, say using its internal clock. Then the first step in the use case becomes again as before:

1. A sensor sends a measured temperature to the system.

With sensor x, temperature t, timestamp y, and r being the room sensor x is in, the first two steps in the textual SSD become:

1. Sensor x ➡ System: Measurement(x, t) ;
2. System ➡ External System: Store(x, t, y, r)

So, the parameters y and r pop up in the second step. They are provided by the system (using its internal clock and the configuration info, respectively).

10.8 Synchronous Feedback from the Actuators

From an engineering point of view, a weak point is that the system adapts the registered state of an actuator as soon as it issued such a command to that actuator, without knowing whether the intended state change actually succeeded; see steps 3–6 in the textual SSD in Sect. 10.6. An extension/improvement would be that the actuator replies with feedback about its status—essentially 'On' or 'Off'—to the system. And only then the system would change the registered state of that actuator. In that case, steps 3–6 in the textual SSD have to be adapted. As an example, the new Step 3 is shown below. Steps 4–6 have to be adapted similarly.

3. **if** t < Hmin of the type of room sensor x is in
then **for each** heating h in the room of x in state 'Off'
  do System ➡ h: 'On!' ;
   h ➡ System: Status(h) ;
   System ➡ System: Make Status(h) the state of h
  end
end

10.9 Asynchronous Feedback from the Actuators

One more issue: It might take a (tiny) while before the actuator gives feedback. But the system has to do other things as well. Therefore, another option is that the system does not wait for an answer and adapts its registered state only once the status feedback from the actuator comes in. That leads to an extra use case, say *Handle status feedback*:

1. An actuator sends its status to the system.
2. The system adapts the registered status of that actuator accordingly.

And the corresponding textual SSD, cast in the form of a definition:

```
define Handle status feedback as
  h ➡ System: Status(h) ;
  System ➡ System: Make Status(h) the state of h
end
```

In steps 3–6 in the textual SSD, these two instructions should now be deleted. For example, Step 3 now becomes:

```
3.  if t < Hmin of the type of room sensor x is in
    then  for each heating h in the room of x in state 'Off'
          do System ➡ h: 'On!' end
    end
```

Note that it is easy to go back from the asynchronous to the synchronous situation because you can simply call *Handle status feedback* within this most recent version of Step 3:

```
3.  if t < Hmin of the type of room sensor x is in
    then  for each heating h in the room of x in state 'Off'
          do System ➡ h: 'On!' ;
             perform Handle status feedback
          end
    end
```

10.10 A Schedule for Threshold Changes?

As the customer base pointed out, it makes sense to have lower threshold temperatures for the heatings at night than during daytime. For example, in an office, say 19 °C from nine till five from Monday to Friday and 15 °C during the other time periods. And, of course, such schedules could be much more subtle. It could be a user wish that the system changes the thresholds automatically in such cases. This could be realized if the system 'knows' the schedule and has an internal clock. Then the question came up: Which kind of schedules for threshold changes should be possible, e.g., based only on the combination of weekday and time during the day, as in the example just mentioned? And to complicate things, some domain experts noted that, ideally, threshold changes might be determined dynamically, based on external conditions or events. For instance, in order to have a temperature of 19 °C at 9:00, it might be necessary to start the heatings (much) earlier, depending on the inside temperature at hand, the outside temperature, the size—and isolation—of the room to be warmed, etc. Then the question arose whether the system itself should know the schedule or that an (intelligent) external system should trigger our system with new threshold temperatures at the right moments, e.g., a system such as Homey (https://homey.app/en-gb/). We realized that the second option is much more flexible and that that external system could easily be replaced by a more advanced/subtle/sophisticated system, provided it has the same kind of interaction mechanism toward our system. We will now work out this second option. So in other words, the scheduling/scheduler will be considered outside the scope of the system to be developed.

In conclusion, another system—but also a human being—should be able to trigger our system with new threshold temperatures. We will use the term 'thresholder' here, instead of 'user'. Suppose that the threshold adaptions are on the level of individual rooms again, not on the level of room types. So, Sect. 10.3 applies again, not Sect. 10.4. Therefore, the 'Room' concept looks as follows:

Room: ! RID, Hmin, Hmax, Amin, Amax /* all four thresholds in Celsius

The use case to update thresholds could run as follows:

1. A thresholder sends (new) threshold values for a certain room to the system.
2. The system adapts those thresholds for that room.
3. The system asks the sensor(s) in that room for the current temperature.

This use case does not need to continue any further here, because once the sensor sends the temperature to the system, the 'old' use case *Handle measurement* starts, and the actuators will be started or stopped accordingly, if necessary, based on the new threshold values.

There are four thresholds per room, but maybe not all thresholds have to be adapted. So, the actor might send less than four thresholds. In the textual SSD, we indicate this by putting the optional parts between '[' and ']'. Since parts might be missing, it must also be indicated which value represents which property, e.g., 'Hmin h1'. The use case does not have explicit parameters, but in the textual SSD, the parameters are made explicit, as usual:

1. Thresholder ➡ System:
   UpdateThresholds(room r [, Hmin h1] [, Hmax h2] [, Amin a1] [, Amax a2]);
2. System ➡ System:
   AdaptThresholds(room r [, Hmin h1] [, Hmax h2] [, Amin a1] [, Amax a2]);
3. **for each** sensor x in room r **do** System ➡ x: SendTemperature **end**

As explained before, after this textual SSD, the system will receive the temperature from the sensor(s), and then *Handle measurement* starts, and the actuators will be started or stopped accordingly (if necessary).

If threshold adaptions would be on the level of the room types, as in Sect. 10.4, then you should change 'room' by 'room type' in steps 1–2 of the use case and the textual SSD, 'the sensor(s) in that room' in Step 3 of the use case by 'the sensor(s) in all rooms of that room type', and '**for each** sensor x in room r' in Step 3 of the textual SSD by '**for each** sensor x in a room of type r'.

10.11 Interactions Between Our System and Its Environment

In summary, Fig. 10.3 gives an overview of the possible interactions between our system and its environment. We replaced the general term 'External System' from the earlier sections by the neutral term 'Data Store'. We recall that the timestamp parameter y in Measurement is absent in some cases and that the parameters h1, h2, a1, and a2 in UpdateThresholds are optional. The actor variables x, h, and a in the overview indicate that there can be several such actors. We note that Fig. 10.3 should not be read as a system sequence diagram!

10.12 Looking Back: Typical Ingredients of an IS and a Control System

Although there is no (need for a) hard distinction between an *information system* and a *control system*, and systems can have characteristics of both, so are 'hybrid', we nevertheless try to indicate their bare essence.

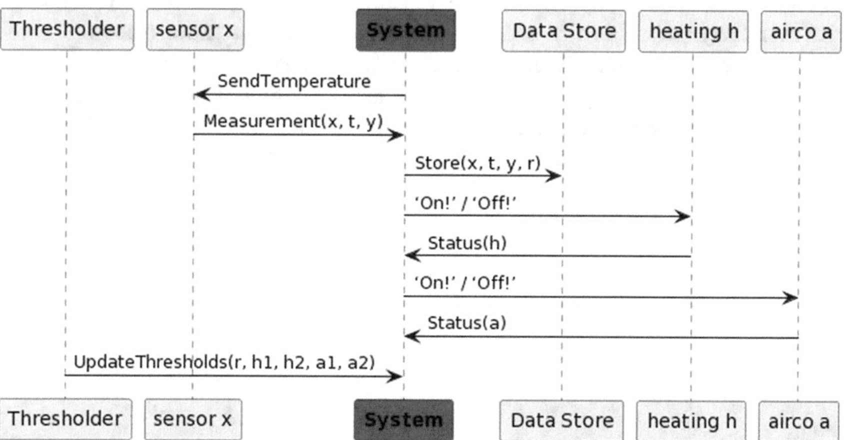

Fig. 10.3 The possible interactions between our system and its environment

Actor ➡ System: CRUD-request;
System ➡ System: CRUD-operation;
System ➡ Actor: Result

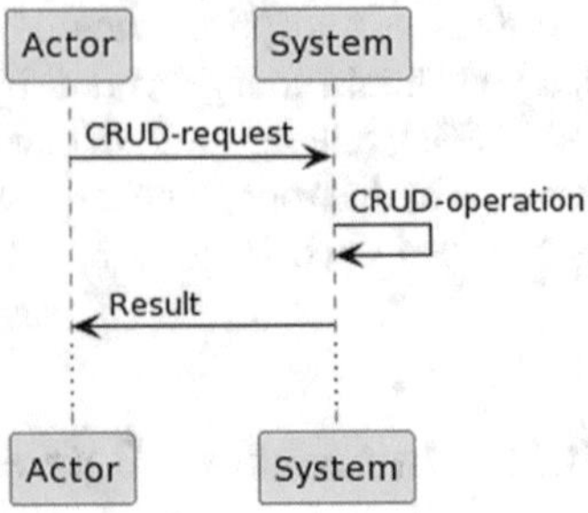

Fig. 10.4 Typical interactions for an *information system*

Sensor x ➡ System: Measurement;
System ➡ Actuator y: Command;
[…]
Actuator y ➡ System: Feedback

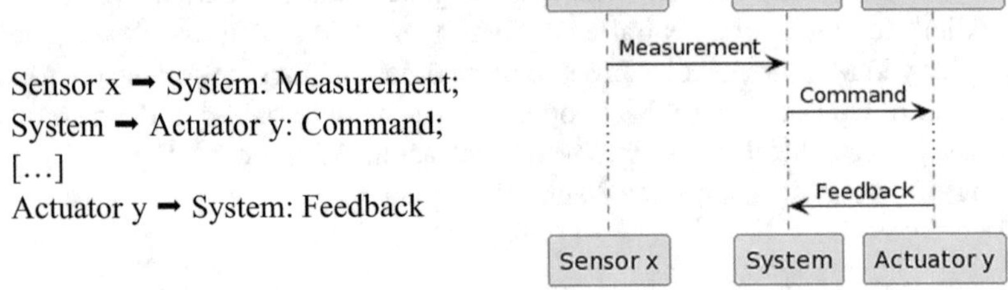

Fig. 10.5 Typical interactions for a *control system*

An *information system* (IS) typically receives a CRUD-request, executes that request, and sends the result back to the original requester. CRUD stands for Create, Read/Retrieve, Update, and Delete.

Typical interactions for an *information system* are depicted schematically in Fig. 10.4.

A **control system** manages the behavior of other systems or devices. It typically receives information—say a measurement result—from any sensor (of which there can be many), subsequently sends a command to one or more actuators to be managed, and might receive feedback from the actuators, immediately (synchronous) or after a while (asynchronous), in the next picture indicated by '[. . .]'.

Typical interactions for a *control system* are depicted schematically in Fig. 10.5.

Appendix: Our Plantuml Tutorial

Throughout this book, we use the open-source tool Plantuml (https://Plantuml.com) as our drawing tool. Actually, **Plantuml** is a *drawing generation* tool: It generates drawings from text (i.e., from Plantuml-code). So, you don't have to drag arrows, rectangles, circles, etc. yourself. This is an important—and big—difference!

Plantuml-code → drawing

This tutorial explains how to generate our graphical SSDs (Sect. A.1), domain models (Sect. A.2), conceptual data models (Sect. A.3), class diagrams (Sect. A.4), and the System represented as Interface + Kernel (Sect. A.5). And although we don't pay much attention to use case diagrams, Sect. A.6 explains how to draw them.

A.1 From Textual SSDs to Graphical SSDs

We can easily turn our textual representations of SSDs into graphical representations by (mis)using the open-source drawing generation tool Plantuml, because its textual specification language for graphical SSDs closely resembles our textual specification language for SSDs. Plantuml turns its textual representations into graphical representations. Therefore, our mapping scheme is

textual SSD → Plantuml-code → graphical SSD

In Table A.1 we inductively define mapping rules from our SSD-syntax to the SSD-syntax of Plantuml (inspired by https://Plantuml.com/sequence-diagram), in order to map a complete textual SSD step by step to Plantuml-code. We define the

B. de Brock, *Developing Information Systems Accurately*,
https://doi.org/10.1007/978-3-031-16862-8

Table A.1 Rules to map textual SSDs to Plantuml-code

	X	P(X)
1	A1 ➡ A2: M	A1 -> A2: M
2	S1; S2	P(S1) <nl> P(S2)
3	**begin** S **end**	**group block** <nl> P(S) <nl> **end**
4a	**if** C **then** S **end**	**group if [** C **]** <nl> P(S) <nl> **end**
4b	**if** A: C **then** S **end**	**group if [** A: C **]** <nl> P(S) <nl> **end**
5a	**if** C **then** S1 **else** S2 **end**	**group if [** C **]** <nl> P(S1) <nl> **else else** <nl> P(S2) <nl> **end**
5b	**if** A: C **then** S1 **else** S2 **end**	**group if [** A: C **]** <nl> P(S1) <nl> **else else** /* not C */ <nl> P(S2) <nl> **end**
6a	**while** C **do** S **end**	**group while [** C **]** <nl> P(S) <nl> **end**
6b	**while** A: C **do** S **end**	**group while [** A: C **]** <nl> P(S) <nl> **end**
7a	**repeat** S **until** C	**group repeat** <nl> P(S) <nl> **rnote over** A_i **#white: **until**** C <nl> **end**
7b	**repeat** S **until** A: C	**group repeat** <nl> P(S) <nl> **rnote over** A_i **#white: **until**** A: C <nl> **end**
8	**for each** E **do** S **end**	**group for each [** E **]** <nl> P(S) <nl> **end**
9	**perform** N	**group perform** <nl> **rnote over** Ai, Aj **#white:** N <nl> **end**
10	S1, S2	**group in any order** <nl> P(S1) <nl> P(S2) <nl> **end**
11	**maybe** S **end**	**group maybe** <nl> P(S) <nl> **end**
12	**either** S1 **or** S2 **end**	**group either** <nl> P(S1) <nl> **else or** <nl> P(S2) <nl> **end**
13	**define** N **as** S **end**	**title** N **\n** <nl> P(S)

mapping *inductively*, i.e., by assigning to each textual SSD its corresponding Plantuml-code in terms of its direct constituents.

For each grammar rule for textual SSDs, the function P defined in Table A.1 assigns to a textual SSD X its corresponding Plantuml-code P(X) in terms of the direct constituents of X. Since Plantuml is 'newline-sensitive', we explicitly add the meta-symbol <nl>, meaning you must enter a newline here (if it wasn't there yet).

In order not to mix up our optionality symbols and the same Plantuml-symbols ('[' and ']'), we wrote out the mapping rules for **if-then** and **if-then-else** separately (rules 4 and 5). Similarly, within the mapping rules 4–7, we separately wrote out the options with and without 'A:'.

In the **repeat**- and **perform**-rule (rules 7 and 9), A_i is the first mentioned (i.e., leftmost) actor of SSD S and N, respectively, and A_j the last mentioned (i.e., rightmost) actor of N. For the **either**-construct (Rule 12), we showed one **or**; for more than one **or** you must repeat the part

else or <nl>
P(S..) <nl>

To arrange some vertical spacing, you might use '\n' telling Plantuml to enter a newline, e.g., as we standard did after '**title** N'. You can use '||10||', for instance, to arrange the size of vertical spacing yourself, but put it on a separate line.

If desired, you can add a separate line 'autonumber' directly after @startuml to automatically add numbers to messages.

Finally, you can put your result between '@startuml' and '@enduml' in http://www.Plantuml.com/Plantuml/uml/SyfFKj2rKt3CoKnELR1Io4ZDoSa70000, and after pressing 'Submit', the graphical representation will be generated.

For more options, see https://Plantuml.com/sequence-diagram.

In order to illustrate all the tSSD-constructs at least once, we composed the following compact, artificial example, consisting of a textual SSD followed by a **define**:

A1 ➡ A2: Za ;
A2 ➡ A1: Zb ;
if C1
then perform N
else either repeat A1 ➡ A2: Z1 **until** C2
    or perform N
  end
end ;
for each E **do** A2 ➡ A2: Z2 **end ;**
A2 ➡ A1: Z3

DEFINE N **as**
  while C3 **do** A1 ➡ A2: Z4 **end ,**
  begin
    if C4 **then** A1 ➡ A2: Z5 **end ;**
    maybe A1 ➡ A3: Z6 **end**
  end
END

Explanation

The textual SSD starts with A1 sending Za to A2 and A2 replying with Zb. If at that moment condition C1 holds, then do N, i.e., the instruction(s) N stands for; otherwise choose between A1 repeatedly sending Z1 to A2 until C2 holds (but doing it at least once) or doing N. After that, A2 does Z2 for each E. Finally, A2 sends Z3 to A1.

Furthermore, the name/abbreviation N stands for the following instruction: In arbitrary order (a) as long as C3 holds, A1 sending Z4 to A2 and (b) A1 sending Z5 to A2 if C4 holds, maybe followed by A1 sending Z6 to A3.

First we apply the mapping rules to each of the two parts. With properly ordered 'participant-commands' in the beginning, as in the first piece, you can enforce the desirable *representation order* of the actors (although it was not really necessary in this case). If you put each result between '@startuml' and '@enduml', then you get the two pieces of Plantuml-code below. Each of the two results can be placed in http://www.Plantuml.com/Plantuml/uml/SyfFKj2rKt3CoKnELR1Io4ZDoSa70000.
After pressing 'Submit', the graphical representation next to it will be generated.

```
@startuml
participant A1
participant A2
participant A3
A1->A2: Za
A2->A1: Zb
group if [ C1 ]
    group perform
    rnote over A1, A3 #white: N
    end
else else
    group either
      group repeat
        A1->A2: Z1
        rnote over A1, A2 #white:**until** C2
      end
    else or
      group perform
      rnote over A1, A3 #white: N
      end
    end
end
group for each [ E ]
    A2->A2: Z2
end
A2->A1: Z3
@enduml
```

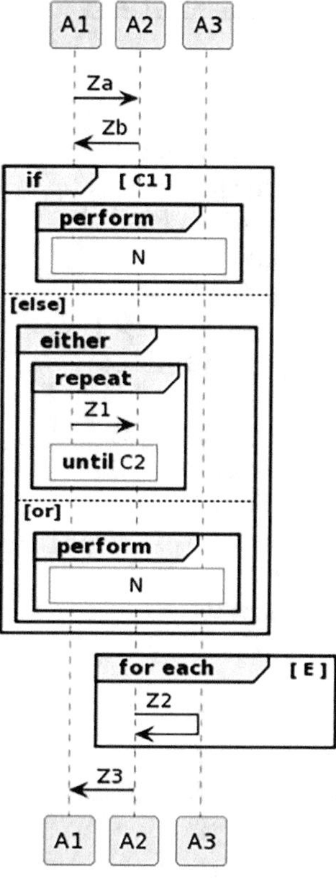

The definition of N

```
@startuml
title N \n
group in any order
    group while [ C3 ]
      A1->A2: Z4
    end
    group block
      group if [ C4 ]
        A1->A2: Z5
      end
      group maybe
        A1->A3: Z6
      end
    end
end
@enduml
```

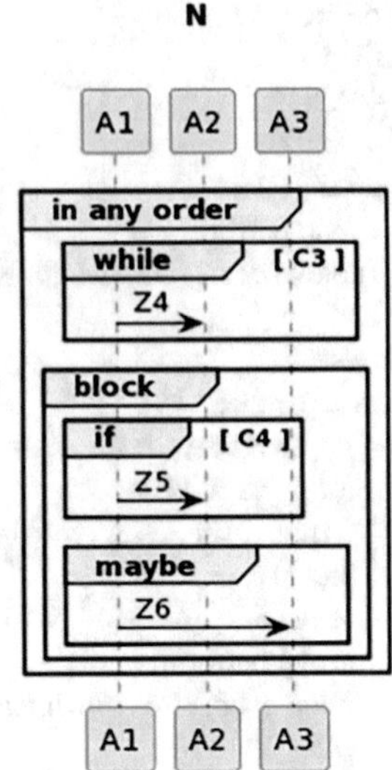

A.2 Domain Models

In Plantuml, a *concept* with its *properties* can be indicated as follows, with the result shown next to it (see https://Plantuml.com/class-diagram):

```
hide circle
hide methods
class Concept {
Property 1
⋮
Property n
}
```

Concept
Property 1
⋮
Property n

Because by default Plantuml draws classes, we added the command 'hide circle' in the beginning to hide the circle © in the class diagrams and the command 'hide methods' to hide the methods-sections.

In Plantuml, an *association* with its *name*, *reading direction*, and *multiplicities* can be indicated as follows:

```
hide circle
hide members
Concept_A "m  "  -  "  n" " Concept B ": xxx >
```

leading to the picture

We used the spaces after 'm' and before 'n' to get the multiplicities *below* the association line. The command 'hide members' (instead of 'hide methods') hides the properties-sections too. The command 'hide empty members' (instead of 'hide members') hides only empty properties-sections. With '-', you get a horizontal line; with '--', you get a vertical line. Use '<' or '>' to indicate the reading direction. If the concept name has spaces in it or should have spaces around it, it should be placed between double quotes (as we did with " Concept B "). This does not apply to property names. Use '\n' to force the next text on a new line.

The following example illustrates most of these options for domain models:

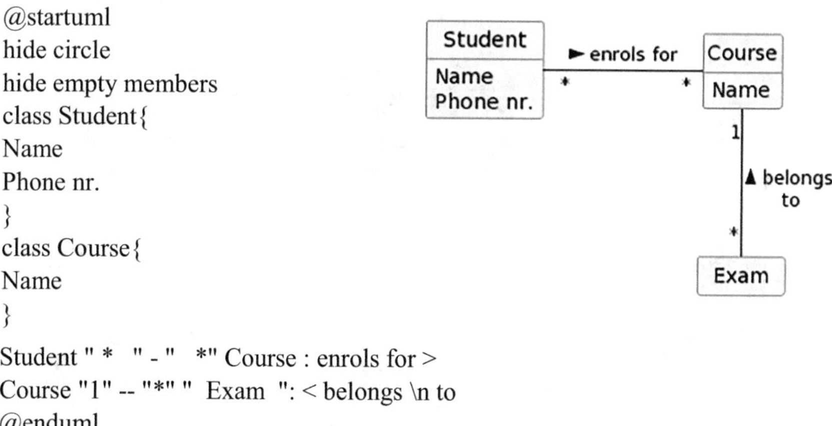


```
@startuml
hide circle
hide empty members
class Student{
Name
Phone nr.
}
class Course{
Name
}
Student " *   " - "   *" Course : enrols for >
Course "1" -- "*" "  Exam  ": < belongs \n to
@enduml
```

A.3 Conceptual Data Models

In a conceptual data model, we use *arrows* instead of *lines with multiplicities*.

Some examples:

<--{ for a 'many-to-1' arrow that goes up (the '{' is for the crow's foot)
-> for a '0/1-to-1' arrow from left to right (no crow's foot)

}..> for a ‘many-to-0/1’ arrow that goes down (0/1 is indicated by the dots)
<. for a ‘0/1-to-0/1’ arrow from right to left (one dot and no crow’s foot)
<|-- for a ‘sub-concept arrow’ that goes up

Formulated more general:

‘--’ is used for a vertical solid arrow.
‘-’ is used for a horizontal solid arrow.
‘..’ is used for a vertical dashed arrow.
‘.’ is used for a horizontal dashed arrow.
‘}’ or ‘{’ is used to indicate the ‘many-side’ (the crow’s foot).
‘>’ or ‘<’ is used to indicate the direction of the arrow.
<|-- is used for a ‘sub-concept arrow’ up.

See https://plantuml.com/class-diagram for further possibilities.

For our conceptual data models, we put properties for which values are optional (i.e., not required) between the brackets ‘[’ and ‘]’ and precede properties referring to concepts with the symbol ‘^’. We indicate uniqueness constraints by ‘!’ or ‘%’ in front of the properties involved, i.e., within each concept, the value (combination) of the property(s) preceded by ‘!’ is unique, similarly for ‘%’.

Figure A.1 contains an artificial example combining all these notational conventions, followed by its Plantuml-code. It also shows how to introduce and use an *alias*, i.e., an abbreviation for a longer name.

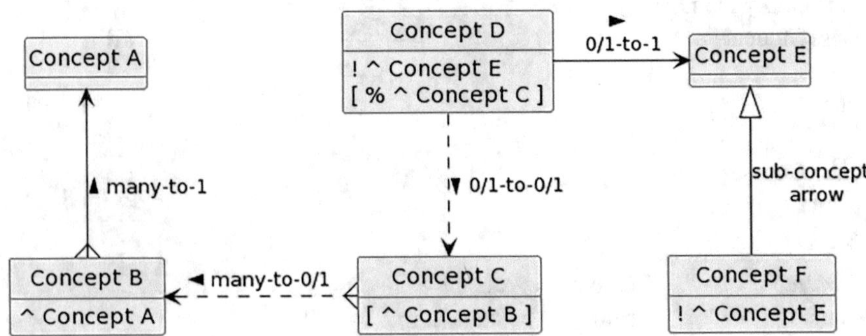

Fig. A.1 Overview of our notational conventions for conceptual data models

```
@startuml
hide circle
hide methods
Class A1 as "Concept A"
Class A2 as "Concept B" {
^ Concept A
}
Class A3 as "Concept C" {
[ ^ Concept B ]
}
Class A4 as "Concept D" {
! ^ Concept E
[ % ^ Concept C ]
}
Class A5 as "Concept E"
Class A6 as "Concept F" {
! ^ Concept E
}
A1 <--{ A2 : many-to-1 <
A2 <.{ A3  : many-to-0/1 <
A4 ..> A3  : 0/1-to-0/1 >
A4 -> A5   : > \n 0/1-to-1
A5 <|-- A6 : sub-concept \n arrow
@enduml
```

A.3.1 Generating a Visualization of a Concrete Graph

A labelled directed graph represented in a conceptual data model can be visualized as well; see Sects. 5.6.4–5.6.6. There are several ways to visualize a labelled directed graph represented in a conceptual data model by means of Plantuml.

One way is to replace every 'entry' of the form

From	To	Label
X	Y	L

by a line 'X-->Y: L' in Plantuml, precede the result by

```
@startuml
hide circle
hide members
class Z
```

(where Z is just any of the occurring nodes), and follow it up with the line

```
@enduml
```

For our example Fig. 5.3, this would result in

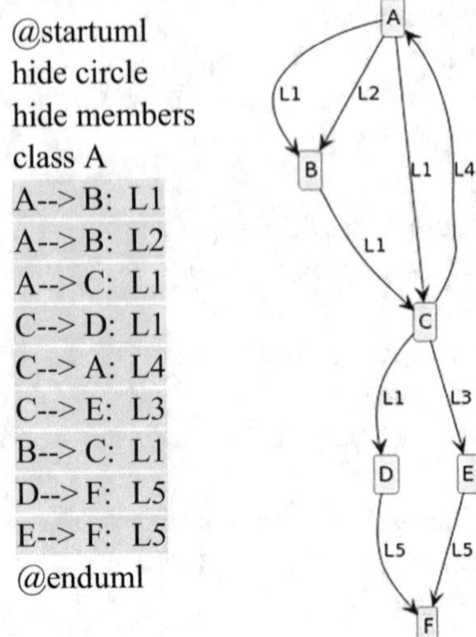

```
@startuml
hide circle
hide members
class A
A--> B: L1
A--> B: L2
A--> C: L1
C--> D: L1
C--> A: L4
C--> E: L3
B--> C: L1
D--> F: L5
E--> F: L5
@enduml
```


Leaving out the parts ': Lx' results in an unlabelled graph. Changing '-->' into '->' results in a graph which is (mainly) horizontally directed, from left to right.

A.3.2 Commutative and Non-commutative Diagrams

To indicate (non-)commutativity of a given diagram, first add a concept, say 'X', with a white background color and a white line color and an enlarged letter 'O' (for a commutative diagram) or enlarged symbol 'ϴ' (for a non-commutative diagram). See the first yellow line in the code. In order to get a (crossed-out) circle in the middle of the diagram, let 'X' refer to a suitably positioned concept, using a white arrow. See the second yellow line in the code.

```
@startuml
hide circle
hide empty members
class A as "Concept A"
class B as "Concept B"
class C as "Concept C"
class D as "Concept D"
C <--{ D: its C
C <--{ B: its C
D <--{ A: its D
B <--{ A: its B
class X as "<size:36> Θ " #white ##white
B <-[#white] X
@enduml
```

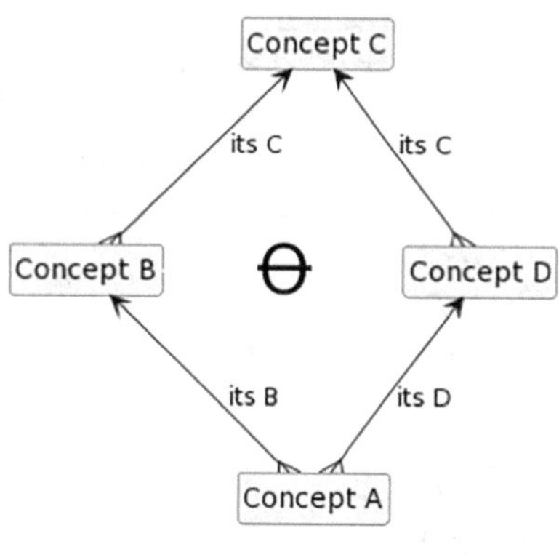


```
@startuml
hide circle
hide empty members
class A as "Concept A"
class B as "Concept B"
class C as "Concept C"
C <--{ B: its C
C <--{ A: its C
B <--{ A: its B
class X as "<size:36>O " #white ##white
B <-[#white] X
@enduml
```

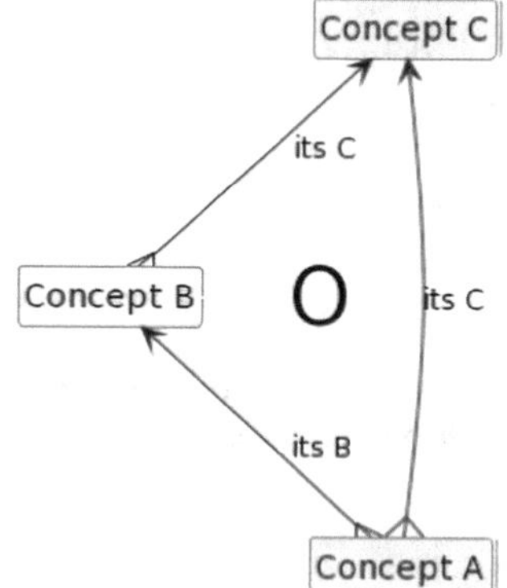

A.4 Class Diagrams

From a conceptual data model, you can easily generate a 'Version 0.0' of a corresponding class diagram, by taking the Plantuml-code for the conceptual data model and simply remove the hide-commands: 'hide circle', 'hide (empty) members', and 'hide methods'. From this Version 0.0 on, methods, derived attributes/fields, managers, etc. can be added.

As an illustration, we now show "Concept E" and its sub-concept "Concept F" from Fig. A.1 with some extra properties and methods. The corresponding Plantuml-code is also shown. Method MethA has no parameters, MethB has one parameter, MethC has two parameters, and MethD has three parameters. The '/' in front of

PropB indicates that PropB is a derivable property, i.e., its value can be computed from the other data. Plantuml automatically separates the 'fields' (i.e., properties) from the methods: Expressions with '(' and ')' are considered methods, and expressions without them are considered fields. So, their order in the declaration is not relevant, as you can see in the declaration of "Concept F".

```
@startuml
Class A5 as "Concept E" {
! E-id
PropA
/ PropB
MethA()
MethB(x)
MethC(y,z)
}
Class A6 as "Concept F" {
! ^ Concept E
MethD(u,v,w)
PropC
}
A5 <|-- A6  : sub-concept \n arrow
@enduml
```

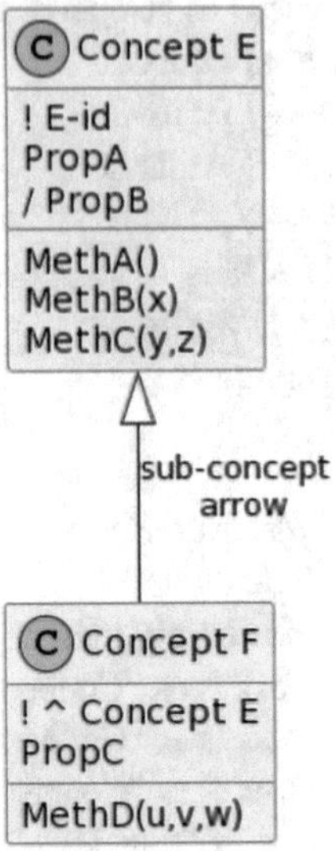

See https://plantuml.com/class-diagram for further refinements, for example, how to override Plantuml's default behavior regarding fields and methods.

A.5 System as Interface + Kernel

In Sect. 6.3, the system was shown as a 'gray box' consisting of an *interface* and a *kernel*. Using the following Plantuml-code, the graphical representation next to it will be generated (where the system is indeed depicted as a gray box):

```
@startuml
participant U as " User "

box "System"
participant I as "Interface"
participant K as "   Kernel   "
end box

U -> I   : A
I -> K   : A′
K -> K   : B′
K -> I   : C′
I -> U   : C
@enduml
```

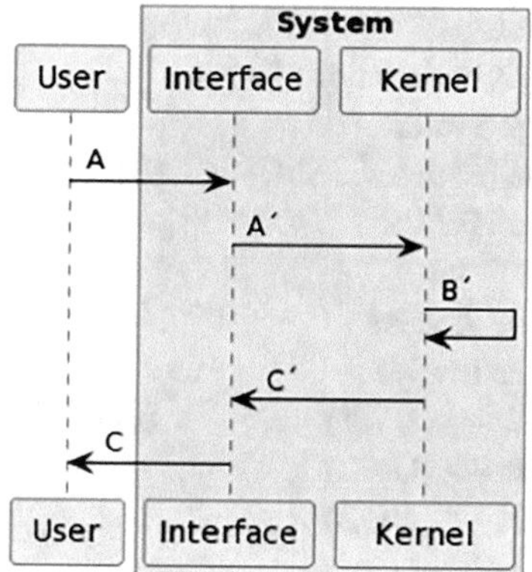

Sometimes the interface can handle the incoming request itself. Then you get:

```
@startuml
participant U as " User "

  box "System"
  participant I as "Interface"
  participant K as "   Kernel   "
  end box

U -> I   : A
I -> I   : B
I -> U   : C
@enduml
```

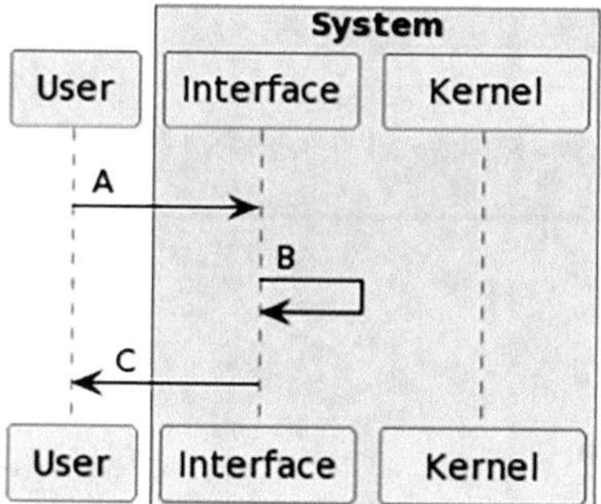

A.6 Use Case Diagrams

We don't pay much attention to use case diagrams; nevertheless, we explain here how to draw them.

Every user story without a benefit part—so, consisting of an *actor role* and a *user wish*—can form an ingredient for a use case diagram. Its SSD indicates the potential secondary actors. Use case names (i.e., *user wishes*) can be put between parentheses in Plantuml. Name of actors are enclosed between colons. By default, an actor is drawn as a stick man. Here we use the keyword 'database' to indicate other systems.

We draw the primary actors left of the system and the secondary actors on the right. For example:

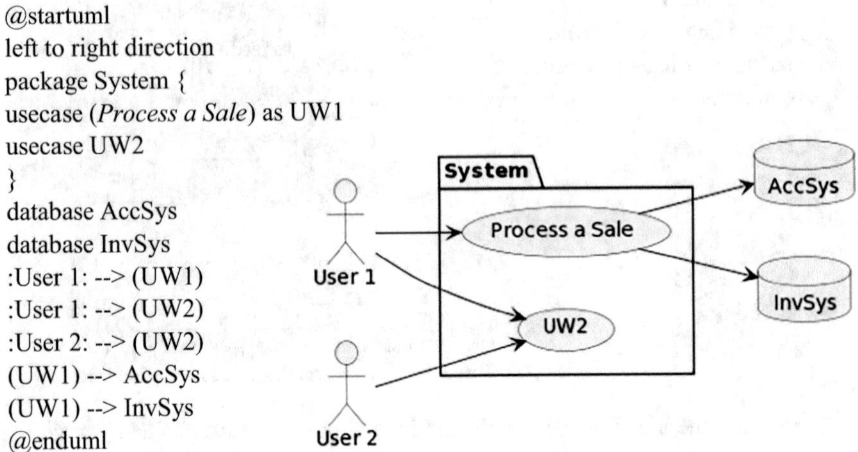

```
@startuml
left to right direction
package System {
usecase (Process a Sale) as UW1
usecase UW2
}
database AccSys
database InvSys
:User 1: --> (UW1)
:User 1: --> (UW2)
:User 2: --> (UW2)
(UW1) --> AccSys
(UW1) --> InvSys
@enduml
```


See https://plantuml.com/use-case-diagram for further possibilities.

Glossary

This glossary contains short informal descriptions of the most important terms as used in this book, including their abbreviations (where applicable).

Each term constitutes a link to the location of its description in the book as well. Their actual page numbers are mentioned in the index.

Agile development Development characterized by frequent user involvement; short, iterative development cycles; self-organizing teams; simple designs; test-driven development; code refactoring; and an emphasis on creating a demonstrable working product with each development cycle

Agile planning Adaptive, 'rolling' planning always staying one stage ahead of the work in progress, on *meso*-level (say 3-month cycles) as well as on *micro*-level (say 2-week cycles)

Alternative Scenario (AS) Another potential 'execution path' of a use case besides its MSS

Assertion Construction in SQL to express constraints *between* rows within one table and 'inter-table' constraints other than foreign key constraints

Asynchronous feedback Feedback 'after a while' (i.e., not 'by return'), and the system under consideration does not wait for it

Auto-increment field Field in a table in SQL that automatically generates a unique number when a new row is inserted in that table

Backus-Naur form Particular notation to specify a grammar

Binary association Association between two concepts in a domain model

Boyce-Codd normal form (BCNF) A concept C in a conceptual data model is in *Boyce-Codd normal form* $\Leftrightarrow$ for each set A of properties of C and each property $b \notin A$ of C: if $A \longrightarrow \{b\}$ in C then A is u.i. within C

CASE Computer-Aided Software Engineering

CASE environment Combination of CASE tools to cover the complete software life cycle

CASE tool Software tool to speed up design and implementation of software applications

CASE workbench Set of CASE tools integrated to completely cover a specific part of the software life cycle

Commutative diagram Diagram in which all directed paths with the same start- and endpoints lead to the same result

B. de Brock, *Developing Information Systems Accurately*,
https://doi.org/10.1007/978-3-031-16862-8

Conceptual data model (CDM) Conceptual structure of the data that the system must be able to retain

Conceptual key Property (combination) which is uniquely identifying within a concept in a conceptual data model and no proper subset of it is

Connextra template Template to express a user story:
As a <role>**, I want to** <user wish> [**so that** <benefit>]

Control system System that manages the behavior of other systems or devices

CRUD Widely used acronym referring to the four general basic functions applicable to *data* in a system: Create, Read, Update, and Delete

CRUDA Extended acronym used in this book referring to five general basic functions applicable to *data* in a system: Create, Read, Update, Delete, and Archive

DevOps Combination of SW-development and IT-operations practices intended to streamline and speed up delivery of (software) applications and services

Domain model Visual representation of concepts, their properties, and their associations that *might* be relevant for the system

Elementary user wish (eUW) 'Wish' of a (future) user which the system should be able to fulfil; typically a 'half-liner' expressed in natural language

Evolutionary prototype Simple, limited version of—a part of—the intended software system, developed on (a copy of) the operational platform

Execution plan Compiled plan for a stored procedure in SQL to execute it optimally

Extension Alternative scenario, i.e., another potential 'execution path' of a use case besides its MSS

External step Step in an SSD not involving **System**

Foreign key Construction in SQL to express a referential integrity constraint

Form Sequence of 'fields', each with an entry to be filled in

Functional requirement (FR) Requirement regarding the system functionality: *What* the system must be able to do, not *how* or *how fast*, for instance

Functionally dependent A set B of properties is *functionally dependent* on a set A of properties within a concept C ⇔ in each state, each pair of instances of C that have the same values for A also have the same values for B

FURPS Commonly used requirements acronym referring to Functionality, Usability, Reliability, Performance, or Supportability requirement

FURPS+ Requirement, be it a FURPS-requirement or another requirement (e.g., design requirement, interface requirement, implementation requirement, physical requirement, legal requirement, ethical requirement, etc.)

Generalization Considering two or more concepts as sub-concepts of a (new) overarching concept

Graphical SSD (gSSD) Graphical representation of an SSD

Homonym A word with two or more different meanings

Incremental development Development where the system is developed (and delivered) 'piece by piece'

Input list Set of similar forms

Input step Step from another actor to **System** in an SSD
Internal step Step in an SSD involving only **System**
Iterative development Development where 'the same piece' of the system will be improved through successive refinements
Iterative process Process that makes progress through successive refinements
Main Success Scenario (MSS) Basic, typical 'standard' scenario of a use case in which everything goes 'well', without complications
Many-to-many association Association in a domain model with on each side a '*' or a '+'
Model-View-Controller (MVC) Software design pattern used for developing user interfaces that divides the related program logic in order to separate internal representations from the ways information is presented to and accepted from the user
***n*-ary association** Association between *n* concepts in a domain model
Non-functional requirement Quality requirement, i.e., requirement not being a functional requirement
On-site customer Customer always available on the development site
On-site developer Developer always available on the customer site
Output step Step in an SSD from **System** to another participant
Pair programming Working in groups of two programmers (one computer, one table, two chairs) where one programmer writes code, while the other reviews that code and thinks about the next step and direction of the work
Parallel development Developing (reasonably) independent subsystems in parallel
Parameterized user wish (pUW) Elementary user wish plus input parameters
Persistent data Data the system must retain, also when it is not 'at work' (i.e., data which is also available after fully closing the application)
Plantuml Drawing *generation* tool to generate drawings from text
Postconditions Conditions holding after execution of the use case. Consist of a specification of the *state change result* (new state in terms of the old state) and of the *output* (also in case of alternative scenarios)
Preconditions (Nontrivial) minimal condition(s) to be satisfied before the use case can start
Primary actor Role that 'calls' the use case. Can be a human being, a sensor, or another system
Primary key Construction in SQL to express a key constraint (consisting of one or more properties)
Primary property Property of a concept that is an element of at least one of the conceptual keys of that concept
Prototype Simple, limited version of—a part of—the intended system, emphasizing only the *functionality* (and *usability*) of the system
Quality requirement Requirement not being a functional requirement
Retrieval Requesting the system for information without changing the state
Scenario integration Integration of all scenarios for a given use case

Search form Form to search for all instances of a concept that satisfy all the criteria expressed in the form

Secondary actors Actors involved in the use case besides the primary actor and the system. Might be human beings, sensors, actuators, and/or other systems

Secondary property Property of a concept that is not an element of one of its conceptual keys

Session data Data the system must retain temporarily only during a 'session', i.e., when the system is 'at work' (as opposed to *persistent* data)

Specialization Distinguishing sub-concepts within a concept

Stored procedure Procedure in SQL consisting of a sequence of SQL-statements mixed with language constructs for control-of-flow

Sub-concept Concept of which each instance is an instance of the other (more general) concept as well

Synchronous feedback Feedback 'by return' and the system under consideration waits for it

System Sequence Description (SSD) Schematic representation of the interactions between the primary actor, the system (as a black box), and other actors (if any), including the messages (with their parameters) between them

Ternary association Association between three concepts in a domain model

Textual SSD (tSSD) Textual representation of an SSD according to a formally defined grammar

Third normal form (3NF) A concept C in a conceptual data model is in *third normal form* ⇔ for each set A of properties of C and each *secondary* property $b \notin A$ of C: if $A \longrightarrow \{b\}$ in C, then A is u.i. within C

Throw-away prototype Simple, limited version of—a part of—the intended software system, not developed on (a copy of) the operational platform

Trigger Stored program in a database which automatically fires/executes when a certain kind of event occurs

Unified Process (UP) System development 'framework'—with variants—that distinguishes a few *stages/phases* and several *disciplines*, combining many existing 'best practices'

Uniquely identifying A property (combination) is *uniquely identifying* within a concept if and only if in any state the same value for that property (combination) cannot occur twice within that concept

Use case (UC) Text in natural language that describes a sequence of actions in one session with the system

Use case diagram Graphical representation of the possible interactions of users with the system

User story (US) Combination of an elementary user wish, a role, and an optional benefit part

Validation Checking whether the specification (still) captures the customer's requirements

Verification Testing whether the implementation works according to the original specification

View 'Named query' in SQL

Waterfall method Development method strictly following a linear development path where each phase closes with an irrevocable report and, in principle, is never reopened

References

[ACM1] Curricula Recommendations: https://www.acm.org/education/curricula-recommendations

[Beck] K. Beck and C. Andres: Extreme Programming Explained: Embrace Change. Addison-Wesley, 2004

[Bro] E.O. de Brock: Foundations of Semantic Databases. Prentice Hall International Series in Computer Science, Hemel Hempstead, 1995

[Bro2] E.O. de Brock: Declarative Semantics of Actions and Instructions. In: B. Shishkov (Ed.): International Symposium on Business Modeling and Software Design, LNBIP Vol. 391, pp. 297–308, 2020

[C&Y] P. Coad & E. Yourdon: Object-Oriented Design. Prentice Hall (Yourdon Press), 1991

[CC20] Computing Curricula 2020: https://www.acm.org/binaries/content/assets/education/curricula-recommendations/cc2020.pdf

[Che] P. Chen: The Entity-Relationship Model – Toward a unified view of data. ACM Transactions on Database Systems, 1 (1), 9-36, 1976

[Coc] A. Cockburn: Writing Effective Use Cases, Addison Wesley, 2001

[Cohn] M. Cohn: User Stories Applied: For Agile Software Development. Addison Wesley, 2004

[Cohn2] M. Cohn: Agile Needs to Be Both Iterative and Incremental.

[Cohn3] M. Cohn: Why the Three-Part User Story Template Works So Well

[CS13] Computer Science Curricula 2013: https://www.acm.org/binaries/content/assets/education/cs2013_web_final.pdf

[Dum] M. Dumas et al: Fundamentals of Business Process Management, 2nd ed., Springer, 2018

[ECTS] European Credit Transfer and Accumulation System: https://education.ec.europa.eu/education-levels/higher-education/inclusive-and-connected-higher-education/european-credit-transfer-and-accumulation-system

[GSE09] Graduate Software Engineering 2009: https://www.acm.org/binaries/content/assets/education/gsew2009.pdf

[IS10] Information Systems 2010: https://www.acm.org/binaries/content/assets/education/curricula-recommendations/is-2010-acm-final.pdf

[JBR] I. Jacobson, G. Booch, and J. Rumbaugh: The Unified Software Development Process. Addison Wesley, 1999

[Lar] C. Larman: Applying UML and patterns. Pearson Education, 2005

[Luc] G.G. Lucassen: Understanding User Stories. PhD thesis, Utrecht University, 2017

[Pla] Plantuml: https://Plantuml.com

B. de Brock, *Developing Information Systems Accurately*,
https://doi.org/10.1007/978-3-031-16862-8

[SET] Summary of Efficacy Table: https://addis.drugis.org/#/users/3/datasets/65f9e23d-6e8d-4ccd-aacd-95b672520ce2/studies/caa8405b-c4f3-47ac-9f20-a7376b37ac63

[SE14] Software Engineering 2014: https://www.acm.org/binaries/content/assets/education/se2014.pdf

[SWE] SWEBOK (Software Engineering Body of Knowledge): https://www.computer.org/education/bodies-of-knowledge/software-engineering

[UML] UML (Unified Modeling Language): https://www.uml.org

[Val] G. van Valkenhoef et al: Quantitative release planning in extreme programming. Information and Software Technology, Vol. 53.11, 1227–1235, 2011

[XP] XP (eXtreme Programming): http://www.extremeprogramming.org

All links were last accessed on the 4th of July, 2022.

Index

The **bold** entries can be found back in the glossary, where each entry has a short informal description and has a link to its introduction in the book as well.

B. de Brock, *Developing Information Systems Accurately*,
https://doi.org/10.1007/978-3-031-16862-8

Printed in the United States
by Baker & Taylor Publisher Services